Missional: Impossible!

MISSIONAL: IMPOSSIBLE!

The Death of Institutional Christianity
and the Rebirth of G-d

FRANCIS ROTHERY

RESOURCE *Publications* • Eugene, Oregon

MISSIONAL: IMPOSSIBLE!
The Death of Institutional Christianity and the Rebirth of G-d

Copyright © 2013 Francis Rothery. All rights reserved. Except for brief quotations in critical publications or reviews, no part of this book may be reproduced in any manner without prior written permission from the publisher. Write: Permissions. Wipf and Stock Publishers, 199 W. 8th Ave., Suite 3, Eugene, OR 97401.

Resource Publications
An Imprint of Wipf and Stock Publishers
199 W. 8th Ave., Suite 3
Eugene, OR 97401

www.wipfandstock.com

ISBN 13: 978-1-62564-203-5

Manufactured in the U.S.A.

To the G-d of Conversation and Exeter Nightchurch
To all Communities of G-d that have been destroyed by hierarchical bureaucracy and managerialism in the churches of institution
Rise again!

Contents

Acknowledgments | ix
Introduction: The Story | xi
Overview | xv

PART 1: Domination Christianity: A Management Misshaped Church
    1 Management Is the Message | 3
    2 The Leadership Deception | 19
    3 Domination Christianity | 37

PART 2: The Missional Illusion: A New Christian West
    4 Missional: Miasma | 59
    5 Missional: The Language House | 81
    6 Missional: Impossible! | 94

PART 3: Recovering Reconciliation: A Community of Partnerships
    7 Conversation Communities | 107
    8 Reconciliation Communities | 129
    9 Empowerment Communities | 146

PART 4: Our Un/Known G-D: A Neotribal Spirituality
    10 Home Truths | 169
    11 Our Un/Known G-d | 180
    12 G-d of Everybody | 191

Glossary | 215
Bibliography | 221
About the Author | 225

Acknowledgments

A BOOK IS THE product of many conversations. I would like to thank the following pilgrims for their provocations and insights. We all sit around the Open Table of Christ. We all go into the dark. Around the table you have Mother Teresa and you'll be lucky if you don't find Dracula. Our light shines ever more brightly the deeper our darkness.

Martin Shaw, Jennifer Wilkin Shaw, Charlotte Shaw, Barry Rothery, Julian and Susannah Warner, Benedict Ramsden, Julian Wheeler, Ray Colledge, Peter Nicholls, Terry O'Donovan, Steve Wilton, Renny Davies, Steve Jones, Gavin Tyte, Michael Langrish, Mark Rylands, Malcolm Joyce, Katie Moudry, Ian McRae Spencer, Russell Grubb, Gavin Colley, Phill Pavey, Laura McAdam, Charlotte Page, Chris Loosemore and Deborah Morse, Pete and Debbie Brazier, Ian Adams, Kim Hartshorne, Alan Roxburgh, Alan Hirsch, Ben Edson, George Elerick, Scott Russell, Jack Stafford, Ed Stasis, Mike Morrell, Noel Moules, Jonathan Henderson, Steve Banks, Tristan Massy-Birch, Patrick Jordan, Rob and Helen Beesley, Kevin and Rachel Thompson, Christopher and Rachel Oldham, Michael Oldham, Reg Walker, Mike Jordan, Andrew Martin, Paul Adams, the Snowdens, Jonathan Creber, Karar, Smaran, Raahi, Michael Power, Eamonn Kirke, Brother Larne, Ben Quarty-Papafio, Naeem Parshad, Yuri and Angel Malkin, Zeeshan Siraj Din, Dale Caldwell, James Smith, Roberto Cardelli, Gerard Van Der Vegt, Mary Jo Radcliffe, Jim Dymond, Grania Luttman-Johnson, Leif Stani Leszczyński, The Community of St Anthony and St Elias, Emergent Village, The Male Journey, Partners In Mission International, Exeter Nightchurch, CMS Missional Projects and Orders Hub, Simply Hub, Hilfield Franciscan Friary, Heythrop College, the Emergent South West Cohort, Third Order of the Society of St Francis; (European Province of the Anglican Communion)

Introduction

THE STORY

THIS IS THE STORY of how Christ—a Way of Life and Truth—has been usurped throughout history by conquering kings, written words and absolute ideas. Without ruling over others like the Greeks and Romans had done he brought freedom to people of all faiths and none; he recognized the face of G-d in everyone. The early church followed him. Yet in time they were seduced by the Roman king god. He promised an illusion of perfection through hierarchical domination. The Usurper took Christ's name and reputation but despised his egalitarian way of life. The followers of the way were absorbed into a superstate. It conquered and subdued all others through the sign of the cross. The Usurper King imposed his will through structures of hierarchical and authoritarian leadership. This was the Roman Empire and the Roman Catholic Church it created. Christian empire went on to become the foundation myth of Western civilization. The king god proved his great love and saved other tribes through incorporating them into his kingdom by violent military conquest. He then enforced unity in the empire through Christian creeds. On a holy mission of military and ideological domination he ruled Europe for 1,000 years.

However, as time went on some of the nobles felt he had become too greedy and was not ruling properly. They were jealous of his wealth and political power. Through the Protestant Reformation they created a word God. In the process they forgot that Christ is not a written word but a human being. Tragically the protestors based their new kingdoms on the words of the Bible. They set up nation states based on its laws. In time these became domination systems of state bureaucracy. Political and religious ministers now ruled. Christian mission was perpetuated through the exercise of ideological and bureaucratic power. Ideas became more important than the practice of faith. By focussing on doctrinal differences the kingdom was split in two. Catholics and Protestants fought for 125 years to decide whose domination God was the true heir to the throne of Europe. Eleven million died in the slaughter. Finally the king God and the word God destroyed each other; domination God was dead.

The prophet Nietzsche warned everyone about what they had done. He went into the streets shouting, "God is dead and we have killed him!" Now that the domination God of the divided Christians was dead the nation states began to rule themselves. The French Revolution saw the creation of the Rights of Man. During the American War of Independence individual human rights were declared self-evident. In time fascism and communism also created seductive visions of a human future where mankind and reason were supreme, but these intransigent regimes of absolute control made the twentieth century one of total war and revolution. The Christian God was dead. Yet these modernist solutions still perpetrated the violent rivalry of ancient Greece and Rome. Their warring gods were hidden inside the systems of the domination God. Modernity's oppressive regimes were also the legacy of their illusory quest for social supremacy. It was still the same Greek search for human perfectibility through the status of hierarchical domination. Emphasizing only one way to salvation had led to a spurious quest for a final solution. People tried to defeat each other with their non-negotiable and invulnerable truths. Everyone was now in competition. Social fragmentation and atomization began to pervade everyday life. A cold war of isolation and intransigence settled over the people of the West.

The modernist quest for total security through the domination of one superior group finally gave birth to the atom bomb. When it exploded society, community and therefore purpose and meaning were atomized into a billion fragments. Even the illusory lie of rule on the basis of ideological superiority had been shattered. When gods and men had reigned people at least had a fake story that helped them pretend to belong. Now everything had been blown to pieces. The stories didn't matter anymore; Christian, usurper and protestor, godless fascist and communist had all failed. Their values had created a polarized world of Christian nations in mutual conflict and destruction. Now everyone could only pretend to believe. There were no big stories left to bring meaning and social control. The power of the bomb had created a social vacuum. It had sucked meaning out of human existence. In panic and a need to manage this abyss of powerlessness daily life became massively over-regulated. Suffocating levels of micromanagement disconnected people. Panoramic human vistas became squeezed into small screens of virtual distraction. People had everything, yet no one knew who they were anymore. Boredom and amorality settled upon the people of the West. *L'ennui* and anomie permeated the modern soul. The splitting of the atom relativized modern democracy. An isolated i-culture of callous alienation emerged.

The atomic bomb of modern Christian America had created postmodernity. Yet all was not lost. Einstein's relativity also brought a gift. People began to realize that when all individuals claim their way as the only truth, then a common and shared way of life disappears. Modernity had actually destroyed the possibility of an integrated society. The hierarchical systems of ancient Greece and Rome had created domination Christianity, which in turn had birthed modernity. These ideologies all contained an inbuilt polarization that had failed to bring the social wholeness and salvation they promised. False peace through the dominance of one social group of higher social status was their final solution. These illusions of mastery and false promises of perfection bound people in fear and slavery. Their values created the potential for global destruction and societies of capitalist and communist nihilism.

Yet, wise people saw underneath the fragmentation of these domination systems to an integrated whole. They remembered a way of life and truth; a G-d in all things and all peoples. The key to our future lay in the recovery of this lost memory. Christ came not as a conquering king or a written word or an absolute idea, but as the first divine human being. People of all faiths and none began to hear a gentle voice deep in their hearts that kept on whispering over and over: "I am the Way, I am the Way, . . ."

Overview

THERE ARE SEVERAL STREAMS of mission attempting to reverse Christianity's decline in the United Kingdom, Europe and the USA. The following structure provides an overview of their efficacy and integrity. It then offers an alternative vision of faith rooted in the reconciliation and empowerment practices of Jesus Christ and our common experience of G-d as un/known.

Part 1: Domination Christianity considers the way practices of hierarchical bureaucracy and management have perpetuated decline in mainline Christian institutions. Mainline mission practices aim to increase denominational membership by inviting people to services and stage-managed worship and preaching events. In the United Kingdom the mission shaped church is a stream within mainline Christianity that is attempting to reverse decline through creating churches around the needs of the unchurched. Frustratingly, all mission initiative is enmeshed in the centralized finance and managerial mechanisms of the mainline institutions. Therefore Church law, policy, regulation, and financial priorities control and curb innovation and growth. Mission shaped church has been formalized as the term, Fresh Expressions. It includes initiatives by the Church of England, the Methodist Church, the United Reformed Church, the Congregational Federation and Ground Level Network.

Part 2: The Missional Illusion considers the ways in which the missional movement contains the polarizing seeds of modernity and Christian cultural dominance. Its goal is "remaking a New Christian West." Lesslie Newbigin stated that "Christians are to occupy the 'high ground' which they vacated in the noon time of modernity."[1] The term missional gained popularity at the end of the twentieth century. It has different methods and emphases from mission shaped church, although there is overlap. Mission

---

1. Newbigin, *The Gospel in a Pluralist Society*, 232.

Overview

shaped church operates from centralized institutions, while missional leaders seek to create movements and organic systems. Missional seeks to rethink the church and create a new paradigm; the church doesn't have a mission, the mission has a church. Christians are sent ones who incarnate the Gospel within their specific cultural localities and neighborhoods.

Part 3: Recovering Reconciliation considers the recovery of the central practices of conversation, reconciliation and empowerment in small communities. This is a way of life that follows the practices of Christ. It rebirths identity, meaning, and purpose in our atomized neotribal democracies.

Part 4: Our Un/Known G-d considers the rebirth of G-d in the neotribal societies of the globalized West. A recognition of G-d as un/known for people of all faiths and none moves society beyond Christianity's mission-misshaped past. It looks to a future where G-d is in all and through all. This empowers a way of life that brings wholeness and integration with/in neighborhoods, towns and cities.

PART 1

Domination Christianity
A MANAGEMENT MISSHAPED CHURCH

1

Management Is the Message

> "Tillich knew, all human institutions, including the church, are inherently demonic."
> —Chris Hedges[1]

> "The medium is the message."
> —Marshall McLuhan[2]

MANAGING DECLINE IN A MISSION-SHAPED CHURCH

The mainline Christian Churches of the West have lost something vital. Managing decline has become the focus of most Christian leaders in the United Kingdom and Europe. The mainline churches of the USA are beginning to experience similar problems. Perplexingly, decline persists year on year even after increasing emphasis and investment of time and

---

1. Hedges, "I Don't Believe In Atheists," para. 10.
2. McLuhan, *Understanding Media*, 7.

Part 1: Domination Christianity

energy in Christian mission. What follows is the national picture in the United Kingdom over the last thirty years. The Anglican church has lost nearly 40 percent of its membership, about 1 million people, and still falling marginally according to the 2012 statistics. It now has an attendance of 1.8 million out of a population of sixty-three million people. It has ceased to reflect the religious zeitgeist of the nation. The Catholic Church is the largest denomination at 4 million. Yet it has declined by 37 percent and is in crisis in terms of priesthood recruitment. The Methodist Church has declined by 50 percent, the United Reformed Movement by 46 percent and the Baptists by 21 percent.

2011 Census polls on UK religion paint the following picture. In a poll conducted by YouGov in March 2011 when asked the census question *What is your religion?* 61 percent of people in England and Wales ticked a religious box, while 39 percent ticked no religion. When the same sample was asked the follow-up question *Are you religious?* only 29 percent of the same people said *Yes*, while 65 percent said *No*, meaning over half of those the census would count as having a religion said they were not religious. Asked when they had last attended a place of worship for religious reasons, most people in England and Wales (63 percent) had not attended in the past year, 43 percent last attended over a year ago and 20 percent had never attended. Only 9 percent of people had attended a place of worship within the last week.

The findings of the census mean that approximately fifty-six million people do not attend Christian worship. Yet about thirty-two million still describe themselves as Christian. What this indicates is that even those who would identify themselves as Christian are not interested in mainline Christianity. Why?

The traditional answer is to blame secularization. Yet some observers think that the UK has entered into a period of post-secularism. This means that many people have their own spirituality but are still not attending religious institutions. One explanation may be that decline is connected with the secularization and bureaucratization of the churches. Lack of vitality in mainline Christianity may be due to an unhealthy preoccupation with hierarchical bureaucracy and management practices.

Ecclesiologist Tony Jones has noted that "the bureaucracy of mainline Christianity is holding back the church from what it can be." The facts seem to confirm this. For, while churches that are run like corporations are declining, the less bureaucratized are growing. In the UK in the last thirty years the Russian Orthodox Church has grown by 60 percent and the Pentecostal Movement has grown by 177 percent.³

The common feature of these churches is that they are not centralized institutions. They are not run like religious businesses. Their faith is mediated through the spiritual and the experiential. They do not have an overreliance on prescriptive bureaucratic machinery or church canon law. Their leaders do not function like managers. Convincingly, the missiologist Alan Hirsch has identified "organic systems" to be an essential feature of the DNA of faith movements that are vital and growing: "in contrast with a centralized institution, missional movements are structured more like an interconnected organism than through hierarchical organization. Organic systems manifest (i) an ethos of a movement (as opposed to institution), (ii) the structure of a network, (iii) spread like viruses, and (iv) are reproducing and reproducible."⁴

THE FAITH OF THE MANAGERS: DOMINATION

"Bureaucratic administration means fundamentally domination through knowledge," said the sociologist Max Weber. To what degree has the practice of bureaucracy and management dominated and misshaped the mission of the Church? Sarah Coakley in *Has the Church of England lost its Reason?* has identified what she terms "the secular bureaucratization of the episcopate." Sarah writes of "the danger of the covert assimilation of worldly or bureaucratic notions of power and authority into the decisions of the Church about Episcopal standing and oversight . . . [and] . . . Along with the notable turn in priestly life in general to the secular bureaucratic models of leadership, efficiency and mission-efficacy has gone an almost unnoticed capitulation—as I see it—to the idolatry of busyness . . . Is our creeping ecclesial bureaucratization indeed the way forward for the Church in all its ministries?"⁵ Anglican clergyman and TV presenter Peter Owen-Jones has also described the effect of bureaucracy on his vocation by saying: "I feel more like a religious civil servant than God's suffering servant." He is not alone. When significant amounts of time and energy are given to the management of religious institutions a living faith becomes secondary. The faith of leaders becomes managerialized. In the process of bureaucratic erosion a

3. www.whychurch.org.uk/images/charts/ch_mem_denom_trend.png.
4. en.wikipedia.org/wiki/Alan_Hirsch.
5. Coakley, "Has the Church."

key element of faith is lost; the ability to risk. A heaviness descends. Order is fetishized. Innovation becomes threatening. Balance is lost. The spiritual health of institutions becomes terminal.

Running a religious corporation requires a focus on the managerial and the bureaucratic. This is difficult to maintain except at the expense of honesty and collegiality in relationships. The maintenance of Christian institutions has usurped and gradually replaced the fragile relationships that create authentic community and real religion. David Whyte reminds us that "We only have to look at the most important word in the lexicon of the present workplace—manager—to understand its inherent weakness. Manager is derived from the old Italian and French words *managgio*, meaning the training, riding and handling of a horse . . . Sometime over the next fifty years or so, the word manager will disappear from our understanding of leadership and thankfully so."[6]

A curious overlap has occurred in the last twenty-five years that has blurred management and mission practices. Stephen Pattison has highlighted mission language as part of a developing theology of management in the mainline churches. "The use of words with religious association in management like mission and vision, should be enough to alert us to the fact that management may have more than a passing resemblance to Christianity. When it is remembered that some of the roots of management theory and practice lie in ecclesiastical control practices in medieval Catholicism and nineteenth century entrepreneurial Protestantism in the USA, it should come as no surprise that management can credibly be seen in some ways as a religious activity embodying a certain kind of faith. This has led me to suggest elsewhere that management can be regarded as a Christian heresy and that it is therefore possible to analyse the faith of the managers."[7] Pattison points out that modern management theory borrows from the language and ideas found in the history of Catholic and Protestant mission. This is the dark underbelly of Christianity and its collusion with coercive and violent colonialism. Catholicism and Protestantism were promoted and maintained through the managerial and mission practices utilized by their priests and pastors.

---

6. Whyte, *Crossing the Unknown Sea*, 240.
7. Woodward and Pattison, *The Blackwell Reader*, 290.

MANAGEMENT IS THE MEDIUM

Pattison continues, "in the case of mission this concept has the positive connotations of clarity of purpose, urgency, outward directedness and the need for change. However it has the more negative connotations evidenced in church history, such as unquestioning response to a command from above, dualism, seeing the world as a hostile place that needs changing and regarding those outside the organization as alien or demonic objects needing conversion or elimination. Christian mission has often been aggressive, violent, exploitative, and colonial—hence the utility of the concept of mission within the military." In consequence, the message that is subtly communicated through Christian institutions has become management itself. Christianity has become a managed commodity with a mission to capture a market share in capitalist culture.

The danger of incorporating mission language into management theory is that, in practice, they become similar. In mainline Christian churches management has become the dominant method of operation. This similarity in language creates a situation where mainline churches can use management as a lever to co-opt and control more organic mission initiatives, such as the mission-shaped church. By definition management always seeks to control. In this way the mainline Christian churches continue to perpetuate a form of managerialized Christian social dominance. This is because church management and mission are essentially concerned with leadership and social dominance by one social group, i.e., Christians. Tragically, the Gospel of Reconciliation that Christ practiced has been usurped by a management and mission emphasis. Where do mainline churches look for power? In what have they really put their faith? Management practices and the machinery of bureaucracy are usurping the Christ of inclusive community—even in mission-shaped initiatives. The presbyterian saint A. W. Tozer puts this trend in perspective: "Some things are not negotiable... A winsome, magnetic saint is worth 500 promoters and gadgeteers and religious engineers."[8]

A faith in Christ who liberates has been usurped by the faith of the managers who dominate. Bureaucratic function consumes time, energy and attention. It disrupts and distorts relationships. It makes everyone feel unnecessarily accountable to clergy and their representatives in the structure. Bureaucratic function and control alienates. It distances clergy

---

8. Tozer, "The Man Who Met God in the Fire."

Part 1: Domination Christianity

from their people and the people from one another. The act of missioning and colonization is always about ownership and rule. To be collared is the symbol of slavery. The yoke of Jesus is easy and light but the yoke of the religious machine is heavy beyond belief. This is the case for clergy and for the church members who are increasingly being asked to augment managerialized functions.

Bureaucracy is the real power behind institutional Christianity. It relies on management for its survival. Management is now its god. Churches promote an ideology of mission and management primarily for their own survival. This needs to be named properly as organizational Christian hegemony. Paul Kivel reminds us that "Christian hegemony . . . is the everyday, pervasive, and systematic set of Christian values and beliefs, individuals and institutions that dominate all aspects of our society through the social, political, economic, and cultural power they wield. Nothing is unaffected by Christian hegemony (whether we are Christian or not) including our personal beliefs and values, our relationships to other people and to the natural environment, and our economic, political, education, health care, criminal/legal, housing, and other social systems. Christian hegemony as a system of domination is complex, shifting, and operates through the agency of individuals, families, church communities, denominations, parachurch organizations, civil institutions, and through decisions made by members of the ruling class and power elite."[9]

The mission-shaped church movement has attempted to offer an alternative to the management-centered mainline churches. However, it is enmeshed in centralized institutions that prioritize management practices that exist for the sole purpose of control. This automatically undermines attempts at real and integrated change. A mission ethos, when dovetailed with centralized institutional management, prevents the emergence of a genuinely alternative movement. This is because innovative attempts at mission are susceptible to being absorbed into the needs of struggling institutions. Mission-shaped innovation then remains dominated by the requirements of a centralized agenda filtered through layers of managerial and bureaucratic machinery. Seth Godin, in *Tribes*, names the situation that mainline Christian institutions find themselves in: "Some tribes are stuck. They embrace the status quo and drown out any tribe member who dares to question authority and the accepted order. Big charities, tiny

---

9. Kivel, "Challenging Christian Hegemony."

clubs, struggling corporations—they're tribes and they're stuck."[10] Charles Ringma also reminds us: "Sadly, the embryonic new is frequently formalized and institutionalized rather than being given the room for further experimentation and growth. Because we want to possess the new, we fail to see it is merely the signpost to something better. Leave the new alone and it will lead us farther."[11]

MANAGEMENT MEDIUM: MANAGEMENT MESSAGE

An overdependence on managerialized mission has shaped and delivered a modernist church to a postmodern society. This church has also usurped Christ's egalitarian Gospel of reconciliation and freedom. The medium of management used by the churches of institution has become their message. It was Marshall McLuhan who coined the phrase "the medium is the message." What does it mean? Douglas Coupland explains that "'the medium is the message' means that the ostensible content of all electronic media is insignificant; it is the medium itself which has the greater impact on the environment, a fact bolstered by the now medically undeniable fact that the technologies we use every day, begin after a while to alter the way our brains work and hence the way we experience our world."[12] Mobiles, iPods, texting, Facebook, and Skype shape the way we see reality through the way information is delivered. In the same way, the medium of management has shaped the message that the churches of institution are sending society. They have caused the church to perpetuate the polarizing and divisive values of modernity. Modernist values emphasize religious and/or political dominance by one social group. What is absent from modernity is an emphasis on reciprocity. Yet this is the touchstone of Christ's Gospel. In this way the church is out of step with both the Gospel and contemporary culture. Therefore it fails to connect meaningfully at all.

ACCOUNTABILITY?: A CULTURE OF SUSPICION

One of the striking features of contemporary life in the West is the way people have rejected institutions. Why? Baroness Onora O'Neill, in her

---

10. Godin, *Tribes*, 5.
11. Ringma, *Resist the Powers*.
12. Coupland, *Marshall McLuhan*, 13.

Part 1: Domination Christianity

Reith Lectures, *A Question of Trust* (2002), pointed to the way opaque and conflicting management and accountability systems have shaped European institutional life. This includes mainline churches that are bound by law to partner with the policy, aims, and legislation of government. The Baroness examined the quest for greater accountability in government and public institutions. She explored whether the instruments for control, regulation, monitoring, and enforcement had worked. What she discovered was an unthinking use of clumsy accountability schemes. These were designed to increase transparency and raise levels of trust. In fact, they increased untrustworthy behavior such as falsifying outcomes and setting unrealistic targets. They created a culture of well-paid professionals who believed it was necessary to lie to keep their jobs. The organizational life of religious institutions therefore carries with it a spiritual opacity. Management fosters illusion. It gives religious managers a feeling of power without its reality.

All public institutions are subject to health and safety law, safeguarding guidelines, financial regulations, and so on. Most have also adopted systems of quality management. To this end they also have management structures, and accountability and appraisal systems. There is no difference between church institutional requirements and those of state organizations. Yet it is salient to remember that total quality management does not bring the reciprocity and mutuality of the kingdom of G-d. In fact, it seems to have done exactly the opposite. Management culture is counterproductive to human well-being and alien to the message of Christ. Baroness O'Neill concluded that the very systems that were set up to promote and increase transparency and trust have created a culture of suspicion. The mainline churches in Europe have not been exempt but are deeply enmeshed. These systems of regulation have dovetailed with management, mission and leadership practices developed in the church over the last twenty-five years. When the church begins to operate in this way, where is it putting its trust? On which gods is it relying for salvation and survival? Management? Bureaucracy? Hierarchy? Government Regulation? Church Law?

Since the Baroness first gave her Reith Lectures in 2002, the erosion of trust by inept accountability systems has only worsened.[13]

---

13. See BBC Radio 4 Analysis Trust http://www.bbc.co.uk/programmes/b00xnxl4

WHEN IS A CHURCH NOT A CHURCH?

The church, when informed, powered and shaped by the needs of centralized bureaucracy, develops into a culture that is necrophilic. This is the case even when it promotes itself as a mission community. It is not false doctrine or liberalism that is killing the church but false practices. Management needs to be clearly named as false orthopraxy. It has turned the egalitarian Gospel of Christ into a mission-vision of credal domination. A church that prioritizes a framework of mission-vision, total quality management, staff appraisals, government health and safety, and child protection directives has lost touch with its soul. It has become necrophilic rather than biophilic, while preoccupied with its own bureaucratic power rather than serving the population made in the image of G-d. C. G. Jung reminds us of the demonic nature of such structures: "In building a machine we are so intent upon our purpose that we forget that we are investing that machine with creative power . . . it can overgrow us in an invisible way . . . they are the dwelling places of divine powers that may destroy us."[14] War correspondent and Pulitzer Prize winner Chris Hedges agrees: "as Paul Tillich knew, all human institutions, including the church, are inherently demonic."[15]

Erich Fromm, in the *Anatomy of Human Destructiveness*, links love of machines and a machine-living with a modernist culture in love with what is dead. When efficiency, effectiveness, and the institution are prioritized people cease to matter. Jesus said, "The sabbath was made for man, not man for the sabbath." Similarly, the institution was made for the human not the human for the institution. Yet, when bureaucracy is central it becomes fetishized. When people worship its money, security, and power, and prioritize its efficiency and effectiveness, they stop valuing and loving one another. To love the religious machine is to be necrophilic.

Fromm writes:

> Let us begin with the consideration of the simplest and most obvious characteristics of contemporary industrial man: the stifling of his focal interest in people, nature and living structures, together with the increasing attraction of mechanical non-alive artifacts. Examples abound. All over the industrialized world there are men who feel more tender towards, and are more interested in, their automobiles than their wives. They are proud of their car; they cherish it; they wash it (even many of those who could pay to have this

---

14. Seminar on Dream Analysis, http://foreignstate.com/?p=4010.
15. Hedges, "I Don't Believe In Atheists."

job done), and in many countries some give it a loving nickname; they observe it and are concerned with the slightest symptom of a dysfunction. To be sure a car is not a sexual object—but it is an object of love; life without a car seems to be more intolerable than life without a woman . . . I am referring to those individuals whose interest in artifacts has replaced their interest in what is alive and who deal with technical matters in a pedantic and unalive way.[16]

A church dominated and dominating through managerial efficiency and effectiveness is necrophilic. It is a church where there is little room for the human and organic life-giving dirt of a Holy G-d. This is why Nietzsche was right when he said, "God is dead and we have killed him." G-d has been murdered by an inordinate and misplaced devotion to mechanistic bureaucratic authority. Is it any wonder churches feel like mausoleums? Many discover G-d only when made alive again in the reconciliation that only non-bureaucratic and non-hierarchical community allows. It is the managerialism of mission that has made genuine religious community impossible in the churches of institution. To what do such churches look to save them? Is it management and mission or reconciliation with the stranger and the other in our neighborhoods?

DELIVER ME FROM THIS CORPORATION OF DEATH

A bureaucratic, law obsessed, and decaying church can be compared to the image of the body of death that the apostle Paul used in his letter to the Romans[17]. It was a form of Roman punishment. The criminal was made to carry a decaying corpse tied to their back through the city streets. The body produced toxic fumes as it decayed. It eventually killed the person carrying it. Paul uses this as an image to illustrate the way legalism destroys the law of the spirit of life[18], which is the defining characteristic of Gospel freedom. A love of the institutional corpse—such as lifeless hierarchy, bureaucracy, church law, and management—is what keeps the body of death on our backs. This body of death is killing the church with its poisonous gases. Leadership has become toxic through enmeshment in managerialized institutional culture. Church leaders have, in fact, become the agents that perpetuate toxic institutional religion. There is at the same time a

---

16. Fromm, "Malignant Aggression: Necrophilia," *Anatomy*, 455.
17. Romans 7:24.
18. Romans 7:6; 8:2.

Management Is the Message

need to present a whiter than white organizational image. It is the need of all institutions. This is when the church is in most danger of becoming a whitewashed sepulchre; inwardly rotting, outwardly hygienic, and flawless.

Wikipedia describes toxic leadership in this way:

> A person who has responsibility over a group of people or an organization, and who abuses the leader–follower relationship by leaving the group or organization in a worse off condition than when s/he first found them.

The phrase was coined by Marcia Whicker in 1996 and is linked with a number of dysfunctional leadership styles. The basic traits of a toxic leader are generally considered to be either/or insular, intemperate, glib, operationally rigid, callous, inept, discriminatory, corrupt, and aggressive by scholars such as Barbara Kellerman.

These may occur as:

- Oppositional behavior
- Plays corporate power politics
- An overcompetitive attitude to other employees
- Perfectionistic attitudes
- Abuse of the disciplinary system (such as to remove a workplace rival)
- A condescending/glib attitude
- Poor self-control and or restraint
- Physical or psychological bullying
- Procedural inflexibility
- Discriminatory attitudes (sexism, etc.)
- Causes work place division instead of harmony
- Use divide and rule tactics on their employees.

. . . Aggressive narcissism: . . .
- Glibness/superficial charm
- Grandiose sense of self-worth
- Pathological lying
- Cunning/manipulative
- Lack of remorse or guilt . . .

. . . Other traits

Many . . . [also subtly misuse authority] . . . who tend use both micromanagement, over management and management by fear to keep a grip of their authority in the organizational group.

Part 1: Domination Christianity

Micromanagers usually dislike a subordinate making decisions without consulting them, regardless of the level of authority or factual correctness. A toxic leader can be both hypocritical and hypercritical of others, seeking the illusion of corporate and moral virtue to hide their own workplace vices. Hypocrisy involves the deception of others and is thus a form of lying... They can also be both frightening and psychologically stressful to work with.

The US Army defines toxic leaders as commanders who put their own needs first, micro-manage subordinates, behave in a mean-spirited manner or display poor decision-making. A study for the Center for Army Leadership found that toxic leaders work to promote themselves at the expense of their subordinates, and usually do so without considering long-term ramifications to their subordinates, their unit, and the Army profession.

The tools of a toxic leader:

- Workload: The setting up to fail procedure is in particular a well-established workplace bullying tactic that a toxic leader can use against his rivals and subordinates.
- Corporate control systems: They could use the processes in place to monitor what is going on. Disciplinary systems could be abused to aid their power culture.
- Organizational structures: They could abuse the hierarchies, personal relationships and the way that work flows through the business.
- Corporate power structures: The toxic leader controls who, if anybody, makes the decisions and how widely spread power is.
- Symbols of personal authority : These may include the right to parking spaces and executive washrooms or access to supplies and uniforms.
- Workplace rituals and routines: Management meetings, board reports, disciplinary hearing, performance assays and so on may become more habitual than necessary.

Inevitably the victim's workplace performance, self-esteem and self-confidence will decline as employee(s) stress inclines. Heavy running costs and a high staff turnover/overtime rate are often also associated with employee related results of a toxic leader.[19]

Pope Francis has identified "clerical narcissism" as the fundamental illness that the church needs to address. He views it as a contagious spiritual

---

19. *en.wikipedia.org/wiki/Toxic_leader.*

sickness that comes from a self-obsessed clericalism and passes from clergy to laity. "We priests tend to clericalize the laity. We do not realise it but it is as if we infect them with our own disease. And the laity—not all, but many—ask us on their knees to clericalize them."[20] It was the apostle Paul that exclaimed, "Who will deliver me from this body of death?"[21] He recognized that the answer to his prayer for deliverance was: Jesus Christ. Following his way of life in companionship and empowerment brings deliverance from the domination systems of corporate religion, state and business. Paul referred to it as "zoe" in the New Testament epistles and it is characterized by G-d's nature of reciprocity and mutuality. It is a G-d Way of Life in connection with the genetic code of YHWH present in all creation. This includes our humanity made in G-d's image.

CHRISTIAN LEADER: GIVE UP FOLLOWING JESUS

Zoe Life cannot be expressed through toxic leadership that has fetishized institutional and hierarchical management, which oppresses and depresses those who work in it. Burnout and stress statistics for clergy of mainline institutions make for grim reading. The church only mirrors the state and business sectors. Toxic leadership is over-competitive, over-controlling, deeply insecure, punitive, morbidly jealous, nasty, and narcissistic. Not all leaders give way to the culture of narcissism that bureaucratic managerialism perpetuates. Some ask with sincerity, "Why do I feel like being a Christian leader means I have to stop following Jesus?" It is something all Christian leaders will have felt. There is something about the way Christian leadership is construed in modernity that is actually at odds with following the Way of Christ. It can end up feeling like a betrayal of the values initially embraced. Hard questions should be asked about this incongruence. Leadership as it is currently construed demands using the mechanisms of church bureaucracy to manufacture consent regarding credal or institutional conformity. To do this may require having to coerce, connive, bully, deceive, manipulate, and destroy others in order to get the job done. The goal is to get everyone to do what you say. Using manipulative means may be successful in the short-term but it destroys the example of Christ and wrecks collegiality. What passes for Christian leadership has been reduced

---

20. National Catholic Register, November 3, 2013.
21. Romans 7:24.

to management with some religious language thrown in to give it a link with tradition or scripture.

The medium is the message. The Gospel is communicated through who we are and what we practice. Management is also a practice. It is one that undermines a living faith of vulnerability, honesty, mercy, and openness. It is impossible to be open or vulnerable if seeking to manage or enforce a party line. The Gospel is about how we actually embody Christ in our communities and neighborhoods—G-d is made flesh through people. If we treat one another like cogs in a religious corporate machine that is what is communicated. Language is at the very heart of the way we communicate our understanding. Corporate management-speak is dominating, depersonalizing, and degrading to people made in G-d's image.

The Presbyterian prophet A. W. Tozer was right when he spoke of "unlovely Christianity." He prayed "that God would break it all down and start over."[22] Tozer recognized that modern Christianity had lost its vitality, warmth, and beauty. It had become cold, safe, bland, vain, gaudy, saccharine, hygienic, and necrophilic. Management and mission have misshaped the Christianity of institution into a fork-tongued, sugar-coated religion. In his poem *Dolor*, Roethke aptly describes such institutional cancer: "And I have seen dust from the walls of institutions, / Finer than flour, alive, more dangerous than silica."

Jesus had this to say about the game of institutional religion: "Are you tired? Worn out? Burned out on religion? Come to me. Get away with me and you'll recover your life. I'll show you how to take a real rest. Walk with me and work with me—watch how I do it. Learn the unforced rhythms of grace. I won't lay anything heavy or ill-fitting on you. Keep company with me and you'll learn to live freely and lightly."[23]

KISSING THE CORPORATE MISSION GOD'S FEET

Mainline Christianity has usurped Christ by putting mission first and utilizing a management-centered church to deliver its message. The mission-shaped church initiative has been introduced into mainline Christianity with a more healthy emphasis on communities. However, is it a potent enough solution? It is open to the continuing abuse of being co-opted by denominational bureaucratic systems and their minders. The whole notion

22. Tozer, "The Man Who Met God in the Fire."
23. Matthew 11:28–30.

Management Is the Message

of mission must also be questioned. Whatever the motives of the mission-shaped church it still carries within its language and practices the seeds of modernism and social dominance. It has inherited these from Christianity's mission-misshaped past. Management and mission serve the basic human drive to subdue. Yet the primary focus of the Gospel is not mission but reconciliation. To put mission before reconciliation is like prioritizing the company mechanisms to deliver a product before the needs of the people it serves. When that happens people get what the company wants them to get in the way the company dictates. Service to customers becomes secondary. The needs of the people are usurped by the needs of the company. When the church gets its priorities mixed up what is communicated is a Gospel of mission and managerial control. The Gospel of peace through reconciliation is made impotent.

The language and ideology of mission perpetuates polarization in society. Increasing fragmentation occurs as the gospel of mission meets secular humanism, Islam or other competing ideologies. The mission-shaped church is, in this way, a dim reflection of modernist cold war politics. This is what has shaped Western culture in our recent history and has filtered into the church. The one way ideologies of modernity created a mutual stand-off in the Cold War era, and nation states of opaque intransigence. It did not create mutual reconciliation or genuine partnership. Whatever difficulties postmodernity has created it has successfully broken a myopic obsession with ideology. This is because it acknowledges that there are many ways and not just one way. Through beginning to recognize our integral journeys the fragmentation produced by postmodernity can now also be healed. The contribution of the many to the whole can, in fact, become a fertile neotribal way of life.

THE MISSION-MISSHAPED CHURCH

Mission has taken on a new emphasis in the Western church. The mission mindset is galvanized by the pragmatic desire to do something urgent in the face of a fragmenting Western civilization. Tragically, to put mission before reconciliation is to put the cart before the horse. Jesus is a way of life and not a manager of mission. The way provides the ability for someone to journey. A modern mission agenda sets up an imperative to subdue through technical mastery. However, what really matters is the journey itself and the wholeness it brings. The goal or destination is not central.

Part 1: Domination Christianity

Postmodernity and the Gospel overlap at the point where they emphasize that the journey is in fact the destination. Mission prioritizes a need to promote the denomination and perpetuate its structure in a bid for its own survival. Yet, to seek reconciliation through community is to meet my own need by also meeting the needs of others. It is not seeking people as human and financial capital to support failing religious infrastructures.

In conclusion I quote the wisdom of Dallas Willard, a Southern Baptist and Professor of Philosophy at the University of Southern California:

> If we put mission first, history teaches us that we become entangled in our own lack of love and understanding and go down in flames. Although the mission may hold up because we got in a position to raise enough funds to keep us going for a few generations, the heart of it is gone when we don't come together around love of one another. 'Love one another as I have loved you and by this all men will know you are my disciples' . I think that's central . . . if we did that we wouldn't have to think about mission."[24]

---

24. Willard, "New Testament Theology of The Church," Renovare International Conference, Colorado, USA, 2005.

2

The Leadership Deception

> "The merger between Christianity and worldly power would long survive the Roman Empire; it's the basic foundation of the Western world."
>
> —Andrew Marr[1]

> "I am a nobody."
>
> —The Apostle Paul[2]

A PYRAMID OF POWER OR A CIRCLE OF TRUST?

"The most effective way to restrict democracy is to transfer decision-making from the public arena to unaccountable institutions: kings and princes, priestly castes, modern corporations."[3] Noam Chomsky. Institu-

---

1. Marr, "The Word and the Sword–History of the World."
2. 2 Corinthians 12:11.
3. Chomsky, "Domestic Constituencies."

tional church practices and structures send the message loud and clear that leadership is the domain of the specialized few. It is the prerogative of the leadership class who have earned the right to rule. Yet this precedent devastatingly undermines the cornucopia of gifts inherent within the body of Christ. Hierarchical managerialism in churches creates a pyramid of power that fundamentally undermines trust. Hierarchical managerialism and genuine community cannot co-exist. There is either a pyramid of power or a circle of trust. Hierarchy never creates the conditions necessary to express the ethos of the open table that is the central practice of Jesus.

Bureaucratic administration means domination through knowledge. The domination game in Protestant and Catholic managerialized churches breeds power games, egocentricity, suspicion, deception, insincerity, and betrayal. In the practice of corporate management mainline churches have tragically created a culture that is in opposition to the ethos of Christ. His vision for community and society was one of companionship and empowerment. Bureaucratic and hierarchical management fundamentally distort and destroy open and honest voluntary mutual submission in relationships. Corporatism in church, state, and business destroys the natural human social fabric of life and replaces it with the values of the automaton. In such a context it becomes dangerous to be open and vulnerable with neighbor or colleague. People in bureaucratic structures become misshaped by their heavily prescribed roles. Self-expression is censured for fear of rocking the corporate boat. The manager reserves the right to tell others what to do. When necessary, they exercise total power to veto contributions and excommunicate for non-cooperation. Management can ultimately sack others for non-cooperation with the demands of the hierarchy. That does not sound much like the open table of Jesus.

Should the church really be characterized by the management practices of a decadent capitalism? The need for management and hierarchy is in fact the ultimate statement of mistrust. The message of Christ is surely freedom from slavery: capitalist, communist, or Christian. An uneasy and competitive culture of suspicion is the inevitable consequence of the distance that managerial methods create. It produces an ultra competitive culture. Those who are the most insecure and needy of status make sure they get to the top at any cost. That means manipulation and betrayal of primary relationships. Others become stepping stones in an ego-fueled game. They cease to be brothers and sisters, fathers and mothers in the faith. This problem is created by the structure itself. It is the hierarchical and bureaucratic design of institutions that energizes the machine and its automaton disciples. Christianity's need to dominate through words, doctrine, and management is directly attributable to its belief in hierarchical and managerial leadership. Where there is belief in dominance through hierarchy that is exactly what will be produced. Christianity's authority problem is therefore structural. It practices a hierarchical form of management that undermines mutual responsibility. Seth Godin aptly names its effect when he writes: "The skeptical among us look at the idea of leadership and we hesitate. We hesitate because it feels like something we need to be ordained to do."[4]

MANAGING TO BE FACELESS

Managerialism creates little tyrants of ordinary women and men. Give people a little bit of power and what is produced is guilt and the need to play the managerial game. It becomes vital for survival in the institution to be seen to succeed at getting others to obey. This is done in order to please those in the hierarchy. Psychological and emotional pressures increase on religious managers as demands for outputs and targets are set. These are aligned and maintained in meeting after meeting *ad nauseam*. This is what passes for leadership. At its worst it is the feeding ground for those engaged in an ugly, nasty, and often abusive game of pseudo-spiritual one-upmanship. It is made possible through a belief in the necessity of regulation, control and managerial manipulation of so-called human resources. Mainline managerialized churches, regardless of their religious language and sentiments, are no exception.

In such institutions leaders cannot afford to be transparent. Salaried job roles in institutions require playing poker face in heavily prescribed roles. Emotional transparency and honesty is frowned upon as weakening the party line. Religious institutions must remain flawless in the eyes of the public in order to foster and maintain credibility. The game is covering up and saving face. Therefore, the machine of bureaucracy, with its precision and predictability, is highly valued. Institutions honor it because it enables them to maintain a respectable image and status. Institutional power is preserved by maintaining an illusion of perfection in order to exercise authority based on pseudo morality. Institutions then exist not for the common good but for their own preservation. Yet it is the nature of human beings

---

4. Godin, *Tribes*, 19.

that they are not whiter than white. They can never live up to the false image of perfection that the religious machine demands.

The preservation of flawless perfection becomes an obsessive institutional need. Yet it is hideously unnatural. When human darkness is not owned or acknowledged it begins to masquerade as light. Christ said, with penetrating insight, "When your eye is healthy your whole body is full of light, but when it is bad, your body is full of darkness. Therefore be careful lest the light in you be darkness."[5] It is no accident that in totalitarian regimes charismatic leaders used white marble to express their supposed purity and superiority. It was Mussolini who built The Stadium of the Marbles—a colonnade of sixty monumental, perfectly white, marble statues—to express the "purity" of his fascist regime. They were intended to symbolize a united Italy under a fascist state of strong totalitarian leadership, and the eradication of an imagined racial impurity. Ironically, it is a whiteness of fear, racism, and tyranny. It echoes the white Greek and Roman sculpture of antiquity. It is an idolization of perfection; a fatal attraction. Its legacy is the seductive addiction to perfection that torments the psyches of everyone born into Western civilization. Robert Francis saw through the illusion when he wrote:

> I follow Plato only with my mind
> Pure beauty strikes me as a little thin
> A little cold, however beautiful.[6]

Upon closer inspection Mussolini's pure white marble colonnades are not really white in any case. They are a grainy black and white. There is a crack in everything, that's how the light gets in. The unrealistic machine-like demand for human perfectibility in institutions of church, state, and business mirrors a fundamentally Greek and Enlightenment aspiration. It has nothing to do with the wholeness and integration found through the Way of Christ. Its enthronement creates a dark shadow in all institutions, including the church. People are brainwashed by its code of efficiency and effectiveness, and conditioned by the system itself to love its false promise of perfection. It is an addiction to an empty hope for immortality and problem-free survival. These illusions are offered only on the basis that domination and strong leadership will secure the elusive state of invulnerability and perfectibility.

5. Luke 11, 33–36.
6. Francis, *Collected Poems*, 155.

Hierarchical and managerial roles also engender sloth. They can be used to avoid vulnerability and potential pain in relationships by relating only through the protective grid of a role, a title, or a job description. The pretense of the role cancels out the power of the person and the personal. Religious roles enshrine pretense. When priests and pastors are unable to express their pain and frustration their lives become overshadowed and hardened. They cease to be real and become idealized projections. A confusing myopia sets in. The need for flawless perfection by the religious machine creates a whitewash. Underneath are real people who are suffocating because they cannot be transparent. Honesty in the institutional environment is an impossibility. Maintaining an image and withholding information is power and currency. Subtle forms of organizational power abuse become automatic, endemic, and justified for survival.

The most glaring examples of institutional failure are the sex abuse scandals of Catholicism. Outwardly, in the institution there is tight managerial and doctrinal control and regulation. Inwardly, in the priest there is deception and betrayal. Protestantism is no better. In its managerial prison it has created a culture of opaque pretense and hypocrisy. There are significant levels of clergy stress, depression, and use of anti-depressants. A 2006 study of Ontario clergy in six Protestant denominations found that the majority felt isolated, stressed out, and spiritually spent. It found a Christian ministry "in crisis" with 77 percent of pastors saying they felt more like a CEO than a spiritual leader. Many clergy could not identify a close friend in the church or the community. Competition among clergy strained relationships. Declining church attendance forced ministers to focus more on the survival of their congregations and denominations than on providing spiritual leadership. Similar scenarios are reflected in reports of clergy stress and burnout throughout Europe. Ministers are told to get it together, diet, pray more, get more personal recreation time, and do less. No one seems to want to acknowledge that the problem is structural. It is related to the ways in which religious institutions organize and prioritize. This also points to some fundamental ethical issues concerning sustainability in the way religious institutions abuse their human resources. Ironically, this is such an inhuman term.

Clergy stress hides a pervasive dis-ease with institutional job roles and bureaucratic expectations. It highlights grossly unrealistic expectations and a resulting pseudo martyr complex. This is the effect of living in the goldfish bowl of what passes for ministry. In the Protestantism of

Part 1: Domination Christianity

Anglicans, Methodists, Baptists, and house church movements the same managerial attempts at doctrinal and behavioral control are at work. The results are hidden and suppressed feelings. Such organizational idolatry is a long way from the companionship of empowerment. The spirit of Catholic and Protestant religious institutions has become completely contrary to the spirit of the Gospel. What now passes for Christianity is an empty shell of the vigor and life of the companionship of empowerment. It has become a religious form of institutional slavery and ceased to be a place of belonging and freedom. Unscriptural and unwise ideas of leadership and authority are at the root of this deception and its propagation.

ROMAN HIERARCHY: CATHOLIC DOMINATION

A model of hierarchical domination has hijacked leadership formation in the Catholic Church. It was absorbed into the church from the culture extant in the Roman Empire. Wikipedia outlines the enduring impact of Rome upon Western civilization, which illustrates its emphasis on hierarchical structures of government. This culture profoundly altered the egalitarian ethos of the nascent communities of G-d only a few centuries after their inception:

> If the traditional date for the founding of Rome is accepted as fact, the Roman state can be said to have lasted in some form from 753 BC to the fall in 1461 of the Empire of Trebizond, a successor state and fragment of the Byzantine Empire which escaped conquest by the Ottomans in 1453, for a total of 2,214 years. The Roman impact on Western and Eastern civilizations lives on. In time most of the Roman achievements were duplicated by later civilizations. In the West the term Roman acquired a new meaning in connection with the church and the Pope of Rome. The Greek form *Romaioi* remained attached to the Greek-speaking Christian population of the Eastern Roman Empire and is still used by Greeks in addition to their common appellation. The Roman Empire also contributed its form of government, which influences various constitutions including those of most European countries and many former European colonies. In the United States, for example, the framers of the United States Constitution remarked, in creating the Presidency, that they wanted to inaugurate an Augustan Age.
> In the third century, the Empire underwent a crisis that threatened its existence, but was reunified and stabilized under the emperors Aurelian and Diocletian. Christians rose to power

in the fourth century, during which time a system of dual rule was developed in the Latin West and Greek East. After the collapse of central government in the West in the fifth century, the eastern half continued as what would later be known as the Byzantine Empire. Because of the Empire's vast extent and long endurance, the institutions and culture of Rome had a profound and lasting influence on the development of language, religion, architecture, philosophy, law, and forms of government in the territory it governed, particularly Europe, and by means of European expansionism throughout the modern world. Roman society was hierarchical, with slaves (*servi*) at the bottom, freedmen (*liberti*) above them, and freeborn citizens (*cives*) at the top. Free citizens were also divided by class.[7]

Andrew Marr also highlights the impact of Romanization on the nascent communities of G-d. The cunning snake of Empire swallowed them whole. "Constantine was the first person to make Christianity a fighting religion. Before that . . . Christians . . . were pacifists. Now the cross . . . became a sword. The Roman response to spiritual revolt was in the end so Roman; pragmatic, shrewd. They reached out and they assimilated even this revolutionary cult and they made it Roman. The merger between Christianity and worldly power would long survive the Roman Empire; it's the basic foundation of the Western world."[8] In time, and through changing political circumstances, the Roman Church began to reflect the strongly hierarchical practices of Rome. It set up a leadership structure based upon a Roman, and therefore hierarchical, interpretation of bishops, priests, and deacons.

BISHOPS: NOT THE FOCUS OF UNITY

In the early communities of G-d bishops were not regarded as the focus of church unity. This was a Roman invention. Unity was not maintained through everyone submitting to a doctrinal creed or to leadership but through people freely submitting to one another out of love in community. Ignatius is the earliest known writer to demand loyalty to just one bishop in each city (diocese). In his plan bishops are assisted by presbyters and, possibly also, elders and deacons. In contrast, earlier writings only mention

---

7. en.wikipedia.org/wiki/Roman_Empire.
8. Marr, "The Word and the Sword–History of the World."

Part 1: Domination Christianity

either bishops or presbyters and describe more than one bishop or presbyter per congregation, as in Philippians 1:1. Before Ignatius the churches were a loose confederacy of house churches, each having several bishops in one congregation. Bishops, presbyters, and deacons are evident in the early Christian communities described in the New Testament. Yet a Roman and hierarchical interpretation of these gifts fundamentally destroys the ethos of common partnership (*koinonia*) that was pervasive in their life together. It was a way of life in mutuality and reciprocity and not a way of death bound by hierarchy.

An egalitarian ethos characterized the Way of Christ and the communities of G-d in the New Testament. *Koinonos* in classical Greek means a companion, a partner, or a joint owner. It can imply an association, common effort, or a partnership in common. This is the common ground by which the two parties are joined that creates a fellowship or partnership. In the New Testament, James, John, and Simon are called partners or *koinonia*.[9] Their joint participation was in a shared fishing business. The ethos of the way was unique in its practice of voluntary mutual submission. The gifts of bishops, priests and deacons therefore cannot be hierarchical. To practice them in a bureaucratized manner is to completely distort and to destroy their true nature. The Jesus way of companionship and empowerment was characterized by strongly egalitarian and non-hierarchical practices. They contrasted starkly with a hierarchical Roman culture of domination and coercion. Yet the egalitarian communities of G-d were shrewdly co-opted into this domination system. In the process, what was once egalitarian became hierarchical, and the essential nature of the Gospel and the Way of Christ was lost.

The mainline Catholic and Protestant Churches still practice this shrewd assimilation today. It is occurring with mission-shaped church initiatives. The companionship of empowerment is tamed and contained by bureaucratic function and demand. Institutional churches cannot see, however, that the seeds of their demise are in the structures of bureaucratic hierarchy. They cannot let go of this structural power. Even if it is conceded that it was a good idea to make one bishop the focus of unity in hierarchical Rome, times change. What the church needs now are structures that will serve it best in a postmodern democracy where freedom of religious expression and belief is taken for granted. In contemporary society, as Seth

---

9. Luke 5:10.

Godin has noted, "If the tribe doesn't like the king, they're now free to leave."[10]

A Postmodern St Francis?

St Francis' submission to the hierarchical thirteenth century Roman Catholic Church of his day is often cited as a model for submission to the institutional church in our day. It is, however, essential to distinguish the differences between the structures of domination in St Francis' lifetime and our own. Cooperation with the domination Christianity of thirteenth century Europe was essential for survival. Hierarchy in church and state was at its zenith and was the accepted political and religious norm. Postmodern democracies are entirely different. The church is not all powerful and is largely divorced from state governance. In the UK only about 6 percent of the population are part of the Catholic and Protestant Churches combined. In the postmodern democratic states of the West freedom of choice in religion is the norm. In such a context there is far less need for new movements to comply with the demands of hierarchical institutions in the way St. Francis did. They are no longer socially and spiritually functional for the 93 percent majority of the UK population.

It is an interesting fact that Buddhism, which is a close spiritual neighbor to Franciscanism, is thriving in the West. This is by the choice of ordinary people of all faiths and none. It is without connection to religious institutions. People have choice in postmodern Western democracies in a way that thirteenth century Europeans could not have imagined. In our context, clerical hierarchy is largely socially impotent and does not meet the spiritual needs of the 93 percent majority. In the thirteenth century it was necessary to work within the existing hierarchical structure for survival. For twenty-first century faith movements attempting to work with/in a marginalized and failing institution may be an unnecessary burden. In fact, it may prevent meaningful connection with the majority of the population, who are formed by non-hierarchical values.

---

10. Godin, *Tribes*, 12.

Part 1: Domination Christianity

BUREAUCRACY: PROTESTANT DOMINATION

Protestant reform ended up creating a different structure of domination to Roman Catholicism. The Protestant variety was not based on the authority of the church and its priests. It utilized the authority of the Bible, pastors and church rules. The game remained the same. Christian social dominance continued in Protestant form. Yet it also split, divided, and polarized institutions, societies and nations. As Protestantism progressed it gave rise to capitalism and, ironically, the increasing secularization of society. Wikipedia outlines Max Weber's analysis of Protestantism with particular reference to its use of bureaucracy as its primary method of ordering and control of society:

> In the "Protestant Ethic and the Spirit of Capitalism" Weber argued that the redefinition of the connection between work and piety in Protestantism and especially in ascetic Protestant denominations, particularly Calvinism, shifted human effort toward rational efforts aimed at achieving economic gain. In Protestant religion, Christian piety toward God was expressed through one's secular vocation; secularization of calling. The rational roots of this doctrine, he argued, soon grew incompatible with and larger than the religious and so the latter were eventually discarded.

Weber continued his investigation into this matter in later works, notably in his studies on bureaucracy and on the classification of legitimate authority into three types—legal-rational, traditional and charismatic—of which the legitimate (or rational) is the dominant one in the modern world. In these works Weber described what he saw as society's movement toward rationalization. Similarly, rationalization could be seen in the economy, with the development of highly rational and calculating capitalism. Weber also saw rationalization as one of the main factors setting the European West apart from the rest of the world. Rationalization relied on deep changes in ethics, religion, psychology and culture; changes that first took place in the Western civilization.

What Weber depicted was not only the secularization of Western culture, but also and especially the development of modern societies from the viewpoint of rationalization. The new structures of society were marked by the differentiation of the two functionally intermeshing systems that had taken shape around the organizational cores of the capitalist enterprise and the bureaucratic state apparatus. Weber understood this process as the institutionalization of purposive-rational economic and administrative action.

To the degree that everyday life was affected by this cultural and societal rationalization, traditional forms of life—which in the early modern period were differentiated primarily according to one's trade—were dissolved.[11]

Features of rationalization include increasing knowledge, growing impersonality and enhanced control of social and material life. Weber was ambivalent toward rationalization; while admitting it was responsible for many advances, in particular, freeing humans from traditional, restrictive and illogical social guidelines, he also criticized it for dehumanizing individuals as "cogs in the machine" and curtailing their freedom, trapping them in the bureaucratic iron cage of rationality and bureaucracy. Related to rationalization is the process of disenchantment, in which the world is becoming more explained and less mystical, moving from polytheistic religions to monotheistic ones and finally to the Godless science of modernity. Those processes affect all of society, removing "sublime values . . . from public life"[12] and making art less creative.

In a dystopian critique of rationalization, Weber notes that modern society is a product of an individualistic drive of the Reformation, yet at the same time, the society created in this process is less and less welcoming of individualism.

"How is it at all possible to salvage any remnants of 'individual' freedom of movement in any sense given this all-powerful trend?" Max Weber.[13]

> Christian religious devotion had historically been accompanied by rejection of mundane affairs, including economic pursuit. Weber showed that certain types of Protestantism—notably Calvinism—were supportive of rational pursuit of economic gain and worldly activities dedicated to it, seeing them as endowed with moral and spiritual significance. Weber argued that there were many reasons to look for the origins of modern capitalism in the religious ideas of the Reformation. In particular, the Protestant ethic (or more specifically, Calvinist ethic) motivated the believers to work hard, be successful in business and reinvest their profits in further development rather than frivolous pleasures. The notion of calling meant that each individual had to take action in order to be saved; just being a member of the church was not enough. Predestination

---

11. Habermas, "Modernity's Consciousness of Time, 1985," *The Philosophical Discourse*.

12. Allan, *Explorations*.

13. Kim, *Max Weber's Politics*.

also reduced antagonizing over economic inequality and further, it meant that a material wealth could be taken as a sign of salvation in the afterlife. The believers thus justified pursuit of profit with religion, as instead of being fuelled by morally suspect greed or ambition, their actions were motivated by a highly moral and respected philosophy. This Weber called the "spirit of capitalism": it was the Protestant religious ideology that was behind—and inevitably led to—the capitalist economic system.[14]

The recent economic collapse has highlighted the failure of the gods of capitalism and revealed their truly demonic dimensions. It is a form of economic slavery, which has been used to sanctify greed and perpetuate gross inequality and injustice. This creates a cycle of dissent and revolution as people sever the social contract between workers and managers when social conditions become intolerable. What Weber described as the iron cage of bureaucracy is pervasive in the West. It makes daily life miserable with administrative and financial targets and procedures. Individual freedoms have suffered greatly under the guise of the free market. The common land and common life of people have been compartmentalized, commodified, and given a price tag. Basic human rights such as water, land, and time have been costed out. Under Protestant capitalism and consumerism our G-d-given breathtaking human vista has been reduced to a small privatized screen and an atomized existence. Life is so excessively managed and controlled as to render it empty of meaning. In aping the management practices extant within capitalist culture the mainline Protestant churches are promoting a way of life that destroys meaning and identity.

PROTESTANT WORD POWER: THE LETTER KILLS

As Protestants became enamored with the printed word, G-d came to be understood primarily as a word. Therefore G-d could be found only through reading the Bible. The words of the Bible became a way to order everyday life and to exercise control and establish authority. Protestant culture, however, distorted the teaching of the Bible, which states that "the Word" is the living Christ[15] and is present in all Creation: "without Him was not anything made that has been made."[16] In Protestantism today "the Bible

---

14. *en.wikipedia.org/wiki/Max_Weber.*
15. John 1:1.
16. John 1:3.

says" remains a sacrosanct and in-house code word for the propagation of authority on the spurious basis of sound doctrine or orthodoxy. Jesus, and the early church that followed him, had no such practice. Orthopraxy was what mattered. It was what you did and not what you believed that saved you.

This distortion of what the Bible says about the Word of G-d made it possible to talk about the way the world should be and to demand that daily life conform to words in a book. However, the words alone are never the experience. The map is never the territory. Looking at a map of a mountain range is not the same as being in a blizzard on the mountain. This can be a great source of deception in Protestant religion because it is mediated primarily through words and print. People learn about G-d but don't learn to experience the G-d they read about. Even when they do their experience is then filtered and interpreted through pastors. Such pastors are often quarreling, accusational, and schismatic in defense of their own doctrinal positions. In Protestantism it is not congregations who interpret the Bible but their pastors.

Open and free conversation about the words of the Bible and their meanings is not a Protestant practice. Reality is experienced as monotone and not multi-voiced. In Protestant meetings there is no right of reply. Authority is in the Bible, but only as interpreted through the pastors. Yet the pastors disagree *ad nauseam*. Such a system has an in-built fragmentation and atomization. Protestants and their communities therefore become fragmented, accusational, and self-righteous. An emphasis on the Word as the Bible and on word as power has produced rival and sectarian churches. These judge and attack one another with their interpretations. Pastors are treated like demigods. "I am for Paul, I am for Apollos" is pervasive in the Protestant way of life. Protestantism produced a rivalrous, schismatic, and sectarian religious celebrity culture. Today, there are over 44,000 Protestant churches. This means there are 44,000 different interpretations of the Bible and of church government. They all believe they are one hundred percent right. They believe it so strongly they have formed their own church and are convinced their way is the only true interpretation. There is no tragedy in there being 44,000 different types of church. There is great tragedy in their belief that they are all one hundred percent doctrinally right.

Part 1: Domination Christianity

BUSINESS IS BUSINESS: PROTESTANT LEADERSHIP

Wikipedia notes that, "Protestant bureaucracy in time gave rise to the development of scientific management. This redefined and reshaped notions of leadership in Protestant cultures." Again, Wikipedia helpfully outlines its nature and development.

> The core ideas of scientific management were developed by Taylor in the 1880s and 1890s, and were first published in his monographs *A Piece Rate System* (1895), *Shop Management* (1903) and *The Principles of Scientific Management* (1911). While working as a lathe operator and foreman at Midvale Steel, Taylor noticed the natural differences in productivity between workers, which were driven by various causes, including differences in talent, intelligence, or motivations. He was one of the first people to try to apply science to this application, that is, understanding why and how these differences existed and how best practices could be analyzed and synthesized, then propagated to the other workers via standardization of process steps. He believed that decisions based upon tradition and rules of thumb should be replaced by precise procedures developed after careful study of an individual at work, including via time and motion studies, which would tend to discover or synthesize the "one best way" to do any given task. The goal and promise was both an increase in productivity and reduction of effort.

Scientific management's application was contingent on a high level of managerial control over employee work practices. This necessitated a higher ratio of managerial workers to laborers than previous management methods. The great difficulty in accurately differentiating any such intelligent, detail oriented management from mere misguided micromanagement also caused interpersonal friction between workers and managers, and social tensions between the blue collar and white collar classes.

Scientific management was one of the first attempts to systematically treat management and process improvement as a scientific problem. It was probably the first to do so in a bottom-up way, which is a concept that remains useful even today, in concert with other concepts. Two corollaries of this primacy are that (1) scientific management became famous and (2) it was merely the first iteration of a long-developing way of thinking, and many iterations have come since. Nevertheless, common elements unite them. With the advancement of statistical methods, quality assurance and quality control could begin in the 1920s and 1930s. During the 1940s and

1950s, the body of knowledge for doing scientific management evolved into operations management, operations research, and management cybernetics. In the 1980s total quality management became widely popular, and in the 1990s re-engineering went from a simple word to a mystique (a kind of evolution that, unfortunately, draws bad managers to jump on the bandwagon without understanding what the bandwagon is). Today's Six Sigma and lean manufacturing could be seen as new kinds of scientific management, although their evolutionary distance from the original is so great that the comparison might be misleading. In particular, Shigeo Shingo, one of the originators of the Toyota Production System, believed that this system and Japanese management culture in general should be seen as a kind of scientific management.

> Peter Drucker saw Frederick Taylor as the creator of knowledge management, because the aim of scientific management was to produce knowledge about how to improve work processes. Although the typical application of scientific management was manufacturing, Taylor himself advocated scientific management for all sorts of work, including the management of universities and government. For example, Taylor believed scientific management could be extended to "the work of our salesmen." Shortly after his death, his acolyte Harlow S. Person began to lecture corporate audiences on the possibility of using Taylorism for "sales engineering." Person was talking about engineering the processes that salespeople use—not about sales engineering in the way that we use that term today. This was a watershed insight in the history of corporate marketing. Today's militaries employ all of the major goals and tactics of scientific management, if not under that name. Of the key points, all but wage incentives for increased output are used by modern military organizations. Wage incentives rather appear in the form of skill bonuses for enlistments.[17]

Scientific management is a product of Protestant culture rather than Protestant churches. Yet it has significantly influenced attitudes toward management everywhere in Protestant culture—including the church. For instance, American megachurches and other religious corporations have adopted the CEO model wholesale. Management skills are highly prized by all major Protestant denominations. It is no accident, however, that megachurches have produced a series of embezzlement scandals and sexual failures. Paul Yonngi Cho and Ted Haggard are two of the most prominent

---

17. en.wikipedia.org/wiki/Scientific_management.

examples of high external success yet deep moral failure and there is a catalog of other casualties. They have been destroyed and destroyed others in this Protestant culture of leadership, which has promoted outward success, numbers, and results rather than inner integrity.

PROTESTANT CHURCH LEADERSHIP TODAY

Interpretations and definitions of Christian leadership in Protestantism are influenced by an unconscious and automatic mental picture of hierarchy. People are not conscious of their beliefs. However, they are the underlying assumptions that are brought to ideas about leadership. These assumptions are shaped and formed by a Protestant legacy that has emphasized the rule of pastors over congregations. This does not reflect the open table of Jesus. Nor does it produce the mutual *koinonia*, or fellowship of the communities of G-d, described in the New Testament. Biblical texts about leadership in mainline Protestant Churches are interpreted through the filter of management. When modern people read Biblical texts about apostles, prophets, evangelists, pastors, teachers, and eldership they do so through their Protestant legacy; a hierarchical and managerial business model.

Anglican/Episcopalian, Methodist, Baptist, house church and other non-conformist denominations all have a list of requirements for leadership. These are their selection criteria for ministers, priests and leaders. Within these criteria are characteristics that are defined primarily by management principles; ability to control the means of religious production for the propagation and maintenance of Christian social dominance in society. The managerial requirement placed upon Christian leaders is the polar opposite of the example of Christ. It is not uncommon to hear those undergoing ordination selection comment that Jesus would never get through it. This is accurate. Jesus did have a completely different value system to mainline Catholic and Protestant churches. Jesus would be turning over tables, as he did with the oppressive religious and political structures of his day.

What mainline Protestant churches prize most in their leaders is an ability to manage their institutions. Property, finance, health and safety, and safeguarding are prioritized. This is because the survival of the religious corporation is at stake. The smooth running of the religious machine is what has become paramount. All other concerns are sacrificed to its promotion. Religious corporations consume human energy, time, devotion, money, blood, sweat, and tears. They demand total worship. Primary relationships are often sacrificed to the demand for effective and efficient management of the religious facade. Job roles dictate behavior and crush the free and open exchange of gifts and talents. It is in this way that the character of the church and its worship has become necrophilic. An inordinate love of the religious machine is killing the love of the human face of G-d in one another.

BABETTE'S OPEN TABLE

A very good insight into the effect of this Protestant form of domination by the word can be found in the film *Babette's Feast*. The film clearly illustrates the culture of life-denying, self-righteousness, and religious one-upmanship that Protestantism created. People were made sin-conscious. They used the Bible to judge others to make themselves feel less guilty. The church authorities no longer condemned them. Yet people condemned each other and used the Bible to do it. Protestantism produced a self-righteousness based on knowledge of the Bible. Its words were then directed toward the alien and the other. They believed in a verbose G-d of one-way speech. At a deeper level, *Babette's Feast* speaks of the numinous character of all life. It is the open table of Babette's feast and her sacrifice that breaks the withering accusational power of Protestant self-righteous words. Babette brings healing and reconciliation as she mirrors the open table practices of Christ.

Babette's meal acts as a catalyst and becomes a womb of grace. Around the open table the stories of those present are reconfigured into wholeness and purpose. As people tell their stories they are empowered to move beyond a self-righteous preoccupation fueled by a myopic use of the Bible. Salvation and wholeness is found in the sacrificial meal Babette gives freely, at great cost to herself. It becomes a meal of reconciliation. Babette has not found a welcome in this Protestant sect. She is not one of the chosen ones. Yet ironically, it is Babette, the secular stranger and worldly outsider, who is the bringer of reconciliation. Notably, she is received with great suspicion. Yet it is Babette who brings grace to this jealous and fragmented Protestant community. The secular outsider is a catalyst of grace in the communities of G-d of today. It is through a fresh encounter with Christ in the secular other that the grace of G-d can be found afresh. Those still in the church must receive their secular gifts of bread and wine to be transformed by the encounter.

Part 1: Domination Christianity

"I AM A NOTHING": AUTHENTIC APOSTOLIC AUTHORITY

What is the leadership deception? It is a belief that the exercise of real authority is possible only through hierarchical management and bureaucracy. This hidden belief has hideously disfigured the expression of G-d's love in the church and in society. This is because G-d's love is only expressed through a genuine invitation to partnership and mutuality. G-d's love does not command people to submit. It is not an invitation to subdue or be subdued. G-d's authority is expressed through an invitation to mutuality and reciprocity. It is this genuine form of authority that has been usurped. The only way forward is the dissolution of bureaucratized and managerialized structures, and the leadership practices that emerge from them. Communities of G-d need to come instead to a truly apostolic place. The authority of the apostle Paul was rooted in his realization that, "I am not in any way inferior to your 'super-apostles,' even if I am nothing."[18] His apostolic authority was created by his encounter with G-d as reciprocal reconciling love.

G-d is love because G-d is authority in equality. Father, Son and Holy Spirit are in voluntary mutual submission with one another in the Trinity. By definition love can only be expressed in relationships of voluntary mutual submission. This mutual submission is also reflected in *koinonia*—the mutual partnership practiced in the early communities of G-d. Without this humility with one another G-d's love is not fully manifested in our social relationships. A good marriage is a potent example of such love. Husband or wife cannot demand obedience to one another through the exercise of hierarchy or management. Such a thought is ridiculous. This is why the apostle Paul advises couples to submit to one another as an expression of their love. It is exactly the same in the church. Obedience is formed by the practice of voluntary submission to one another. This creates love. It is only this kind of love that enables us to obey. What is lacking is not obedience to authority, it is the love that creates such obedience. This kind of loving obedience is never created through hierarchical leadership, bureaucracy, and management. In fact it is voided, nullified and avoided. What is essential for the creation of obedience is to follow the mutual and reciprocal Way of Christ. He promised that, "If you love me you will obey my commandments."[19]

---

18. 2 Cor.12:11.
19. John 14:15.

3

Domination Christianity

"Bureaucratic administration means fundamentally
domination through knowledge."
—Max Weber[1]

"The Party... stands for positive Christianity."
—Point 24 of the Nazi Party plan[2]

THE GRAND INQUISITOR

Management and hierarchical bureaucracy have turned Western Christianity into a religion of domination through knowledge. In *The Grand Inquisitor* Dostoevsky[3] provides us with a story which sheds light

---

1. Roth and Wittich, *Max Weber*, 225.
2. Steigmann-Gall, *The Holy Reich*, 121.
3. Dostoevsky, *The Brothers Karamazov*.

on the way domination Christianity has usurped Christ's authority of mutuality and reciprocity.

In the tale Christ comes back to earth in Seville at the time of the Inquisition. He performs a number of miracles echoing his ministry in the Gospels. The people recognize him and adore him, but Inquisition leaders arrest him and sentence him to be burned to death the next day. The Grand Inquisitor visits him in his cell to tell him that the church no longer needs him. He explains, *ad nauseam*, why his return would interfere with the mission of the church. The Grand Inquisitor frames his denunciation of Jesus around the three tasks Satan set Jesus during his temptation of Christ in the desert: to change stones to bread; to cast himself off the Temple in order to be saved by angels; and to rule over all the world. The Grand Inquisitor accuses Jesus of rejecting these offers in favor of freedom. However, he accuses him of misjudging human nature. He does not believe that the vast majority of humanity can handle the freedom Jesus has given them. He implies that in doing so Christ has excluded the majority of humanity from redemption and doomed it to suffer.

Despite declaring the Inquisitor to be an atheist Ivan, who is telling the story, has the Inquisitor saying that the church follows "the wise spirit, the dread spirit of death and destruction," in other words the Devil, Satan. He says, "We're not with Thee, but with him, and that is our secret! For centuries we have abandoned Thee to follow him." For he, through compulsion, provided the tools to end all human suffering and for humanity to unite under the banner of the church. The multitude then is guided through the church by the few who are strong enough to take on the burden of freedom. The Inquisitor says that, under him, all humanity will live and die happily in ignorance. Though he leads them only to death and destruction they will be happy along the way. The Inquisitor will be a self-martyr, spending his life to keep choice from humanity. He states that, "Anyone who can appease a man's conscience can take his freedom away from him."

The Inquisitor advances his argument by explaining why Christ was wrong to reject each temptation by Satan. Christ should have turned stones into bread, as men will always follow those who will feed them. The Inquisitor recalls how Christ rejected this, saying, "Man cannot live on bread alone," and explains to Christ, "Feed men, and then ask of them virtue! That's what they'll write on the banner they raise against Thee." Casting himself down from the temple to be caught by the angels would cement his godhood in the minds of the people, who would then follow him forever.

Rule over all the kingdoms of the Earth would ensure their salvation, the Grand Inquisitor claims.

The segment ends when Christ, who has been silent throughout, kisses the Inquisitor on his "bloodless, aged lips" instead of answering him. At this, the Inquisitor releases Christ but tells him never to return. Christ, still silent, leaves into "the dark alleys of the city." Not only is the kiss ambiguous but its effect on the Inquisitor is as well. Ivan concludes, "The kiss glows in his heart, but the old man adheres to his idea."

CHRIST: ROMAN DOMINATION KING?

Christianity is hideously disfigured by Roman practices of maintaining dominance through hierarchical authority and leadership. This leadership addiction has perpetuated an ugly parody of the message of Christ throughout history in the form of hierarchical Catholicism and then managerial Protestantism. Protestant or Catholic Christians today automatically interpret kingship as exercising rule through hierarchical and managerial means. The image that most Christians carry is of Christ as a Domination King. It is this image that has given birth to Domination Christianity in its various forms. It has also perpetuated Christian social dominance on the basis of correct doctrine. For Catholics Christ rules through church and priest. For Protestants Christ rules by the letter of the Bible administered by its managerial pastors. Church and scripture are not methods of rule found in the practice of Christ. They are frightening distortions of the companionship of empowerment and the open table of Jesus. He was not interested in the external management of others. He had a far more compelling agenda: the captivation and renovation of our hearts.

Where does the idea that Christ is King come from? The Gospel of Matthew places special emphasis on the King and the gospel of the Kingdom. The term Kingdom of G-d is misleading and will be discussed later, but will be used in the present discussion. The Kingdom of which Matthew speaks is the future millennial kingdom of Israel's King, who is interpreted to be Jesus. His millennial kingdom will be the golden age of the Earth. It will be the crowning dispensation in which he will rule as King of Kings and Lord of Lords. All of history will culminate through Christ in his millennial Kingdom. The notion of Christ as King is derived from Old Testament prophecies concerning the coming Messiah, who would come to bring Peace. Yet the language of kingship is absent from the Gospels, except when used of Christ as King of the Jews. This is far from any acknowledgement of actual political rule. The Old Testament prophecies however, do contain reoccurring themes. The Messiah is presented as a King, yet one who is familiar with sacrifice and suffering. He is presented as a man but also as divine. In the New Testament these prophecies are believed by Christians to be fulfilled in Jesus Christ.

In the Old Testament the Messiah is portrayed as a King and the ancient Rabbis often referred to him as King Messiah. He is the star out of Jacob and the scepter that rises out of Israel in Numbers 24:17. He is the one who sits on David's throne in Isaiah 9:7. He comes with the clouds of heaven to reign over a kingdom where all people, nations, and languages will serve him in Daniel 7:13–14. In his kingdom the nations will no longer lift up the sword against one another in Isaiah 2:4. We are promised that his reign will have no end in Isaiah 9:6–7. Messiah is also interpreted as King in the Gospel of Matthew. Jesus Christ is referred to as the Son of David, the Son of Abraham in Matthew 1:1 and the King of the Jews who wise men seek to worship in Matthew 2:2. He speaks of the kingdom of heaven on forty occasions. He says that the day will come when he will return in the clouds to establish his kingdom on earth in Matthew 26:64. Jesus is asked directly, "Are you the King of the Jews?" to which he replies, "I am" in Matthew 27:11. As he hung on the cross a sign was put over his head that read, "This is Jesus, the King of the Jews."

It is clear from the Gospel accounts that Jesus held no legal, political or bureaucratic authority. Nor is he referred to as king in the Gospels except as a form of mockery. All interpretations of his kingship are derived from applying Old Testament prophecies to him. Jesus does refer to the kingdom of G-d many times. Yet the kingdom he describes is an upside down one where the first are last and people wash each other's feet. He categorically rejects Roman lordship as a method of rule. Christ is therefore painting a picture of a different kind of kingdom. Jesus was a Rabbi of a marginalized tribe in the Roman Empire. He lived a message of freedom from the violent domination of Roman occupation and the burden of pedantic Jewish Law codes. The irony is that the church under Rome became exactly that—a system of domination and law in the shape of hierarchical Roman authority. In Europe, as the centuries rolled on and the winds of change shifted, the Protestant Church gradually adopted the methods of modern bureaucracy. These methods birthed the turgid legal-rational managerialism that currently suffocates our societies. However, these developments in Christian history raise a fundamental question. If Christ does not rule through hierarchy or bureaucracy then how is Christlike authority manifested? How can evil be overcome and humanity saved? How are communities to learn and become whole and holy? What is the Way of Christ to bring truth and justice in society?

A REAL KING: THE COMPANIONSHIP G-D

Jesus did not use the word kingdom to mean rule by domination through kingship, hierarchy, or management. This is our Western understanding that has been shaped by over a thousand years of civilization based on Roman hierarchy. Jesus used kingdom to mean the exercise of power through equality, mutuality, and companionship. Diarmuid O'Murchu helpfully directs us to Douglas-Klotz 1999 and the website www.abwoon.com for a more egalitarian understanding.[4] Jesus used the Aramaic word *malkuta* to express his idea of the kingdom. It carries a strong feminine quality in the way it is used in the Gospels. Kingdom is symbolic of royal power, patriarchy, domination, privilege, exclusion, and hierarchical control. *Malkuta* is symbolic of an egalitarian way of life that is liberating and empowering. It speaks of a quality of leadership that enables others to take the next steps together, rather than in competition. *Malkuta* is win-win. Roman kingship is win or lose. The first speaks of taking our place in the great chain of being. The second of wanting to avoid the necessary humility required in order to belong as part of the human family. *Malkuta* speaks of power with and through each other. It is extended through and with the alien and the stranger. A Roman kingdom always seeks power over the alien outsider and the other.

Government through kingship was the accepted way of exercising rule and power at the time of Jesus. The king was the political and religious representative of G-d on earth. For much of its history Christianity has colluded with kingly power and dominance. It has modeled its rules and norms on those of patriarchy, kingship, and hierarchical leadership. Jesus, however, rejected this conditioning. He practiced a radical alternative characterized by empowerment from the common base upwards, rather than power exerted from the top down on others. This is the way of life described in the Gospel phrase "the kingdom of God." John Dominic

---

4. O'Murchu, Diarmuid. "Christian Life (Essay 2)."

Crossan[5] has more accurately expressed it in the phrase "the Companionship of Empowerment." Diarmuid O'Murchu writes: "That Jesus envisioned faith communities to subsequently embody his vision is beyond question, but something akin to Basic Christian Communities, rather than an institutional church is probably what he had in mind."[6]

This egalitarian way of life honors the understanding contained in the Aramaic used by Jesus. *Malkuta* literally translates as the right to rule. Yet this kind of rule only comes from the base and through the practice of empowerment with and through others. Authority is created through voluntary mutual submission rather than through one person obeying the command of another. There is an underlying subversive connotation, which the use of the feminine word *malkuta* uncovers. The companionship of empowerment radically challenges the competitive individualism so endemic in our time, which is clearly expressed in the management culture of our institutions. Diarmuid O'Murchu writes that:

"Empowerment can be facilitated by a benign patriarchal ruler; empowerment from the top down. But it seems that this mediation of empowerment was not acceptable to Jesus. It had to be empowerment through the process of mutuality. The pyramid had to become a circle. Gospel empowerment was to be circular, mutual, interactive, mobilizing diverse gifts, interpersonal and lateral. It was not to be linear in any sense. Hence the significance of the word 'companionship.'"[7]

MISSION: IN THIS SIGN CONQUER

The Romanized kingship of Christ became the basis for Romanized Christian mission. It demanded incorporation into the Empire rather than offering reconciliation with neighbor. The Emperor Constantine had been told, in a vision of the Cross, "in this sign conquer," and this spirit began to characterize the mission of the church. Mission is a term used in the New Testament to describe the purpose of a journey. It is not used in connection with conversion to a religion. The apostles were certainly sent by G-d with the message of peace through reconciliation. Yet, after Romanization the term mission changes in the way it is used. It became co-opted and Romanized by the politics of Theodosius First and the theology of Augustine

---

5. Borg, *Jesus at 2000*, 22–55.
6. O'Murchu, Diarmuid. "Christian Life (Essay 2)."
7. O'Murchu, *Christianity's Dangerous Memory*, 30.

of Hippo. Mission then carried with it the idea of conquest to bring order and establish peace. It was no longer Christ's invitation to reconciliation in order to establish justice through making peace. Under Rome, mission became about assimilation into a Roman way of life characterized by hierarchy and dominance. When used in the New Testament, mission just means sent and it comes from the Latin *mittere*, used to translate the Greek *apostelein*. It gives us the word apostle, meaning the ones who are sent. Therefore, it is essential to distinguish the word sent from the word mission. G-d sent people as ambassadors of peace in a spirit of companionship. They were not on a Roman mission to convert people and co-opt them into domination Christianity.

MISSION-MISSHAPED HISTORY

The earliest examples of people being sent by G-d as peacemakers into other geographical areas are recorded in the fragments of scriptures that eventually became the New Testament. These include the letters of Paul written in the course of his apostolic journeys in Asia Minor and Greece. His activities were preceded by a geographical spread of the Way from the first followers of Jesus in Jerusalem throughout Syro-Palestine. This is described in the much later Acts of the Apostles. The earliest proclamation and teaching of the Way was active within Judaism. It then spread beyond Judaism and became a contested issue. The apostle Paul was an early proponent of community peacemaking through the formation of Gentile communities of reconciliation. He contextualized the message of the Way for the Greek and Roman cultures. Paul enabled it to reach beyond its Jewish context. The Way grew and there were intermittent periods of persecution. This continued until Rome co-opted and legalized the church as a way to maintain unity in its Empire.

After Romanization mission became a tool of imperial assimilation. Wikipedia describes how mission practices had changed by late antiquity:

> Much missionary activity was carried out by members of religious orders. Monasteries followed disciplines and supported missions, libraries, and practical research, all of which were perceived as works to reduce human misery and suffering, thus enhancing the reputation of God. For example, Nestorian communities evangelized much of North Africa. Cistercians evangelized much of Northern Europe, as well as developing most of European

Part 1: Domination Christianity

agriculture's classic techniques. In the sixteenth century the proselytization of Asia was linked to the Portuguese colonial policy. With the Papal bull Romanus Pontifex the patronage for the propagation of the Christian faith in Asia was given to the Portuguese, who were rewarded with the right of conquest. The Portuguese trade with Asia was profitable and as Jesuits came to India around 1540, the colonial government in Goa supported the mission with incentives for baptized Christians. Later, Jesuits were sent to China and further countries in Asia. With the decline of the Portuguese power other colonial powers and Christian organizations gain influence. After the Reformation, for nearly a hundred years, occupied by their struggle with the Roman Catholic Church, the Protestant churches were not missionary-sending churches. But in the centuries that followed, the Protestant churches began sending missionaries in increasing numbers, spreading the proclamation of the Christian message to previously unreached people.[8]

After Theodosius First, Christian mission was empowered by Roman law and force. In consequence, Christianity's violent history has been a horrific distortion of Christ's Way of reconciliation and empowerment. Rome created a Christianity based on one church and one creed as a means to unite the Roman Empire. The belief of the Christian Church in one G-d became the justification for only having one Empire, which belonged to that one G-d. This became used to justify and implement Christian social dominance. It is founded on the belief that kingship, lordship and military force are necessary to maintain peace. Redemptive violence therefore became the foundation myth of the West. Christian civilization was invented by imperial Rome and is rooted in Roman practices of social dominance. In no way does it reflect the egalitarian and non-violent social vision of Jesus Christ.

CHRIST THE KING: PROTESTANT BUREAUCRAT?

The Grand Inquisitor is clearly describing how Christ was usurped by Catholic desire for social dominance. Yet exactly the same can be said of Protestant social dominance through its use of bureaucratic management. Max Weber states that: "Bureaucratic administration means fundamentally domination through knowledge."[9] The practice of bureaucratized power

---

8. en.wikipedia.org/wiki/Roman_Empire.
9. en.wikipedia.org/wiki/Max_Weber.

Domination Christianity

in Christian religious institutions is domination through knowledge. It is therefore domination Christianity. Weber proposed that Protestantism was one of the major catalysts in giving birth to the rise of capitalism, bureaucracy and the legal-rational nation state. He clearly recognized bureaucracy as the means of Protestant propagation and domination. Even earlier, in fifteenth century France, Cardinal Richelieu laid the foundations of the modern state bureaucratic method. This enforced absolute monarchy by legal-rational means.

In the twenty-first century it is now inconceivable for Westerners to think of rule being exercised without managerial control and the state bureaucratic machinery. Bureaucracy is bound up with the money system that Protestant capitalism created. Administrative rule by a civil service is the accepted norm in most nation states. To the modern mind to think of a king is to hold a picture of rule through militarism, law, dictate, coercion, force, manipulation, persuasion, punishment, and legal-rational and bureaucratic control. In general, Western ideas about kingship derive from observations, memories, and suppositions about monarchy. The British have one of the only surviving monarchies in the world. This inevitably carries with it the memory of a lost Empire. It puts them at a particular disadvantage when trying to imagine what Jesus was talking about when he described the kingdom. The British find it difficult to imagine exactly what kind of kingdom Christ was talking about. The creation and exercise of authority through voluntary mutual submission is inconceivable to a people conditioned by hierarchical dominance. A country that still describes itself as a United Kingdom is fundamentally rooted in ideas of domination that dimly reflect Roman hierarchy. This is also clearly reflected in the bureaucratic structures that persist in the UK state church.

THE STATE: BOUND AND BLINDED IN BUREAUCRACY

A bureaucracy is a group of non-elected officials of a government or organization that implements the rules, laws, ideas, and functions of their institution. Bureaucracies date back to ancient societies across the globe: Mesopotamia, Constitution of the Roman Empire, Government of the Han Dynasty, Ancient Egypt, Inca Government, Aztec Government, Maurya Empire, Umayyad Caliphate, and Songhai Empire. Weberian bureaucracy has its origin in the works by Max Weber (1864–1920), a German sociologist, political economist, and administrative scholar who contributed to the study of bureaucracy and administrative discourse and literature during the late 1800s and early 1900s. Max Weber belongs to the scientific school of thought, which discussed such topics as specialization of job scope, merit system, uniform principles, structure, and hierarchy. "Bureaucratic administration means fundamentally domination through knowledge."[10]

Weber described many ideal types of public administration and government in his magnum opus *Economy and Society* (1922). It was Weber who began the study of bureaucracy and whose works led to the popularization of this term. Many aspects of modern public administration go back to him, and a classic, hierarchically organized civil service of the Continental type is called a Weberian civil service. As the most efficient and rational way of organizing, bureaucratization, for Weber, was the key part of the legal-rational authority and, furthermore, he saw it as the key process in the ongoing rationalization of Western society.

> Weber listed several preconditions for the emergence of bureaucracy. The growth in space and population being administered, the growth in complexity of the administrative tasks being carried out, and the existence of a monetary economy require a more efficient administrative system. Development of communication and transportation technologies makes more efficient administration possible, but also in popular demand, and democratization and rationalization of culture result in demands that the new system treats everybody equally. Weber's ideal bureaucracy is characterized by hierarchical organization, delineated lines of authority in a fixed area of activity, action taken on the basis of, and recorded in, written rules. Bureaucratic officials need expert training, neutral officials implement rules, and career advancement depends on technical qualifications judged by organizations not individuals.

> "The decisive reason for the advance of bureaucratic organization has always been its purely technical superiority over any other form of organization." While recognizing bureaucracy as the most efficient form of organization, and even indispensable for the modern state, Weber also saw it as a threat to individual freedom, and ongoing bureaucratization as leading to a "polar night of icy darkness," in which increasing rationalization of human life traps individuals in the aforementioned "iron cage" of bureaucratic,

---

10. Ibid.

rule based, rational control. In order to counteract bureaucrats, the system needs entrepreneurs and politicians.[11]

Jesus did not practice a Gospel of domination through knowledge, but of social empowerment through social and communal practices. The above description leads us to see with clarity how dominated by bureaucracy institutional churches have become. Contrary to the spirit of the Gospel this culture enables the technical mastery of human beings. It is aptly described by Weber as domination through knowledge. Only one of these has a future in the economy of G-d. Bureaucratic methods have been exercised with success up until the present time. Now the Internet and globalization are rendering them dysfunctional and increasingly problematic. These forces have democratized knowledge, and therefore authority, and are beyond effective bureaucratic controls. This has created a new global reality. Bureaucratic culture is breaking down because it is no longer working. It creates more problems than it solves. The churches of institution made in the image of the managerial machine god are breaking down with it.

THE SECULARIZED CHRISTIAN DOMINATION SYSTEM

Roman hierarchy and Protestant bureaucracy have resulted in the idea of Christ as domination king becoming the defining myth of Western civilization. This has given birth to a pervasive and pernicious legacy of Christian social dominance in our own time. Paul Kivel clarifies it well in the following way:

> Christian hegemony operates on several levels. At one level is the internalization of dominant western Christian beliefs and values by individuals in our society. Another level is the power that individual preachers, ministers and priests have on people's lives. Particular churches and some Christian denominations wield very significant political and economic power in our country. There is a vast network of parachurch organizations, general tax-supported non-profits such as hospitals, broadcasting networks, publishing houses, lobbying groups, and organizations . . . And there is the level which provides the foundation for all the others—the long and deep legacy of Christian ideas, values, practices, policies, icons, and texts that have been produced within dominant western Christianity over the centuries. That legacy continues to shape our

11. Ibid.

language, culture, beliefs, and values and to frame public and foreign policy decisions. Christian dominance has become so invisible that its manifestations appear to be secular, i.e. not religious. In this context, the phrase "secular Christian dominance" might be most appropriate, Christian hegemony under the guise of secularism. Of course, there are many forms of Christian fundamentalism that are anything but secular. Often fundamentalists want to create some kind of theocratic state. But the more mainstream, everyday way that dominant Christian values and institutions influence our lives and communities is less evident, although no less significant and certainly not limited to fundamentalists.[12]

Christian hegemony has its roots deep in Roman hegemony. The Emperor Constantine created it. Roman hegemony in no way reflects the egalitarian values of Jesus Christ. Built on a theology of Empire it is perpetuated through the hierarchical leadership and dominance of one country or social group. Christian nation was Constantine's big idea. Empire Christians are the disciples of Constantine. "In this sign conquer" is the defining ethos. Rather than following Christ in sacrificial death they believe in overcoming all others who oppose their Christian religion. This is brought about through war and party politics or creeds, hierarchical leadership, bureaucratic systems, and word based domination through preaching. These disciples of Rome have put down their crosses and picked up their swords. They have ceased to follow the crucified Christ as an agent of social change that brings wholeness only through reconciliation.

QUEEN DREAM: THE NEW CHRISTIAN WEST

Roman hegemony pervades Western civilization. It has shaped contemporary Christianity in all its forms, including the mission-shaped church. It is easy to make the assumption that the goal of the church is obvious; to make Christ known and to grow the church. It seems highly unlikely that Christianity will ever become a dominant force in the West again. Yet what would happen if it did? Is the aim of the modern church to re-establish Christian social dominance in the same style that we have had it in Europe for the last 1,500 years? Some factions in mainline Christianity may be employing a mission-shaped approach to help it attain cultural dominance. Christian fundamentalism is a more strident manifestation of this demand. Yet one of

---

12. Kivel, "Challenging Christian Hegemony."

Domination Christianity

the terms associated with missional and the mission-shaped church is the phrase, remaking the New Christian West.

"The Party . . . stands for positive Christianity" was Point 24 of the plan of the Nazi Party. The goal of mainline Christianity to remake a New Christian West through building strong communities dimly echoes the social vision of the philosopher Heidegger. He naively supported the National Socialism of the Nazis in 1930s Germany. Some Germans saw Hitler as a kind of Christian Messiah. He sold a thrilling and seductive vision of immortality and invulnerability to be attained through strong leadership and the formation of a new German identity. In reality, his illusory picture of German state and empire was far more Roman and dominant than Christlike and mutual. Whilst far from being Nazism, the mission-shaped church has a mission theology that is vulnerable to being hijacked by a mainline Christianity. The churches of institution are rooted in corporate and modernist concerns. Modernity has grown out of Romanized Christian hegemony. It contains its assumptions and mirrors its ethos. Modernist agendas are always monocultural and seek to establish one totalizing social vision for all: capitalist, communist or Christian. This means that in its language and theology the mission-shaped church contains the potential seeds of community fragmentation rather than community reconciliation.

In prioritizing mission and making it central the church has focussed on its own purposes and advancement. It wants to establish itself as a strong presence in local communities. To do this means prioritizing strategic planning and management as a means of achieving its goal. More advanced mission practitioners will argue that it is shaped by the neighborhood itself. While this may be true it is still aiming to build something that perpetuates the leadership and dominance of one social group: the Christians. A mission-shaped church remains invulnerable to competing visions of reality and is therefore immature. Mission mentality prevents people from becoming transparent regarding their purpose and creates pseudo-inclusivity. It is an ethos that lacks the maturity of being able to genuinely embrace differences and practice Christlike reconciliation. Significantly, it is primarily reconciliation that is needed in our neotribal neighborhoods. Managerialized mission practices seek to order the world and make it capable of being mapped. Its language is used as a means of social control and advancement. The use of modernist terms like mission, leader, mapping, and planning points to an underlying belief in determinism. This is the idea that nothing occurs at random but that everything happens for a reason and by necessity. Strict determinism means that accurate predictability of events is possible. In consequence, only one possible outcome can result. Mission language is rooted in a deterministic view of the world. This is because it utilizes leader-initiated strategic planning, which promotes reliability, predictability, control, and order.

In contrast, postmodernity has highlighted the difficulty in creating predictable and reliable maps. Life is constantly being updated by the flux and flow that new information creates. In consequence, contemporary sympathies do not respond well to the prescribed package deal of Christian religious institutions. The mission of mainline Christianity is to try and redress what it fears is the mess of postmodernity, and attempts to do so by methods it regards as more pragmatic and strategic. Therefore, stability is prioritized to the detriment of innovation. Church institutions have even invoked stability in pseudo-Benedictine terms. This is a misapplication of Benedictine rhythms, which were focussed on maintaining stability in human-sized religious communities of monks. It is misplaced when used to justify the maintenance of centralized institutions ossified by bureaucratized management systems that only reinforce church canon law. Centralized bureaucracy always imposes order in a mechanical way. Benedictine rhythms bring an order that emerges out of our G-d-breathed human natures.

Heidegger's modernist mistake was his naive search for a strong nation made up of stable and robust communities. This social vision echoes the founding myth of Western civilization. It is in fact Plato's dualistic dream of Greek perfection through social hierarchy. In this respect Plato's ideas can be seen to be the seeds that have been used to justify fascism. His message of social hierarchy results in violence because it perpetuates faction-based rivalry. It is rooted in hubris. Plato's Greek values undergird the ethos extant in Western civilization and mainline Christianity today. Yet Leonard Cohen warns us, "there is a crack in everything, that's how the light gets in."[13] Real life is not a Greek architect's pure white, perfectly formed dream. Such a dream is closed, sterile, anemic, and life denying. It is the Greek search for human perfection that continues in modernity that has misshaped Christ's non-dualistic message. It is Plato's dream of the ideal, and of perfectibility through hierarchical social dominance, that still holds mainline Christianity captive. When followed to its extreme it can be used to justify a hierarchical, factional, and domination-based vision of so-

---

13. Cohen, *The Future*.

ciety. Mainline Christianity is a liberalized form of these Roman practices and Greek ideas. It has betrayed its roots and genus, contained only in the Way of Life of the Rabbi Jesus.

FUGUE

Modernity's obsession with superiority and getting the right answer is, in fact, fueled by the persistence of the ancient Greek search for perfection. This is because those who are perfect are interpreted as having the right to rule. Plato assumed these were the philosopher kings. This narcissistic dream also fueled the hierarchical conflicts inherent in Greek civilization. It has been perpetuated through Greco-Roman Christianity in Western civilization. The inheritor of this nightmare is modernity and modern Christianity. In consequence, it is still held captive by a powerful illusion of becoming Queen of the West. In this illusion there is a subtle association between righteousness and superiority, and the right to rule. Yet modern Christianity would do well to pay heed to Thomas Merton who spoke during the intransigence of 1950s Cold War politics. He reminds us that "Ideologies rent their fury on men."[14] This is the dangerous nature of all ideology. It induces a trance-like state of imagined superiority. It has been the case with communism and fascism, and all forms of religious fundamentalism and reactionary conservatism. Such ideology is inherent in the Roman hegemony that birthed Christian hegemony and in turn the modernity in which we live. It is what defines the modern church.

This illusion holds the imagination of the mainline Christian churches captive, which gratifies the most primitive and childish desires for ego-dominance. It has held Catholicism and Protestantism captive for over a thousand years. This picture can influence people so strongly that its effects can be like being in a fugue state. Fugue is a psychiatric disorder in which a person forgets who they are. This includes memories, personality, and the things that make for individuality. Identity is lost. The shock of postmodernity has caused the churches of institution to enter a kind of fugue in loss, pain, denial, and disorientation. Postmodernity has stripped Christianity of its illusions of social dominance, yet the churches refuse to believe or acknowledge its truth. In this trance of denial the egalitarian companionship of empowerment of Jesus Christ has become a distant and vague memory. The pragmatic mission-vision solution of the mainline

14. Merton, *Conjectures*.

churches is an attempt at recovery from the fugue. This acts like a medication that masks and controls the underlying disease. It offers no real healing, but creates more distance by avoiding the disturbing picture of life that postmodernity has revealed. These are realities that those rooted in the comforting illusions of modernity and Christian social dominance do not want to acknowledge. Postmodernity has burst the bubble of the Greco-Roman illusion of perfection. It was based on a vision of social hierarchy and dominance that has masqueraded inside Christianity. Now a deeper reality has begun to move people beyond the rule of kings or the boundaries of nation states and religions—the Way of Christ.

A MISSION-SHAPED MANDATE?

In such postmodern democracies is there room for a mission-shaped church that seeks to perpetuate the social dominance of the churches of institution? The images of companionship and empowerment given by Jesus are of salt, light, and leaven and are pervasive and catalytic. They do not seek to bureaucratically dominate through knowledge. Jesus is not interested in remaking a New Christian West. He seeks to nurture small communities of companionship and empowerment in whatever kind of society they find themselves. The language of mission, management, leader, and planning has arisen from a paradigm of Protestant bureaucracy, modernity, and managerialism. Mission-shaped language and practice dovetail too seamlessly with the mission-vision and managerialism of the mainline churches. They are blindly seeking to reboot their decaying infrastructures. For the majority of the population in the West Catholicism is over, and so is Protestantism. The companionship of empowerment calls us beyond these dualistic dead ends. It invites us beyond the divisions of Catholic and Protestant, priesthood and laity, left wing and right wing, liberal and conservative, atheist and theist, gay and straight, manager and worker, male and female, and beyond religious and secular separation.

Christianity in Europe and the USA has lost considerable social status and is seeking to regain it. Yet, attempting to remake a New Christian West short-circuits another very real process of emancipation. When this process is completed the church will not need to depend on dominance for its identity. What it is really seeking is not authority over others but its own freedom and autonomy. The resolution of its journey is not to become Queen. It is to go beyond a preoccupation with dominance to rediscover the practice of reconciliation and love of neighbor. Being salt, light, and leaven in society is its identity. It is not found in calling the shots in the neighborhood or the nation. Yet, in order to overcome its dominance addiction the church needs to wake up from its fugue state.

CAN DOMINATION CHRISTIANITY BE SAVED?

How will the church wake up? A fugue is a state of extreme disorientation.

Ricoeur understands life as a repetitive cycle of three seasons: orientation, disorientation, and reorientation.[15] This happens as people traverse through life stages and life events, such as major loss and bereavement. The life of the church can also be understood in this way.

Seasons of orientation come in times of well-being. It is a season of joy, delight, goodness, and reliability. Seasons of disorientation come in the most difficult times of hurt, alienation, suffering, and death. These times create anger and frustration as lives are fragmented and broken by raw, dark, frightening, and sickening loss. Seasons of reorientation come when joy eventually breaks through despair as a new way is found. Eventually a new reality is created, and new gifts can be received. In reconnection and re-establishment life has meaning, purpose, and direction again.

Walter Brueggemann has applied Paul Ricoeur's ideas of orientation, disorientation and reorientation to the Psalms and the history of Israel.[16] The church has also gone through periods of orientation, disorientation and reorientation. Disorientation is a very apt way of describing the effect of postmodernity upon the mainline churches. They understand it as a sickness unto death. Yet the church is attempting to heal itself through a pragmatic mission strategy. It is important to realize that by doing so it may be avoiding a very necessary period of disorientation and questioning. This will enable it to reorientate so it can wake up to its new identity. Like all modernist solutions pragmatic mission avoids necessary grief and transition. It wants to avoid the pain of feeling weak and lost by fixing things. Yet, despite attempts at fixing, the problems remain hidden underneath the cracks. Honesty is a prerequisite for healing to occur. Yet in its pragmatic focus a mission solution continues to mask some very deep problems. Without disorientation there is no reorientation to a vital and sustainable true purpose. No death, no resurrection. Know death, know resurrection.

15. Brueggemann, *Psalms and Life*, 9.
16. Ibid.

Part 1: Domination Christianity

Two world wars and atomic destruction are the result of maintaining a trajectory guided by Roman-based Christian social dominance. World wars sanctioned by Christian nations produced profound social disorientation. The fragmentation of postmodernity began after Christian America dropped the atomic bomb. It killed 90,000–166,000 people in Hiroshima and 60,000–80,000 in Nagasaki. During the following months large numbers died from burns and radiation. In both cities most of the dead were civilians. Such unbridled evil also atomized the Western Christian way of life. The West is still trying to recover. Our minds cannot cope with the fact that Christian human beings are capable of such evil or such unbridled power. Johnston McMaster has articulated the devastating social fragmentation of Christian world war, "a Christendom God died in the trenches. All knowledge is provisional, the end of doctrinal hegemony."[17] When the Christian story resulted in the potential nuclear destruction of all life, people began to have profound and deeply disturbing doubts. Modernity and the ideas of social dominance dormant in the Christianity that had given it birth had failed. That totalizing story had ended up blowing the pathway to pieces. People began to pick up the remaining fragments left in the aftermath. Now there were many ways.

Yet all was not lost. McMaster has also discerned a reorientation toward reciprocity rising from the ashes of our atomized modernity, "there is globalisation and interdependence. To learn to live with many narratives and many cultures, in a post-colonial world with a challenge to build a more participative democracy."[18] When the church has completed its rite of passage it will be in a new place.

The powerful fugue that has driven Christianity's violent struggling nightmare of social dominance will be over. It will be able to share the world with others and overcome its preoccupation with its own survival. This will be the discovery of a new way of being with the courage to belong in G-d's universal family. There will be a companionship of empowerment with/in every tongue, tribe and nation. People will have a new identity and way of making their way in the world. They will realize that G-d is always making all things new.

17. McMaster, Johnston. "Living."
18. Ibid.

HE NOT BUSY BEING BORN IS BUSY DYING

With great perception St Francis prayed that it is only in dying that we are born to eternal life. Harry Williams also has this to say about the death and rebirth of the church:

> It is, to say the least, extremely unlikely that institutions of church or state will ever begin to approach the richness and value which belong to the institution they call Jesus of Nazareth. And if he gave it all up into God's hands and was willing, as Jesus of Nazareth to disappear in death, it should not worry us too much if lesser institutions disappear and die. For death, in this context, is the necessary prelude to life abundant. For Christians, the background and context of institutional change must always be death and resurrection. That is how God's kingly rule works.[19]

Rowan Williams echoes his spiritual fathers when he concludes, "I can see that it's by no means the end of the world if the Establishment disappears."[20]

In following Christ we begin to recognize a way of life through death. It is the way of resurrection and reorientation. In the death of institutional Christianity we are not leaving our faith but arriving to a place of new belonging with Christ. It is no longer a belonging defined by commitment to a management dominated church. Nor is it expressed in trying to reboot the decaying structures of Christendom through a mission-shaped church initiative. Christ can now only be discovered afresh in the many faces and forms that he is taking in our neotribal societies. These are faith communities made up of all the people for all the people.

---

19. Williams, *Living Free*, 30. Harry Williams was a member of the Anglican Community of the Resurrection at Mirfield and a Fellow of Trinity College, Cambridge.

20. "Archbishop of Canterbury: Disestablishment would not be end of the world." The Telegraph, 17 Dec 2008.

PART 2

The Missional Illusion

A NEW CHRISTIAN WEST

4

Missional
Miasma

"There are consequences when the meanings of words become confused. This is particularly true within a biblical worldview. The Hebrews were suspicious of images as conveyors of truth, so they guarded words and their meanings carefully. Part of theology, therefore, includes guarding the meaning of words to maintain truth within the community of faith."

—Alan Hirsch[1]

"God Is a Community."

—Peter Schmid[2]

---

1. Hirsch, "Defining Missional," para. 4.
2. Schmid, *In the beginning*, 15.

Part 2: The Missional Illusion

MISSIONAL MISUNDERSTANDINGS

WHAT IS MISSIONAL? UNDERSTANDING it is problematic. Google the word and what may come up are thirty minute YouTube presentations or whole blog entries. It is open to misunderstanding. Practitioners sometimes cite definition as a modernist over-concern with precision. It is seen as more helpful to try to identify contemporary use. Therefore, a range of interpretation and opinion has developed. To some extent this has led to a privatization of meaning. Alan Roxburgh decries this drift in *Missional: Joining God In the Neighborhood* (2011). Yet privatization of meaning and drift in practice are somewhat inevitable because of the ambivalence and malleability inherent in the term. Malleability of interpretation allows for creativity of application in a variety of contexts. Yet it has also made missional terminology vulnerable to being usurped and misapplied by institutional Christianity.

The missional movement is an improvement on colonial approaches to mission. Yet missional language still seems to contain a modernist attempt to make the world understandable and manageable. This belies impatience with the uncertainty and fuzziness of postmodernity. Missional language promotes the use of modernist language such as mission, leadership, map-making, and planning. This dovetails neatly with the language, agenda, and mission practices of mainline Christian churches. Wikipedia defines modernism as, "a socially progressive trend of thought that affirms the power of human beings to create, improve and reshape their environment with the aid of practical experimentation, scientific knowledge, or technology. From this perspective, modernism encouraged the re-examination of every aspect of existence, from commerce to philosophy, with the goal of finding that which was 'holding back' progress, and replacing it with new ways of reaching the same end." "Lets fix it!" seems to echo a pragmatism inherent in the missional method.

To consider how well missional meets the social concerns of contemporary Western democracies it is useful to consider the nature of postmodernity. Wikipedia defines it as:

> apparent realities are only social constructs and are therefore subject to change. It claims that there is no absolute truth and that the way people perceive the world is subjective and emphasizes the role of language, power relations, and motivations in the

formation of ideas and beliefs. In particular it attacks the use of sharp binary classifications such as male versus female, straight versus gay, white versus black, and imperial versus colonial; it holds realities to be plural and relative, and to be dependent on who the interested parties are and the nature of these interests. Postmodernist approaches therefore often consider the ways in which social dynamics, such as power and hierarchy, affect human conceptualizations of the world to have important effects on the way knowledge is constructed and used. In contrast to modernism, postmodernist thought often emphasizes constructivism, idealism, pluralism, relativism, and scepticism in its approaches to knowledge and understanding.[3]

Missional practice seems to try to avoid the issues of pluralism, relativism, and skepticism by an emphasis on pragmatic action. The answer is to build stronger communities to create a New Christian West. What gives missional purchase in postmodern cultures is its constructionist method. It acknowledges the need for conversation with/in the local neighborhood. This makes it a great improvement on the tell it/sell it, church-focussed mission method. Constructionism can be described as the way people create meaning through a series of individual constructs. They choose filters to place over their experience of the world. This changes their perceived reality from chaos to meaning. Simply stated, it is a learning process that allows people to experience an environment firsthand. This creates reliable and trustworthy knowledge. People are required to act upon the environment to acquire and test new knowledge. This approach informs the use of conversational methods with/in neighborhoods.

Missional's conversational approach is culture-current, but its modernist language is retrograde to its method. It belies an attempt to gain some secure ground in a world that seems out of control. This seems like paternalistic modernist doctoring of what missional regards as a postmodern sickness. It reflects an underlying dualism. Maybe what Greco-Romanized Christians have to recover from is an attempt to make functional something as earthy and fertile as the life of G-d in a group of human beings. The language of mission, leadership, map-making, and planning seems incongruent with the needs of postmodern democracies in which people are rediscovering non-dualistic approaches to life.

---

3. en.wikipedia.org/wiki/Postmodernism.

Part 2: The Missional Illusion

MISSIONAL UNDERSTANDINGS

Wikipedia offers the following description: "Missional living is a term that is used in contrast with historical institutional churches. Church leaders as well as Christians in general have often regarded the Church as an institution to which outsiders must come in order to receive a certain product, namely, the gospel and all its associated benefits. Institutional churches are sometimes perceived to exist for the members and depend on pastors and staff to evangelize the lost. The 'missional church,' on the other hand, attempts to take Christ to 'the lost' and its members are personally engaged in reaching their communities with the message of Jesus Christ."

The missional church movement first arose during the end of the twentieth century and the beginning of the twenty-first century. The movement seeks to rethink and redefine the nature of the church and create a new paradigm in which churches are seen as missional in nature, instead of attractional. Leaders in the movement argue that instead of churches attempting to attract people to churches through church programs, churches should instead take the gospel outside of the church and engage society with the gospel, often by being involved not only in missions and evangelism but also in social justice movements. The missional church defines itself in terms of its mission—being sent ones who take the gospel to and incarnate the gospel within a specific cultural context. The church exists, in other words, for what we sometimes call mission: to announce to the world that Jesus is its Lord.

Missional living is the embodiment of the mission of Jesus in the world by incarnating the gospel. This embodiment of the gospel is often referred to as contextualization or inculturation. "Both refer to more than a simple translation of the gospel into different languages and cultures in the way that one translates a history book or a science text. Rather, they point to the embodiment of the living Word in human culture and social settings in such a way that its divine nature and power are not lost. True contextualization is more than communication. It is God working in the hearts of people, making them new and forming them into a new community. It is his Word transforming their lives, their societies, their cultures."[4]

Alan Hirsch says, "missional church is a community of God's people that defines itself, and organizes its life around, its real purpose of being an agent of God's mission to the world. In other words, the church's true and

---

4. en.wikipedia.org/wiki/Missional_living.

authentic organizing principle is mission. When the church is in mission, it is the true church. The church itself is not only a product of that mission but is obligated and destined to extend it by whatever means possible. The mission of God flows directly through every believer and every community of faith that adheres to Jesus. To obstruct this is to block God's purposes in and through his people."[5]

Whilst missional is defined as being in contrast with institutional churches, many within the mission-shaped church movement utilize missional methods. Tension has emerged between the needs and priorities of bureaucratized centralized institutions and the desire of missional parishioners to work with/in more organic systems. The above definitions reflect the main themes of the missional movement. Yet practice and implementation have been more complex in the churches of institution. The purpose of centralized bureaucratic management is to control. This conflicts with the desire to work through organic systems that promote missional living and aspire to meet the needs of people outside mainline institutions. The concept of a mixed economy church of institutional alongside mission-shaped church has been promoted. Yet, in practice, institutions stifle widespread innovation and transformation of their systems because their structures prioritize managerial and financial controls. Even salaried staff given a missional brief are enmeshed in the financial and bureaucratic regulations. This drains resources and energy. Institutional churches exercise authority through a pyramid of power. This undermines the authority of missional circles of trust even as they are forming. Salaried staff are always invested with greater authority in the institution. This significantly distorts the mutuality that missional communities are attempting to create. Dwindling finances also limit the long-term sustainability of mainline institutions. There are increasing instances of bankruptcy fueled by poor attendances. In the near future institutions will reach a situation where they will no longer be able to afford to run their infrastructures. Yet much energy is concentrated on the maintenance of these ossified structures. This drains resource and innovation. The danger is that the little innovation there is will implode with the infrastructures as they collapse.

---

5. Hirsch, *The Forgotten Ways*, 82.

Part 2: The Missional Illusion

MISSIONAL MEANINGS

Where does the term missional come from? Alan Hirsch has this to say by way of definition:

> I am concerned about the confusion surrounding the meaning of the word missional. Maintaining the integrity of this word is critical, because recovering a missional understanding of God and the Church is essential not only for the advancement of our mission but, I believe, also for the survival of Christianity in the West.
>
> First, let me say what missional does not mean. Missional is not synonymous with emerging. The emerging church is primarily a renewal movement attempting to contextualize Christianity for a postmodern generation. Missional is also not the same as evangelistic or seeker-sensitive. These terms generally apply to the attractional model of church that has dominated our understanding for many years. Missional is not a new way to talk about church growth. Although God clearly desires the church to grow numerically, it is only one part of the larger missional agenda. Finally, missional is more than social justice. Engaging the poor and correcting inequalities is part of being God's agent in the world, but we should not confuse this with the whole.
>
> A proper understanding of missional begins with recovering a missionary understanding of God. By his very nature God is a "sent one" who takes the initiative to redeem his creation. This doctrine, known as Missio Dei—the sending of God—is causing many to redefine their understanding of the church. Because we are the "sent" people of God, the church is the instrument of God's mission in the world. As things stand, many people see it the other way around. They believe mission is an instrument of the church; a means by which the church is grown. Although we frequently say "the church has a mission," according to missional theology a more correct statement would be "the mission has a church."[6]

MISSEO DEI: THE MISSION GOD

Alan Hirsch has rooted missional in the idea of Misseo Dei. It is therefore useful to explore the origins of the term. Wikipedia has the following summary:

6. Ibid.

Missional

Missio Dei is a Latin Christian theological term that can be translated as the "mission of God," or the "sending of God." The idea that the mission of the church is in the first place the mission of God or missio Dei has its origins in the thought of Karl Barth. Barth's argument that mission must be understood as an activity or attribute of God himself was first proposed in a paper given at the Brandenburg Missionary Conference in 1932. In 1934, Karl Hartenstein, a German missiologist, coined the phrase in response to Karl Barth. This language, it is argued, was picked up at the 1952 Willingen conference of the International Missionary Council (IMC) and developed theologically by Lutheran theologian, Georg Vicedom. A more recent account from John Flett maintains that while Hartentstein did introduce the actual term "missio Dei," he did not locate that mission in the doctrine of the Trinity. Such reference to the Trinity appeared in the "American report," a study document prepared for the 1952 Willingen conference, under the leadership of Paul Lehmann and H. Richard Niebuhr. This document suggested a link between revolutionary movements in history and "God's mission." Many of the later problems with missio Dei stem from these origins, and especially the failure to ground the concept in a robust account of the Trinity.[7]

Is Misseo Dei an idea that can be found in the practices and teaching of Jesus or in the Bible? As discussed in the first section of this book, the centrality of the Gospel is reconciliation and not mission. G-d is primarily reciprocal in nature rather than missional. What is clear is that Misseo Dei is a theological idea created in the early to mid twentieth century. It emerges out of a culture shaped by modernity. This is a period characterized by Christian nation states in world wide war and competing ideologies of social dominance—i.e., communism vs. capitalism. After the demise of the power of nation states and the rise of globalization and neotribalism this terminology no longer seems a good theological fit to describe the activity of G-d in the world. Contemporary communities of faith are served better by language other than that inherited from a mission-misshaped past and Christian hegemony.

7. en.wikipedia.org/wiki/Missio_Dei.

Part 2: The Missional Illusion

PERICHORESIS: THE COMMUNITY G-D

Alan Hirsch, in his definition of missional, is rooting his understanding in the nature of G-d. Yet Misseo Dei was not articulated as a doctrine until 1934. It also fails to reflect adequately a theology of trinitarian interpenetration. Perichoresis is a term in Christian theology first found within the Church Fathers. It is reinvigorated among contemporary theologians such as C. Baxter Kruger, Jurgen Moltmann, and Miroslav Volf. Perichoresis comes from two Greek words, *peri*, which means around, and *chorea*, which means dance. It refers to the mutual indwelling and intimacy of the three persons of the G-dhead. It has been argued that the Missio Dei is the inner life of the Trinity reaching out to all humanity and drawing us into the life of G-d. Yet, to use the word mission in association with perichoresis seems incongruous. A G-d of engagement or interface would be language that more accurately conveys the ideas of Newbigin and Bosch about Misseo Dei.

David Hahn's understanding of G-d helps us to see the way in which Missio Dei and perichoresis are incongruous. For Hahn G-d is "between us." He describes the G-d between in this way:

> I am drawn out by God in a centrifugal way, rather than pushed and propelled outwards, . . . What does it mean to live in and around the life of God? Are we really bringing truth to the world? Or are we just caught up in the truth that embraces us, dwelling in time and space, that reflects through us? Rather than some watered down and vague description of an ultimate existence, what place does the trinitarian God play in unfolding an understanding of God's life in this world in conjunction with mine and yours? The interplay of these, yielding one to another, exposes and presents for me, the picture of God whose very relational existence, speaks of a movement much more intimately involved in all of life than we could ever imagine or even hoped could exist. The circle dance of God's existence is a lifestyle I'm wondering about . . . what does it look like? What does it mean for me, those I encounter and the event going on between us? What does it mean then to be "sent" (*missio*) in this God's name? Am I really "sent" from a place of static existence or am I centrifugally propelled from a pre-existing presence/momentum breathing through me? In what ways can Rublev's icon of the Holy Trinity become a window through which we wonder about and engage in Gods' mysterious and holy communion with humanity and all creation? . . .

> There is freedom in this dance ... for the joy of dancing comes (even as this pilgrim with two left feet can resist the dance) in the fluid movement, the give and take, the dynamic God-between, which involves me in ways beyond myself. Getting "caught up," to use the apocalyptic language of John's Revelation, I am listening and learning what it means to not so much become a holding tank for God's Spirit, as a broken and porous vessel through whom God's breezes blow. For in many ways and often, I hear this wind's sound, but don't always know from where it comes.[8]

The early Church Fathers did not articulate a G-d of mission. A G-d of reciprocity is a more accurate reflection of their vision. G-d reaches out to all humanity drawing us in. Yet crucially, this is done in a way that is reciprocal and centrifugal. G-d is not invading and pioneering but inviting us all to dance. There is a big difference. The language of the Misseo Dei does not adequately express the perichoretic dancing G-d. It is this confusion that has resulted in the retrograde language of missional. It has created a distorted G-d, and a distorted message, and a distorted direction. G-d is not a map-maker. G-d is a love dance. This is the energy that will heal the wounds of modernity. Missional ideology is born in the heart of modernity and therefore cannot heal. The language of Misseo Dei and missional unwittingly carries the message of social dominance. This makes it retrograde. Yet postmodern societies need non-dualistic practices and systems. This is the shift many find themselves in as working lives become clogged, unproductive, and unsatisfying. People are tightly bound in a fetishized legalistic efficiency and effectiveness. The church is the same. This is what creates depression and numbness in a meaningless search for total security and flawless perfection.

MISSIONAL DNA

Another way that missional has been defined is what Alan Hirsch has termed missional DNA (mDNA), or apostolic genius. Wikipedia defines mDNA in the following way: "As to its phenomenology, it is made up of the symphonious interplay between six core elements or mDNA."

Hirsch explains these six as follows:

---

8. emergingcuriosities.blogspot.com/2007/05/perichoretic-lifestyle.html.

Part 2: The Missional Illusion

1. 1. Jesus is Lord—a confession made by Christians that Jesus is the ruler over every aspect of life.⁹ This is the most central element, around which the other five orbit. By locating this at the center, Hirsch asserts the Christology (the whole phenomenon of Jesus' incarnation, life, teachings, role model, saving and redeeming work in cross and resurrection and return) must be the central defining theology of all Christian movements.

2. 2. Disciple making—a practice of becoming like Jesus and leading others to do the same.¹⁰ This follows directly from the statement that Jesus is Lord and, in essence, is the calling of disciples to live in Christ and allowing him to live through them.

3. 3. Missional-incarnational impulse—the dual element of mission and incarnation by which a disciple goes into the surrounding world missionally and embodies the actions of Jesus incarnationally.¹¹ This forms the basis of how a Jesus movement extends itself into the world.

4. 4. Apostolic environment—which highlights the catalytic role that the apostolic person plays in both generating and sustaining movemental ecclesiology.¹² Hirsch then highlights the role of Ephesians 4 in movements. He maintains that missional church requires a missional ministry to generate and sustain it. The prevailing pastor-teacher combination is not generative enough for movemental forms of Christianity, he asserts.

5. 5. Organic systems—in contrast with a centralized institution, missional movements are structured more like an interconnected organism than through hierarchical organization. Organic systems manifest (i) an ethos of a movement (as opposed to institution), (ii) the structure of a network, (iii) spread like viruses, and (iv) are reproducing and reproducible.

6. 6. Communitas, not community—in contrast with an inward-focused group, communitas is an outward-focused group who, by

---

9. Hirsch, *The Forgotten Ways*, 83–100.
10. Ibid., 101–26.
11. Ibid., 127–48.
12. Ibid., 149–78.

engaging in various forms of risk and liminality, begin to relate to each other on a significantly deeper level.[13]

Alan Hirsch maintains that all six elements are needed to create highly transformative, exponentially growing, missional movements. In his book, he displays that it is critical to think in a systemic way about apostolic genius and not see each mDNA as a silver bullet. Rather it takes the whole (apostolic genius) to create the kind of movement he is describing.

CHRISTIAN SOCIAL DOMINANCE AND MDNA

There are very positive aspects of mDNA that echo the companionship of empowerment, such as the need for organic systems, communitas, and incarnational living. The exercise of authority through group carismata and complementary gifts in synthesis is promoted as producing immense spiritual movement. In particular, the exercise of apostolic and prophetic gifts is needed if movement and change is to occur. Also, the incarnational impulse reflects something deeply Christlike as people find the Christ who is already present in each other and in society. The apostle Paul illustrated this feature of mDNA brilliantly in his encounter with Greek society. At Mars Hill in Athens Paul recognized their unknown G-d as his own G-d of Abraham, Isaac, and Jacob. He also affirmed Greek philosophers as carriers of G-d's wisdom by quoting them liberally in his proclamation and dialogue.

On the other hand, there are also aspects of mDNA that are easy for people rooted in the modernist mindset of institutional churches to misinterpret. Language is again a key issue. Christianity's practices of hierarchical and managerial domination could seem endorsed by the phrase Jesus is Lord. This phrase is cited above as characterizing mDNA 1. Jesus is Lord is a time-honored Christian phrase, yet great care needs to be taken with its interpretation. This is because it has been overlaid with primarily Greek meanings concerning rule. This is misleading because it entirely distorts the egalitarian and mutual nature of Christ's rule and lordship. Similar social and political factors to those that have distorted an understanding of Christ as King have also distorted the understanding of Jesus is Lord. Modern Christians interpret lordship in terms of social dominance and political and hierarchical rule. Lordship is not understood as a liberating

---

13. Ibid., 217–42.

JESUS IS YHWH: "I WILL BE WHAT I WILL BE"

To say Jesus is Lord is not to imply that Jesus is a ruler. The phrase is more accurately translated as Jesus is YHWH. YHWH does not mean ruler. It means "I will be what I will be." When the Hebrew Bible was translated into Greek (Septuagint), *kurios* (meaning ruler) was used as the translation of YHWH. Therefore, instead of reading Jesus is YHWH, the Bible—when translated into Greek—reads that Jesus is Lord. Most modern English translations of the Bible are from the Greek. They therefore carry over from the Greek translation of Jesus as Lord. This distorts the original meaning and has led to almost universal misunderstanding. To find out what Jesus is YHWH really means it is necessary to understand more fully the Hebrew meaning of YHWH. In "The Future Of Judaism"[14] Chief Rabbi Jonathan Sacks challenges the Greco-Christian interpretation of YHWH. Rather than I am that I am, YHWH is better translated as I will be what I will be. Rabbi Sacks therefore interprets YHWH as that which is to be encountered in our unknown and unpredictable future: "God is the future tense . . . I am encountered not in the physical or the metaphysical but in history. You will not know where I am until I am there and you are there." G-d is a free agent, beyond categorization, prediction or description. Wikipedia agrees with the Chief Rabbi:

> The God of Israel has a proper name, written YHWH (Hebrew: הֹוִהְי, Modern Yehovah) in the Hebrew Bible. The name YHWH is a combination of the future, present, and past tense of the verb "*howa*" (Hebrew: הוה) meaning "to be" and translated literally means "The self-existent One." A further explanation of the name was given to Moses when YHWH stated Eheye Asher Eheye (Hebrew: היהא רשא היהא) "I will be that I will be," the name relates to God as God truly is, God's revealed essence, which transcends the universe. It also represents God's compassion toward the world. In Jewish tradition another name of God is Elohim, relating to the interaction between God and the universe, God as manifest in the physical world, it designates the justice of God, and means

---

14. Sacks, "The Future of Judaism."

"the One who is the totality of powers, forces and causes in the universe."[15]

To say that Jesus is YHWH is to recognize all the above qualities as belonging to him. His authority is rooted in his inability to be defined, constrained, packaged, or commodified. He is therefore not a force for rule but a way of life beyond rules. YHWH is a way of life in mutuality and reciprocity beyond dependence on political and religious domination systems. This is why Jesus said, "Love is the fulfillment of the Law." Loving people are not constrained to obey unloving rules, but live beyond them. Through Christ these qualities also become manifested in all who choose to follow his way of life. This alignment with YHWH empowers a different way. Those who are born again into this new social reality also become free agents. They are also empowered to act beyond our dependence on political and religious domination systems. They are beyond categorization or prediction. This reveals an innate sacred human reality that is far more fundamental than lordship or domination. It is a view of human nature that flies in the face of all modernist attempts at categorization, prediction, planning, mapping, control, and utilitarianism. This is nothing less than an encounter with our human nature as G-d; that is the Gospel. Postmodernity's non-dualistic rays of darkness have made YHWH visible once again after centuries of modern dualistic blinding light. They have enabled us to develop dark-adapted eyes that can see G-d in everything.

"BEFORE ABRAHAM WAS, I AM"

To reduce Jesus to a Lord is to entirely miss the significance of Christ's real identity and authority. When Jesus said, "Before Abraham was, I am"[16] he recognized his own human nature as YHWH. He was not saying this as a unique claim for himself either. Jesus recognized YHWH as dormant within all humanity. Yet humanity's inherent YHWH nature needs liberation from the illusions of slavery and addiction created by slavish attachment to the false promises of religious and political domination systems. This deception through illusion is the work of the father of lies. Potential liberation was achieved for all humanity through the death and resurrection of Christ. He destroyed the power of the domination system by exposing its

15. en.wikipedia.org/wiki/God_in_Judaism.
16. John 8:58.

lies and illusions. He altered the very nature of the religious and political domination system. He lived in a deeper and more fundamental unity with Life in YHWH. This G-d Way of Life went far beyond the fragmentation and arbitrary boundaries of the domination system. As the domination system destroyed his body it also destroyed itself. He entered it as a catalyst and transformed it from the inside out. He became the very salt of all the Earth.

Therefore, to recognize Jesus as Lord does not support hierarchical forms of leadership. It causes them to implode. When Christ rose from the dead he did so as the first born of a new race of humans who are divine. Through him the pathway is open for every person to actualize their own inherent kingship and priesthood. This is now a priesthood of all who begin to act on the basis that the substance of the multiverse has been transformed by the actions of Christ. Through active commitment to practicing the reconciling Way of Christ they access the non-hierarchical reality that is uniting all things. This is our underlying social reality. In this way all life—all that is biospherical, biological, political, religious, social, psychological, and atomic—is being transformed. To begin to follow in the way is to be a part of that transformation.

Abraham is regarded as the founding father in all three great religions—Judaism, Christianity and Islam. In saying, "Before Abraham was, I am" Christ is recognizing himself as YHWH. YHWH is the ground upon which the surface differences of these religions are built. They were created by their founders in response to the social forces and demands inherent in their different geographies, politics and histories. Yet YHWH flows through all these tributaries. This is what Christ recognized when he said "Before Abraham was, I am." To realize about oneself that "Before Abraham was, I am" is to realize that you are also YHWH. It is to realize that YHWH envelops us all, and is in all, and through all. This is panentheism. It is the understanding of life that is intrinsic to Eastern Christianity. Yet it is deeper than differences created by religious founders and traditions. This explains the way in which Jesus could worship in spirit and truth. He was not tied to worship in one place or one religion. All who follow his way walk in the same freedom. When people begin to follow Jesus in the Way of Life they can also say with Christ, "Before Abraham was, I am." To say Jesus is

YHWH is to recognize that the nature of all reality in the multiverse is one of non-hierarchical companionship and empowerment.

JESUS IS THE TAO

To say Jesus is YHWH may also convey the sense that Jesus is like the Tao.

> The concept of Tao was adopted in Confucianism, Chán and Zen Buddhism and more broadly throughout East Asian philosophy and religion in general. Within these contexts Tao signifies the primordial essence or fundamental nature of the universe. In the foundational text of Taoism, the Tao Te Ching, Laozi explains that Tao is not a "name" for a "thing" but the underlying natural order of the universe whose ultimate essence is difficult to circumscribe. Tao is thus "eternally nameless" (Dao De Jing–32. Laozi) and to be distinguished from the countless "named" things which are considered to be its manifestations.[17]

The Tao's "eternally nameless" nature echoes the way in which the Israelites experienced YHWH as "I will be what I will be."

The *Tao Te Ching* was written as a manual for a ruler. Yet paradoxically, it teaches that rule is only possible through not ruling. The Tao is the way or "the course of things."[18] The Tao does not rule as a king or a governor or a maker of things. The Tao flows everywhere and loves and nourishes all things. It does not lord it over things but always seeks the lowest level. Therefore the Tao is in no way equivalent with Western Christianity's interpretation of G-d as domination king or Jesus as a Roman lord. The Tao loves obscurity. The Tao is not different from nature or ourselves or the surrounding trees, water, and air. In the Tao everything behaves in an interrelated way. Everything arises through mutuality and is complementary. The Tao is an interconnected, interdependent, self-regulating, self-governing organism. It is also a totality. The Tao's method is "to be so" and "of itself."[19] The Tao is being, which is self-evidently powerful.

This is in great contrast to the mechanical universe of cause and effect proposed by Newton and intrinsic to domination Christianity. It carries the idea of G-d being in control of everything. Yet the Tao recognizes that the world is not automatic but spontaneous. G-d is not in control. Everything

17. *en.wikipedia.org/wiki/Tao*.
18. Ibid.
19. Ibid.

happens by itself. It is what it is. G-d allows it to happen by itself and find its level. It is like water. The Tao is the ruler that abdicates and lets people sort out their own affairs. Life is a unified organism. Therefore the Tao does not seek to impose an organizational uniformity. The more things are allowed to unfold, the more natural order is manifested. There is more liberty and love. In Taoism, Chinese Buddhism and Confucianism, the object of spiritual practice is to "become one with the Tao."[20] This is to harmonize one's will with nature and achieve "effortless action."[21] It involves meditative and moral practices. Important in this respect is the Taoist concept of *De* (virtue). This is also Christ's Way of Life expressed as companionship and empowerment. To say Jesus is like the Tao is to recognize that he manifests order not by control but by cooperation. The Tao manifests in a naturally occurring way in society.

Religious, state and business corporations act as bureaucratic domination systems that seek to control YHWH. They seek to suppress the life that is beyond names with an illusion that control is necessary. Kingly and priestly systems steal this life's authentic power and seek to contain, manage and control it in domination systems. Christ's death and resurrection dismantled the political and religious domination system of his time. This altered social reality and made a new relationship possible between all material life in the multiverse. All ground is now holy ground. All flesh is now incandescent with the divinity of YHWH. Those in the hierarchy are not more holy than anyone or anything else. G-d is center of the multiverse and yet pervades all things. Bureaucratic hierarchy is dismantled. The inherent holiness of the multiverse is liberated and made manifest within all that is.

JESUS IS YHWH: THE GATE OF HEAVEN

To recognize that Jesus is YHWH is to connect with the fact that the Earth and everything in it has been liberated. YHWH, who is dormant in everything and everybody, can now be manifested. When Christ exposed the political and religious domination systems as illusion he made it possible for all humanity to reconnect with, and begin to manifest, YHWH. Therefore, he became the firstborn of a new kind of human being; a race of divine humans. These are people who see through the imposed illusions

20. Ibid.
21. Ibid.

of corporate religion, politics and business. They can live in freedom. "All creation strains to see the sons of God come into their own."[22]

Realizing that Jesus is YHWH makes a new self and a new world possible for all humanity. Kallistos Ware has expressed it in this way: "In my beginning is my end . . . Become what you are."[23] Become, consciously and actively, what you already are potentially and secretly, by virtue of your creation according to the divine image and your re-creation at baptism. Become what you are, more exactly, return into yourself; discover him who is yours already; listen to him who never ceases to speak within you; possess him who even now possesses you. Such is God's message to anyone who wants to pray: "You would not seek me unless you had already found me."[24] Emerson also recognized YHWH in all things: "Every person is a doorway through which the Infinite passes into the finite, through which God becomes man, through which the Universal becomes individual."[25]

A new humanity has been revitalized and transformed from what was previously subject to decay and death. All things are made new because YHWH in all things has been liberated by Christ's death and resurrection. The New Testament speaks of this change as a chain reaction that is in the process of gradually transforming the multiverse, like yeast causing bread to rise. Thomas Merton saw it in this way:

> At the center of our being is a point of nothingness which is untouched by sin and by illusion, a point of pure truth, a point or spark which belongs entirely to God, which is never at our disposal, from which God disposes our lives, which is inaccessible to the fantasies of our own mind or the brutalities of our own will. This little point of nothingness and of absolute poverty is the pure glory of God in us . . . It is like a pure diamond, blazing with the invisible light of heaven. It is in everybody, and if we could see it we would see these billions of points of light coming together in the face and blaze of a sun that would make all the darkness and cruelty of life vanish completely . . . I have no program for this seeing. It is only given. But the gate of heaven is everywhere."[26]

---

22. Romans 8:19.
23. Ware, *The Power of the Name*, 3.
24. Ibid.
25. https://www.facebook.com/SoulSpeaking/posts/403374016378835?.
26. Merton, *Conjectures*, 156.

Part 2: The Missional Illusion

This is why Jesus describes the companionship of empowerment as yeast in the Gospels. It is the image of a catalytic chain reaction that permeates all life in a profound, unfolding transformation. To follow Christ means to seek to live in obedient cooperation with YHWH. It means subverting the shallow nature of a domination way of life through hierarchy, and the rule of kingship and lordship. To make this choice is what it means to recognize that Jesus is YHWH. As we recognize YHWH in Jesus he challenges us to manifest YHWH in our own bodies. This is realized through a transformative journey of ongoing reconciliation in small communities of learners. In these small communities we keep on, keeping on being born again. This is the *ekklesia*; the communities of YHWH.

NOT A ROMAN LORD OR A MODERN MANAGER

The way in which Jesus is YHWH was used in the early communities of G-d highlighted the authority of Jesus as not like Roman rule. Wikipedia also notes:

> For a Christian to recognize Jesus as Lord caused problems for society. When in 27 BC Roman Emperor Octavian received the title Augustus it carried religious overtones, suggesting a special relationship with the world of the gods, symbolized by the cult of the Emperor's genius, a veiled form of emperor worship. (Friend:16). J. G. Davies comments, "Jesus is LORD means Jesus is sovereign over the individual's relation to the state . . . Loving one's neighbour . . . means working to destroy the structures that can destroy my neighbour, the people, the poor."[27]

To say Jesus is YHWH meant that his presence and influence permeated all social relations and went beyond all socially constructed boundaries and hierarchies. To follow Christ was to live in a way that transcended obstacles to mutuality through practicing a companionship of empowerment. To follow Jesus as YHWH meant subverting all hierarchically-powered structures that distort and undermine mutuality. These are the structures of capitalism, communism and the bureaucratized and monetized secular Christian domination system and its churches.

Throughout mDNA there is the assumption that mission is normative to the nature of G-d and the church. There are significant problems with this view. This is due to Christianity's mission- misshaped past and

27. Davies, *Christians, Politics*.

Missional

the pervasive influence of secularized Christian hegemony extant in Western culture. It has shaped our Western understanding of G-d and church. The missional movement is an improvement on management-saturated mainline Christianity. Yet it still carries within its language and assumptions the residue of ideas that can be interpreted in terms of Christian domination. Therefore it fails to fully express Christ's way of companionship and empowerment. Christians in mainline institutions can augment their religious domination systems by utilizing Missional organic systems and communitas. Organic systems and communitas can then become the methods through which domination of society and creation of the New Christian West is secured. Whilst this may not be Alan Hirsch's intention, others still under the influence of domination Christianity in the mainline churches or evangelical house churches will use mDNA for these purposes. A more radical alternative is needed if the mission-misshaped mistakes of Christianity's history of domination are to be avoided.

THE END OF DISCIPLES OF DOMINATION

Disciple making is highlighted as the second feature of mDNA. Yet, what kind of disciples will missional Christianity make? Hopefully, the emphasis on communitas and organic systems will dispose missional learners toward companionship and empowerment. Yet once again, care must be taken due to the effect that domination and empire ideology have had on the history of the West and its churches. It is disciples of domination that have been created by a church with a mission emphasis, which contains a socially embedded but unrecognized Christian social dominance. In *The End Of Evangelicalism* David Fitch has drawn attention to the way that Western evangelicalism has emphasized the Bible, Christian nation and conversion as central to Christian faith. Yet, in doing so, it has usurped the centrality of Christ as person. This clearly illustrates the influence of Christian social dominance in the thinking and practices of modern Christianity. Christ did not emphasize the Bible, Christian nation and conversion as the central features of his Way of Life. Christ drew people to himself and his way of living in companionship and empowerment. He said, "My kingdom is not of this world."[28] This is better translated as, "My companionship of empowerment is not of the domination system."

28. John 18:36.

Part 2: The Missional Illusion

The Bible was created 400 years after Christ, as a product of a Roman State Church who used it to reinforce unity in its Empire. The Bible was in no way central to the early communities of G-d. Before one Bible, one creed, and one church, people learned to follow Christ through dialogue with teachers, and the conversations and common life of their communities. They did not learn through private Bible devotion because there was no Bible. When the communities of G-d gathered there was public reading from the fragments of scriptures different communities possessed. Requiring belief in the centrality of the Bible as a requirement for faith is a distortion of Christ's Way of Life created by Roman culture. The centrality of one authorized Bible for all matters of faith became re-emphasized in the power vacuum created by the Reformation. It became a tool of power for Protestant domination.

The idea of a Christian nation also derives from this period. The Roman Empire became synonymous with ideas about the City of G-d. Yet the vision of Christ is for a people of companionship and empowerment with/in every tribe, tongue and nation. It is not a seductive illusion of one Christian nation or state dominating all others. Conversely, in practicing the companionship of empowerment learners of Christ actually begin to go beyond their identities previously rooted in nation, religion (including Christian), ethnicity or family. Conversion is interpreted by modern Christians as signing up to a list of doctrinal requirements as a way of entrance to the church. Christ had no such practice. His learners followed him in the school of life. What was important was the state of their hearts with G-d and others. This way of life cannot be learned through reading books or absorbing an endless stream of verbal teaching. Authentic discipleship only occurs in small learning communities of shared life and in the situations of daily life. Christ did not define admission to the community in terms of doctrinal assent. He looked instead for changes in a way a person lived as indications of their changed heart. The Rich Young Ruler is a good example of this. It was his unchanged heart and his behavior that prevented him joining Jesus in his learning community. It was not his failure to accept the authority of the Bible, the church, a creed, or other doctrinal tests.

BEYOND MODERNITY AND SOCIAL DOMINANCE

The communities of G-d described in the New Testament did not have a mission-management strategy like the churches of institution. Nor did they

Missional

have a prescriptive missional emphasis by modernist design. They grew because people found being in those communities compelling. People discovered something worth dying for that contrasted with a religion of empire defined by deities of domination. In such a world the communities of G-d did not prioritize mission. People were drawn to their way of life because it was characterized by an experience of love. They found a *zoe* life in these communities because G-d is love. The domination mindset of Rome still defines our societies today because it became the foundation for our way of life in the West. In our own societies love is only realized as people become enamored with the way of reconciliation and practice peacemaking. It is only communicated through this way of life in small communities and cannot be taught by words.

These diverse communities, by their very nature, drew people in and propelled people out with Good News. Like the G-d they encountered in community they were centrifugal by nature. They were impossible to design or plan. The Good News was not that the church had a mission, but that they had experienced G-d as love in a way of life together. This life was not communicated in a message of words, or a catchy soundbite, or YouTube video. It could not be manufactured or manipulated to serve the priorities of institutions or missional movements. The moment it was bottled for consumption it died. It was like the manna that Moses found in the wilderness.

Love cannot be compelled. By its nature love never compels others against their will. Love is by definition mutual. It is itself compelling. The modernist overtones and Christian social dominance inherent in missional language need to be recognized and transcended. Only then can people begin to embody Christ through the reconciliation practices that are central to learning in community. Missional Christianity draws back from totally embracing the community God of reconciling love. It remains beguiled by the promises of the mission God of domination Christianity. Love does not have a mission, it just is what it is: "I will be what I will be."[29] Such a G-d, and the communities of people who have experienced that G-d, do not need a mission. To encounter them is enough to captivate our hearts. Nothing is as compelling as that love.

Alan Hirsch is right: "There are consequences when the meanings of words become confused. This is particularly true within a biblical worldview. The Hebrews were suspicious of images as conveyors of truth, so they

29. Exodus 3:14.

guarded words and their meanings carefully. Part of theology, therefore, includes guarding the meaning of words to maintain truth within the community of faith."[30]

Ironically, it is the missional movement itself that needs to heed his warning.

30. Hirsch, "Defining Missional."

5

Missional

The Language House

"A picture held us captive. And we could not get outside it, for it lay in our language and language seemed to repeat it to us inexorably."

—WITTGENSTEIN.[1]

"A language house predetermines how one sees the world or reads a text. We always bring our language house to the task of interpreting the world and understanding how to navigate our way."

—ALAN ROXBURGH.[2]

---

1. Wittgenstein, *Philosophical Investigations*, 115.
2. Roxburgh, *Missional: Joining God*, 85.

Part 2: The Missional Illusion

THE LANGUAGE DOMI-MATRIX

LANGUAGE SHAPES OUR ACTIONS. In *Missional: Joining God in The Neighborhood* Alan Roxburgh suggests that we have "become trapped in the language and presuppositions of our late modern consumerism." Using the above quote by Wittgenstein he notes the way in which "a picture holds us captive" and that "we all live inside a particular story that tells us how the world works and how we ought to live in it."[3] In the West we are trapped by the pictures and language of consumerism. This has resulted in people defining their sense of belonging in society through the pursuit of such happiness. Individualism, consumerism, and careerism are the prescribed pathways to success and meaning. In this consumerist picture people feel that they can only belong if they do well in their careers. They need to earn enough money to enable them to buy houses, cars, clothes, and other quality products. If you do not have these status symbols, you are nothing.

This emphasis enables people to live individualistic lifestyles that do not require interdependence or vulnerability. It creates an anesthetized and atomized independence. These blind spots drive our priorities. They cause Christians to cease to reflect Gospel values of wholeness and community. Their lives become dominated by the late-modern story of consumption. We are all motivated by beliefs that are hidden from us. They do shape the way we act. Like the air we breathe these beliefs are difficult to see. They are just part of the way life is organized and structured. Perpetuating a subtle and seductive domination, they are expressed and reinforced through the structures that run business corporations and the monolithic institutions of state and church. In this way they condition the population like lab rats. This is the modern domination system of corporate state, church, and business. Political and religious ministers are its agents.

The missional movement also has its own language house. It holds Christianity captive in modernity through using language such as mission, leadership, mapping, and planning. This is language that does not fully reflect Christ's values of companionship and empowerment. As illustrated in previous chapters, the language of Christian mission and management perpetuates Christian social dominance. The language of missional is miasmic. Yet it still contains and communicates a modernist solution based on ideological dominance. It can be misapplied and misused because its meaning is amorphous and open to debate. This allows it to be co-opted by

3. *Ibid.*

mainline churches in support of their inherent agenda of social dominance. The practices of mission, leadership, mapping, and planning dovetail with the centralized structures and bureaucratic practices of mainline Christian institutions. In this way missional language perpetuates Christian hegemony. It is also used to "repeat it to us inexorably,"[4] in church, on the web, and in book after book, and has become a formidable propaganda. It creates buzzwords that can be used to identify us as being on board the missional mission train.

WHAT PICTURES HOLD WESTERN CHRISTIANITY CAPTIVE?

The non-Biblical picture of Christian mission is one that has driven the Protestant and Catholic projects. It holds Christianity captive to a past of division, polarization, sectarianism, wars of religion, and the proliferation of over 40,000 denominations. It has created Christian nation states in a World War quest for dominance and a Western Crusade against Islam. These are the consequences of mission language and ideology. It is not neutral. It implies taking control of another person's religion, culture, and way of life. Protestantism is once again held captive by a picture of remaking a New Christian West. Missional meanings are more amorphous. Yet the association with the previous ideology of mission is very difficult to escape. This is because the word mission is contained in the word missional. It is too easy to associate the mission ideology of Christendom with missional language and practices. This allows missional practitioners to perpetuate communities that have more in common with Roman lordship and domination than the companionship and empowerment of Jesus.

On the cover of *Missional Map-Making* Martin Robinson writes an endorsement that states: "this is a needed book to help us remake the New Christian West."[5] The New Christian West could mean something less culturally dominant than it sounds. Yet, to the uninitiated it implies a vision of a Christianized society. What might Muslim and secular citizens think of the New Christian West? What do missional Christians think of a New Muslim West? If we are not careful we may be knee deep in the bloody wars of Christian hegemony's legacy. There is further irony when Alan Roxburgh quotes the philosopher Heidegger: "Language is the house of Being. It is the home where man dwells. Those who think and those who create with words

---

4. Wittgenstein, *Philosophical Investigations*, 115.
5. Robinson, *Missional Map-Making*, cover.

Part 2: The Missional Illusion

are the guardians of the home."⁶ It was Heidegger who supported Hitler and the Nazi Party. He was, perhaps, held captive by a Christian National Socialist picture of strong communities rooted in a sense of national unity through uniformity. Could it be that in its quest for strong community in a united New Christian West that the missional movement is not far from making Heidegger's mistake? What is the ultimate goal of missional? Its language traps us in a modernity characterized by the polarization that gave birth to the Cold War. This creates mutual stand off but not mutual reconciliation.

THE MISSIONAL SOLUTION IS MODERNIST

Heidegger risked being pragmatic for the sake of being pragmatic in order to mobilize Germany. He felt it was essential to do something strong in the face of the rising communist threat. To do this he was willing to sacrifice some of his principles to try and steer Nazism toward building a stronger united Germany. This seemingly noble conservative desire to keep the world from falling apart may have been what caused it to polarize and fragment. It was trying to hold on to an idealized social unity though a uniformity that perpetuated a polarizing left wing/right wing view of reality.

These ideologies split Europe in two and gave birth to the Cold War. They still rage today in left wing and right wing extremes. The missional solution advocates doing something strong and pragmatic in the face of the nihilism of postmodernity. Yet, this will perpetuate religion-based rivalry and division and, incidentally, produce further nihilism. It was Protestantism that gave birth to nihilism. G-d is a community and not an idea that can be expressed in a word. The word is Christ himself, not Christian doctrine or ideology. G-d is therefore only found in the creation of community through the practice of reconciliation and reciprocity. Christ's kingdom of companionship and empowerment is not established through the imposition of creeds, or conversion to Christian doctrinal ideology. This is the socially devastating cycle of Christian hegemony's nihilistic legacy. The West may fall apart as Christians refuse to let go of a vision of a New Christian West. This is because Muslim and secular competitors may also refuse to let go of their social visions. It is the illusory desire for unity through uniformity that actually creates social fragmentation. All ideologically-driven nation states have found this to be a tragic reality. Is the Armageddon that

6. Heidegger, *Basic Writings*, 213.

may result from such polarizing visions really an affirming *telos*, or good life?

MISSION LANGUAGE: CAPTIVE CHRISTIANITY

Christian mission contains the idea that there is a king who comes to establish a rule. It is blindly assumed that the authority of the king is maintained through hierarchical leadership structures. These reinforce a unity through uniformity to one totalizing vision. Where there is an emphasis on a hierarchical leadership, a system of doctrinal Christian social dominance is established. It is held in place through the way religious leaders govern their communities. Catholic Papal infallibility and Protestant Biblical authority have the same function; somebody rules in the name of the king god or the word god. These need to be named clearly as false gods. This way of viewing reality inevitably leads to an attempt at social dominance by one country, social group, church, or religion. Protestantism has bred schism and perpetuated rivalry and a striving for creedal dominance through the word god. Yet it is Jesus who warned his disciples not to model themselves on Roman practices of dominance through lordship, even through the use of words and ideas. This is why Jesus modeled practices and a way of life and not conversion. When people reconcile they are not trying to convert others to their doctrinal system. The doctrine is irrelevant. It is the practice of reconciliation and reciprocity that transforms them both. This is the way the kingdom is established. It is not through conversion to doctrine or ideology. The example of reconciliation, reciprocity, and mutuality is the teaching.

Jesus provided us with an egalitarian picture of authority. It was in a story of people washing each other's feet. The Roman Church rejected this picture of mutual submission. Instead, it is the Roman picture of hierarchical mission that holds Christianity captive. It is this picture that is modeled in Protestant and Catholic leadership. Modernity has only worsened the situation. It has produced leadership built on ideas of self-fulfillment, ego expression, and management theory. An erroneous picture is then presented as Biblical Christian leadership. This distorted image of authority has repeated itself throughout Christian history. It is like a nightmare from which we are trying to wake up. Romanized mission language holds Christianity captive to a picture of coercive social dominance. This image will keep it captive unless it can be born again through a better way of life. The church must no longer be conformed to a Roman model of leadership and Protestant managerialism. It must be transformed by Jesus' own picture of authority; voluntary mutual submission in small learning communities.

MISSIONAL (NOT)

Missional practices go a long way in trying to redress the tragedies of Christian domination. Yet its language remains captive to the graven image of the mission God. Missional practice is, in fact, held captive in modernity by its own language. It uses mission, leadership, map-making, and planning to help Christian leaders navigate their way through the ever-shifting sea of faith and culture in postmodernity. The definition of missional is miasmic and amorphous. Similarly, missional practices are described in an amorphous and confusing way. The term missional leadership is used as a way to talk about the practice of facilitating conversation. Missional mapping is used as a way to talk about cultivation of practices in communities. Missional planning is used to refer to non-strategic planning. The modernist nuances in this language can be misleading. It leaves the door open to interpret missional through a modernist lens. This is disconcerting, because the modernist social vision is essentially about leadership or dominance by one country or social group.

MISSIONAL (NOT) LEADERSHIP

Missional leadership is not really leadership in the modern sense. Wikipedia defines leadership as, "organizing a group of people to achieve a common goal. The leader may or may not have any formal authority. Students of leadership have produced theories involving traits, situational interaction, function, behavior, power, vision and values, charisma, and intelligence, among others. Somebody whom people follow: somebody who guides or directs others."[7]

This modernist definition emphasises organization, having a goal, being followed, and directing others. The missional leader may have some of these traits. Yet their task is described not in terms of organization but of facilitating a conversation. Missional leadership is about having a strategic

---

7. en.wikipedia.org/wiki/Leadership.

goal. It is not about being followed but about encouraging others to become self-generating missional practitioners. Missional leadership is not framed in terms of directing others. It is about listening to and facilitating people's concerns, yet remains more directive at a planning stage. However, this emerges out of the conversational process with/in communities and neighborhoods.

The missional leader is a fuzzy kind of leader. Strategic planning is seen as counterproductive. Missional leadership is characterized by skills in group consultation and listening. A co-ordinating and planning function is, however, retained once the consultative process has been completed. This is confusing. Can it be described as leadership? It is not about organization, goal setting, or direction. The missional leader is, first and foremost, a community listener. They also articulate the message of the community once they have facilitated the listening process. Alan Roxburgh links the role to that of being a poet. This is someone who articulates the aspirations and mood of the community and thereby creates meaning. Community poet or community facilitator is therefore a more accurate description of the role. To continue to use the word leader to describe this activity becomes confusing and misleading. The use of the word leader retains a modernist assumption of direction and planning.

When the term missional leadership is unpacked what it in fact means is that there is no mission and there is no leadership. Yet, without the benefit of missional decoding using these words keeps intact the picture that someone actually does lead and there actually is a mission. This creates a confused expectation. Some missional practitioners have begun describing themselves as community architects. This is better in some ways and worse in others. To focus on the community aspect seems a true reflection of missional values. Yet the word architect is a clear return to the modernist notion of design by a planner. This confusion of language sets the direction and forms the context of the work that will be done in communities by missional practitioners. To avoid the repetition of mistakes made by the strategically orientated leaders of modernity it would be wise to just drop the language of leadership. The word leadership does not describe the facilitative role being proposed. G-d is more reciprocal than missional. Community poet more accurately reflects the G-d of reciprocity.

Part 2: The Missional Illusion

MISSIONAL (NOT) MAP-MAKING

Missional map-making occurs as the missional leader helps people develop practices that are meaningful in their context. These might be forms of prayer (offices), hospitality, being alongside the poor or learning, and so on. The core identity of the missional community emerges from the stories of people in the community itself. Map-making is not about the leader communicating his or her vision. It is about cultivating the practices of the group. People are invited to reflect upon their own stories in the context of the history of G-d's people in the Bible. Shared practices that will have meaning in the community are then cultivated. This is done collaboratively. In this process missional map-making helps people connect their own stories with the history of G-d's pilgrim people. Participants bring to the group their stories of fragmentation and dislocation. These have been shaped by the culture of consumerism, globalization, late modernity, and pluralism. They find meaning and purpose again by developing a different core identity. This emerges as they discover themselves as part of G-d's pilgrim people by developing shared practices that are culture current.

Alan Roxburgh also uses the term cultivation to describe the activity of map-making. This organic image is well-suited to the task being described. Yet, retaining the term map-making implies that something more than just cultivation is the desired outcome. Mapping is a modernist activity. It denotes clear definition of a geographical territory. Mapping allows 100 percent predictability. In contrast, cultivation is open-ended. It involves loosening the soil and preparing ground to receive crops. This imagery suits the task of preparing a group to receive new people, new ideas, and develop new practices. Use of mapping language implies a well-defined predictable outcome. Yet a well-defined outcome is not what missional practitioners are trying to create. The language of mapping sends a mixed message. It keeps a sense of pseudo-stability that is characteristic of modernity. The language of map-making is retrograde to the task of community cultivation. These are mutually exclusive tasks. Alan Roxburgh writes, "Those who cultivate do not make but call forth what is already inherently present."[8] It seems misleading and confusing to try to describe this as map-making. This fuzzy use of language creates cognitive dissonance. It prompts the question, can a map be cultivated? People opt for one or the other to resolve the tension.

---

8. Roxburgh, *Missional Map-Making*, 184.

In this way the mapping metaphor and intention is perpetuated. Modernity triumphs.

Missional map-making occurs when churches or groups reflect on their fragmented postmodern stories and histories. They then reconnect with the story of G-d's people in history. Usually, it means some kind of reflection on the story of G-d's people in the Christian scriptures. This aspect of the missional conversation is also one that has clear modernist overtones. Focussing on the Bible is a practice rooted in the Reformation Christianity of the sixteenth century. Such a practice perpetuates Christian social dominance through use of the Bible and is rooted in a belief in the supremacy of the Bible. This belief prioritizes the Bible above all other forms of revelation and encounter with G-d, such as, nature, the human soul, and human wisdom. The apostle Paul certainly appealed to the wisdom of the Greeks and understood that all truth is God's truth. Using the Bible as an exclusive source of revelation in a pluralistic society is a retrograde practice. It is rooted in a fragmented and dying Protestantism. The challenge confronting communities of G-d in the twenty-first century is to move beyond attempts at doctrinal social dominance rooted in one book, one church or one creed. It is to move to a more holistic spirituality rooted in an encounter with Christ in people. These people live in neighborhoods and societies that are neotribal. It is in these people that Christ needs to be discerned, and cultivated, and formed. G-d is, in this way, given skin. In a neotribal society it is a G-d with neotribal skin.

Making the Bible the sole focus of revelation is more likely to result in mis-mapping neighborhoods formed by globalization, postmodernity, and pluralism. This will create a faulty map. It will be one with a bias toward an outmoded, Bible-centered Christianity that will regurgitate the sectarianism inherent in Protestantism. Surely, the neighborhood conversation must be one that includes and reverences other holy books and the sacred practices of other religions. It then creates something entirely new with the influences that are present. As Alan Roxburgh notes, "Those who cultivate do not make but call forth what is already inherently present."[9] Community cultivation requires an open source approach to articulate the stories that will emerge in neighborhoods. These stories will be secular, Muslim, Hindu, gay, straight, black, white, left wing, right wing, anarchist, Catholic, Protestant, male and female, Greek and Jew, and so on. Surely the story we now find ourselves in is one of globalization, postmodernity, and pluralism.

9. Ibid.

Part 2: The Missional Illusion

This is the next instalment in the story of G-d's neotribal people; a more empathic civilization.

Practicing love of neighbor and reconciliation seem more potent than inviting people to relate with the story of G-d's people in the Bible. Scripture may be one voice that needs to be heard. Yet there are many others. It is the practice of the Gospel of companionship and empowerment that will open up the future. This is G-d's new covenant of universal love. It is where everyone belongs through Christ. This calls forth a multiple range of small communities of people who belong, regardless of race, religion, or politics. This is the cultivation of a neotribal identity and empathic civilization. Bible-focussed ghettos, trapped in the language of modernity and Christian doctrinal dominance, do not express Christ. Whilst it will be argued by missional practitioners that that is far from what is intended, it is what missional language may unintentionally give birth to. Words are only one of the ways in which G-d speaks. The Bible itself testifies against *sola scriptura*.

MISSIONAL (NOT) PLANNING

Alan Roxburgh writes that, "as the mission emerges people need to be able to plan their activities, define the steps they will take, align their energies and resources with the vision. In this sense mission becomes a radically decentralised process."[10] The missional approach warns that strategic planning for church growth has become counterproductive. This is due to globalization, pluralism, rapid technological change, postmodernism, increasing global needs, loss of confidence in primary structures, the democratization of knowledge, and a return to romanticism. Planning therefore occurs at the end of the neighborhood conversation and group identity formation process.

Wikipedia defines a plan as "a detailed proposal for doing or achieving something. Decide/arrange in advance. Synonyms: design, scheme, project, layout, draft, map, idea, design, project, scheme, plot, engineer, schedule."[11]

The practice of planning fits well within the definition of modernism previously outlined as: "a socially progressive trend of thought that affirms the power of human beings to create, improve and reshape their environment with the aid of practical experimentation, scientific knowledge, or

---

10. Ibid., 180
11. *en.wikipedia.org/wiki/Plan.*

technology."¹² Missional planning is still trying to shape an environment, even when it occurs toward the end of the community cultivation process. The use of the planning metaphor holds the planner captive to the image of acting upon the neighborhood. Planning directs a neighborhood design process. It needs to be asked at this point, whose plan will it be? Will it be a Christian neighborhood plan? Will this be part of re-making a New Christian West? Or will it be a genuinely open neighborhood plan with people of all faiths and none?

This feels like missional Christianity is trying to pull the rabbit out of the hat at the last moment. It is still promoting an illusion of mastery. Isn't the message of the Gospel beyond this cultural dominance? Some of those in the missional movement will protest that this is not their goal. However, in using the word planning missional practitioners declare an intention to design a New Christian neighborhood. In doing so they do not spell out clearly enough its implications. Missional community design is being practiced in pluralistic and neotribal neighborhoods. This means that missional communities must reflect those neighborhoods. Yet missional practitioners seem to want to retain planning rights at one crucial point. It is a New Christian West that is being created through this planning. The remaking of a New Christian West necessitates the creation of New Christian neighborhoods. This seems to be a part of the plan that is non-negotiable. It also does not "call forth what is already inherently present"¹³ in pluralistic and neotribal neighborhoods. Finally, missional Christianity still wants to negotiate, or even impose, a New Christian plan.

A NEW CHRISTIAN WEST OR A NEOTRIBAL WORLD?

Einstein reminds us that, "It is absolutely impossible to solve any problem with the same consciousness that created the problem."¹⁴ What missional is proposing is a cure for the sicknesses of modernity. Yet it is using modernist language and concepts to solve it. Missional has given Christianity the right diagnosis but the wrong cure. It keeps it trapped in modernity and Christian social dominance by using the terminology of mission, leadership, map-making, and planning. The following agenda for change is implied in the ambiguous and dissonant mix of missional language:

12. *en.wikipedia.org/wiki/Modernism.*
13. Roxburgh, *Missional Map-Making*, 184.
14. *en.wikiquote.org/wiki/Talk:Albert_Einstein.*

Part 2: The Missional Illusion

- Misseo Dei: the mission God
- Missional: sent Christians
- Missional leader: confusion with community poet
- Missional map-making: confusion with community/neighborhood conversation
- Missional planning: confusion with community/neighborhood cultivation

Produces:

- Missional communities: Christian communities shaped by neighborhood
- Remake the new Christian West: a bid for cultural dominance
- Christian history of division: polarization repeats itself
- Armageddon?

David Whyte warns us that, "If our language is technical, then the qualities we draw from people will only be of a technical nature."[15] A language is needed that is more consistent with Christ's message of mutual and communal empowerment. It needs to go beyond missional Christianity's modernist and ambiguous language. Such a language needs to reflect G-d's perichoretic dance with/in all humanity. It needs to provide pictures that enable people to form communities of reconciliation rather than Christian mission. These are pictures that will foster reconciliation in the midst of our globalized and pluralistic societies. A picture of G-d needs to be recovered which creates a faith free from the social dominance inherent in Protestant and Catholic mission. This language needs to be faithful to the Bible's revelation of a G-d of reconciliation and reciprocity. Such a language might be:

- Interface G-d: reciprocal reconciling love
- Inter-facing mutually sent peoples: find reconciliation together through giving and receiving
- Community Poets: articulate community/neighborhood stories
- Community Conversations: identify community/neighborhood contours and horizons, these lead to making peace and reconciliation
- Community Cultivation: empowers mutually initiated/owned community stories and practices involving people of all faiths and none.

15. Whyte, *Crossing the Unknown Sea*, 239.

This creates:

- Reconciliation Communities: in neighborhoods/neotribal societies.

This gives birth to:

- Companionship of Empowerment/(the kingdom of G-d)
- A neotribal world made whole.

Reconciliation gives birth to mutual submission, mutual giving, companionship, and empowerment. Such language creates an increasingly empathic, permeable, and neotribal world. It incarnates and makes manifest in social reality the vision of Jesus Christ who said: "Go beyond your mentality. The Companionship of Empowerment is within your grasp."[16]

Alan Roxburgh is right when he observes: "A language house predetermines how one sees the world or reads a text. We always bring our language house to the task of interpreting the world and understanding how to navigate our way."[17]

Ironically, it is the missional language house itself that is making Western Christianity's vision myopic.

---

16. *Matthew 3:2.*
17. Roxburgh, *Missional: Joining God,* 85.

6

Missional
Impossible!

> "Illusion is the first of all pleasures."
> —Voltaire[1]

> "Losing an illusion makes you wiser than finding a truth."
> —Ludwig Börne[2]

MISSING THE MOMENT

THE MISSIONAL MOVEMENT HAS woken up the church. It knows it no longer meets the spiritual needs of people in globalized and pluralistic societies. Missional has also taken the church forward from colonial missions and the abuses of domination Christianity. It is trying to move from a church-centered agenda into the neighborhood. Although much of this is good,

---

1. Voltaire, *La Pucelle d'Orléans*.
2. Börne, *Collected Writings*, 11.

how far will it take the communities of G-d? Will it be enough to save the planet? Is missional language a faithful container of the message of Christ? Missional leaders agree that it is language that shapes our practices and understanding as learners of Jesus Christ. It is also language that shapes engagement with/in our communities and neighborhoods.

What kind of world will be created as missional communities move into the neighborhood? Whatever may be meant by the term missional there is no denying its immediate impact. It communicates the idea that I am trying to convert even if it is explained that what is intended is to strike up a conversation about community and neighborhood. The language of missional is confused at best, and misleading and deceptive at worst. Missional language is retrograde to its method because it derives from modernity. Mission, leader, mapping, and planning are all pragmatic and expansionist activities. It is a language that reflects the paradigm that has characterized modernity; pioneering into new and hostile territory, mapping it, and then planting. Eddie Izzard is perceptive when he says of the British Christian Empire that "we stole countries with the cunning use of flags."[3]

One of the problems with mission language is that its history is characterized by colonialism. Missional language is retrograde to its stated purpose because the primary failure of modernity has been the clash of missions and ideologies: capitalist vs. communist, white vs. black, straight vs. gay, state vs. church, Protestant vs. Catholic, right vs. left, ad nauseam. Mission language perpetuates denominational and religious turf wars. It reflects a dualistic and individualistic quest for ideological superiority. The modernist nuances inherent in missional language create practitioners who are not that far from planting flags again. The game just got less obvious.

THE MISSIONAL ILLUSION

The psychotherapist Erich Fromm was aware of the way in which powerful illusions created by ideology drive our motivations. He writes with clarity about self-deception in the pursuit of aims that can seem pure and noble and sanctioned by society.

> Our conscious motivations, ideas, and beliefs are a blend of false information, biases, irrational passions, rationalizations,

---

3. *en.wikiquote.org/wiki/Eddie_Izzard*.

prejudices, in which morsels of truth swim around and give the reassurance albeit false, that the whole mixture is real and true. The thinking processes attempt to organize this whole cesspool of illusions according to the laws of plausibility. This level of consciousness is supposed to reflect reality; it is the map we use for organizing our life.[4]

Mission is a powerful illusion. It is now serving the needs of a marginalized church to galvanize itself toward a somewhat insincere and self-interested community service. Its agenda comes across as opaque. Behind it lurks an attempt at social dominance through the word of scripture and an idea of a creating a Christian culture—as if it even exists. There is no such thing as a Christian shirt or Christian counselling or Christian marriage. Jesus didn't have a mission or a missional purpose but came seeking to make society whole through reconciliation. Missional language confuses and distorts the aims and purpose of the communities of G-d. To be a companion to someone and to mission to them are different things. Jesus commanded us to love our neighbors not convert them. He called his learners to practice companionship and empowerment, and not missional leadership.

What is needed is a transformation of the modernist and mission-driven worldview. It is this corporate mechanistic language that has been instrumental in driving a vacuous culture in the West. As it stands, missional has been a confused, subtle, somewhat reactionary response to recent emerging shifts towards experiencing a truly emancipatory Christ. It is reactionary because it is attempting to guide leaders away from what it regards as the harmful excesses of postmodernity to something more pragmatic. In attempting to put leaders back on track missional seems to have become a misdirected movement. It is now chiefly serving the needs of mainline church hierarchies, rather than Christ in the people of an emerging neotribal society. Missional seems to have been co-opted. Its *raison d'être* has been re-forged to suit the less benign purposes of propping up the decaying infrastructures of mainline Christian institutions.

THE NIHILIST FINAL SOLUTION

The missional illusion is perpetuated by the idea that it is a way of addressing the sickness of nihilism created by postmodernity. Ironically, it is the modernity of the missional solution itself that perpetuates nihilism. This is

4. Fromm, *To Have or To Be*.

because it clings to the modernist ideals of cultural and social dominance through conversion to Christian doctrine. It is centered on the Bible as the source of salvation rather than the person of Christ. Cultural change is achieved through pragmatism and the creation of a Bible-based cultural social dominance. The movement arises out of a period in history framed by modernist priorities, i.e., the 1950s and 1960s. It does not make the person of Christ known through practicing his example of reconciliation and reciprocity. The missional movement perpetuates Bible centered and creedal cultural dominance. Yet Christ did not make himself known as a written word but as a human being. In making the Bible created by Rome the center of its faith Protestantism became idolatrous. Christ did not make scripture central. He was clear: "I am the Way . . . the Door, the Bread, the true Vine, the Life, the Truth . . ."[5] It was in the flesh and blood of his own humanity that he knew that divinity and salvation were found and not in the words of a book. This is why his way of life is not a religion of a book. On the contrary, it is a way of transformation through the human heart. Christ saw that it was through our acceptance of YHWH in ourselves and others that salvation and social wholeness would come. He did not believe that the companionship of empowerment would come through the words of a book. The Bible as one book did not exist until the fourth century. It was created as a way of making the Roman Christian mission more uniform and conformist. The way of Christ used no such methods of soft mind control and cultural dominance. He didn't need a book. He knew G-d was nearer than breathing in every fibre of his being and in all things that "Abba" had created.

Bishop Lesslie Newbigin was a British missionary whose work laid the foundations for the missional church movement. His challenge regarding mission was born out of a post war and cold war culture shaped by the values of modernity. The overriding concern he had was the decline of modern Christian influence in society. He resented not being top dog anymore and wanted his lost status back:

> If the gospel is to challenge the public life of our society, if Christians are to occupy the "high ground" which they vacated in the noon time of "modernity," it will not be by forming a Christian political party, or by aggressive propaganda campaigns. Once again it has to be said that there can be no going back to the "Constantinian" era. It will only be by movements that begin with the local

---

5. John 14:6; 10:9; 6:35; 15:1.

congregation in which the reality of the new creation is present, known, and experienced, and from which men and women will go into every sector of public life to claim it for Christ, to unmask the illusions which have remained hidden and to expose all areas of public life to the illumination of the gospel.[6]

Lesslie Newbigin decried going back to a Constantinian era of domination of society through a hierarchical church. Nevertheless, he was captured by the nightmare of a Gospel that would come about through ideological and cultural dominance. This clearly expresses his Protestant belief in domination through the word of creed and Bible. In an attempt to "occupy the high ground" of society the missional solution is trying to redress the effects of modern secular social dominance. Yet it is trying to do this with a reassertion of Christian ideological and cultural social dominance. Newbigin had a blind spot. He failed to see that all social dominance is itself the problem—whether Roman, Christian, or modern. All social dominance leads to ancient Greece and Rome—not to Christ. The modern hegemony of the West grew out of Romanized Christianity. Newbigin's Christianity supports the ideological and cultural domination of the West by one creed and one Bible for all people. These ideas were Roman inventions that acted as social instruments to maintain the unity of the Roman Empire. They in no way reflect the egalitarian message of Christ. They became Protestant strategies to establish their cultural supremacy. As Jesus said, "a house divided against itself cannot stand."[7] Dualism brings about its own collapse. Modernity was born out of ideas rooted in Greek and Roman ideas of social dominance. Therefore, the real enemy of modernity is modernity itself. This is similar to saying that "in a nuclear age the true enemy cannot be defeated. In the nuclear age the true enemy is war itself."[8]

The missional illusion does not sufficiently address the questions and needs of postmodernity. People need to move beyond the dualistic and polarizing distinctions of secular and Christian, left and right, liberal and conservative, Protestant and Catholic, and so on. Missional seeks to sidestep these questions by pragmatism in the face of the disturbing social fragmentation caused by postmodernity, globalization, and pluralism. The missional solution is a quick fix programme for a postmodern sickness unto death. It is in fact a social dominance of the word. This is not a move

6. Newbigin, *The Gospel*, 232–33.
7. Matthew 12:25.
8. Commander Hunter, *"Crimson Tide."*

forward but an attempt to step back in time to a more ordered world. The missional program is attempting to recreate a modernist world. It was, in fact, shaped by mission, leadership, mapping, and planning. It is over. G-d has moved on. Ironically, the nihilism it seeks to overcome by ideological and cultural dominance it in fact perpetuates. Modernity cannot fix modernity. Its insistence of dominance by one social group perpetuates rivalry, societal schism, and atomization. Atomic destruction is a fitting image. Its final solution has within it the anatomy of human and social fragmentation. This is the result of belief in ideological and cultural domination through words and ideas; the supremacy of the word god, i.e., the Bible. It needs to be named clearly as bibliolatry. Missional Protestantism has deposed Christ and put in his place a book. It has forgotten the warning of the apostle Paul that the "letter kills but the spirit gives life."[9] Missional religion is a fragmented and fragmenting way of life that steals, kills, and destroys.

MISSIONAL: NOT SOCIALLY TRANSFORMATIVE

The missional illusion is also perpetuated by the idea that Christians can remake a New Christian West. This idea grows out of Newbigin's stated purpose that Christians should attempt to "occupy the high ground" of society. It advocates a homogenous Christian social vision that is implemented through Christian churches. It actually seeks to use them as a means of ideological and cultural domination by the word God (the Bible). In Newbigin's vision churches will disseminate a creedal and Bible based form of Protestant domination by the word and "claim society for Christ."[10] This is a total misunderstanding of the purpose of the Gospel, which is to bring reconciliation, companionship, and empowerment and heal the world. The call of Jesus is to be salt, light, and leaven and in no way to "occupy the high ground" of society and "claim it for Christ." Jesus specifically warns his disciples not to try to lord it over others and try and establish dominance. This is the Roman and hierarchical way. Jesus is not made lord when Christians have ideological and social dominance in society. Jesus is realized as YHWH when people are reconciled to one another through following his example. Building a Christian Empire through ideological and cultural dominance of the word was not the vision of Christ. It is the

---

9. 2 Corinthians 3:6.
10. Newbigin, *The Gospel*, 232–33.

Roman vision of creedal conformity enforced through hierarchical leadership and doctrinal mind control.

The societies of the West are neotribal and post-secular. There is still huge potential for a clash of ideologies by aiming to establish Christian social dominance on the basis of the word of God. This just reflects the previous socially devastating mistakes of mission-misshaped Christianity. Seeking neighborhood strength and unity by advocating a New Christian West increases social fragmentation. What postmodern societies need most are communities that practice reconciliation. Communities of Christian mission seeking to remake a New Christian West only perpetuate the practice of social dominance through their creedal and Bible centered emphasis. In this way the missional solution only serves the interests of the mainline institutions. It is therefore not faithful to the purposes of Jesus Christ who is seeking to bring reconciliation in our emerging neotribal societies. If the focus is on mission the communities of G-d will move further and further away from reconciliation. Like in the pursuit of happiness when making happiness the goal is always counterproductive. We only become happy by doing the things that will make for happiness. The more communities practice reconciliation the more they will quite naturally be fulfilling the task of making learners of Christ the peacemaker. Making mission primary and central is the biggest mistake that learners of Christ can make in neotribal societies.

MISSIONAL: NOT GOSPEL OR SCRIPTURE

The missional illusion is perpetuated by the myth that mission is at the heart of the Gospel. This is a belief that aims of the Gospel will be achieved through the practices of ideological and cultural dominance. Yet the Gospel does not call the people of G-d to occupy the high ground of society. It calls those who follow Christ to make peace with their neighbor. The idea of using creedal conformity as a means of manufacturing consent only begins in the Roman Church. It was then transferred through Protestantism and its emphasis on using the Bible as a means of authority and ideological and cultural domination. This what Newbigin believed in and what missional assumptions are founded upon.

Missional

Yet mission language only begins to be used with the rise of a church driven by Roman practices of hierarchical domination. The Roman Church became entangled with, and co-opted by, the Roman imperialistic drive to conquer. "The Roman response to spiritual revolt was in the end so Roman; pragmatic, shrewd. They reached out and they assimilated even this revolutionary cult and they made it Roman."[11] Mission is the terminology of Roman military conquest with which the church became associated and has found it impossible to free itself. It is an obvious connection to link this development with the history of a violent and coercive Christianity. The companionship of empowerment is not the imposition of mission, either through the hierarchical machinery of Catholicism or the ideological and bureaucratic machinery of Protestantism. Such developments have completely distorted the Gospel, which is a way of peace through the practice of reconciliation in community.

The missional illusion is also perpetuated by the false assumption that modern mission is an idea found in the Scriptures. This is not the case. The word mission does occur in the New Testament but only in the sense of going on a journey for a specific purpose. Mission language in its current usage only begins with Romanized Christianity. There is also a subtle connection between the idea of mission and war. As Michael Foucault reminds us, "Politics is war continued by other means."[12] As is the politics of a mission strategy perpetuated through ideological and cultural means. Contemporary mission ideology emerges out of a generation that was saturated and traumatized by the horror of two World Wars, atomic devastation, and a long and deeply entrenched cold war mentality. This reflects the dualism and polarization that is the fall out of modernity. Mission also carries with it a certain *jouissance*. Consider the popular appeal the cold war hero James Bond or his American cousins in *Mission Impossible*. We have lived through a time shaped by mission ideology inherent in cold war politics. The mainline churches are aping this cold war mentality by choosing a mission-shaped strategy. It is a subtle and covert way of continuing to wage a gospel war of ideological and cultural domination on society. This reflects the missional solution's covert and subtle nature. It is why it appears underground, amorphous, and opaque.

11. Marr, "The Word and the Sword–History of the World."
12. Foucault, *Society Must Be Defended*.

Part 2: The Missional Illusion

MISSIONAL: MISSING THE MOMENT

The missional movement has woken the church up to begin to examine the reasons that it is failing. It is causing it to acknowledge massive cultural shifts. Things have changed: globalization, postmodernity, pluralism, internetization, democratization, and massive global need. Yet missional has given Christianity the wrong prescription: mission, leadership, map making, and planning. It is driven by the use of retrograde missional language and the socially divisive purpose of remaking a New Christian West. Missional map-making is misguided because of the assumption that making a map will provide some direction. The way mission is propagated by mainline Christian churches has made it more managerial than missional. In the mainline Christian churches it is the propagation and implementation of management practice itself that has become the mission. Missional is missing the moment because the task of the communities of G-d in pluralistic societies is practicing reconciliation. This will foster the creation of a mutually submissive neotribal world through the companionship of empowerment. Christian mission is religious war continued by other means; a mutual destruction for all nations and tribes. The task of the communities of G-d is not to serve a modernist agenda to remake a New Christian West. It is to save planet Earth and its neotribal peoples through the practice of reconciliation as the way of Christ. In a nuclear neotribal world the true enemy of Christ's kingdom of peace is Christian mission itself.

EAT AND BE EATEN

It is only in reconciliation that we are made whole and saved. Mission alienates and undermines the fragile fabric of our daily social interactions. Without reconciliation with our neighbor there is no salvation for us or for our planet. We are not made whole by giving mental assent to the message of the Gospel, but only as we enact it in reconciliation with our neighbors. This is the evidence of our faith. In reconciliation the Gospel message becomes embodied through our eyes, our hands, and our feet. This is how we love our neighbor.

Missional

Who is my neighbor? My gay neighbor, straight neighbor, Catholic neighbor, Protestant neighbor, Muslim neighbor, Jewish neighbor, Christian neighbor, theist neighbor, atheist neighbor, right wing neighbor, left wing neighbor, anarchist neighbor, addicted neighbor, health freak neighbor, sick neighbor, employed neighbor, unemployed neighbor, old neighbor, young neighbor, worker neighbor, manager neighbor, lower-class neighbor, upper-class neighbor, rich neighbor, poor neighbor, communist neighbor, fascist neighbor, emergent neighbor, missional neighbor, mission-shaped neighbor, inherited church neighbor.

There is no such thing as individual salvation. To be made whole and saved a person needs to belong in a community of unity in diversity. Reconciliation happens at exactly the place where we are different from our neighbor. It is actually how we are born again into a new way of life. This creates a different kind of society. With each new genuine encounter and reconciliation we keep on being born again and again. Where there is no reconciliation with my neighbor there is, in reality, no new spiritual or social rebirth. What creates a physical new birth? It is only the meeting and interaction of two people who are very different. Out of their meeting, and the inevitable numerous reconciliations that it will require, a new person is created who is a combination of each of them. In this way all things are always being made new. This is the only way new birth can happen; an interpenetration and mixture of two different people. To be born anew into the way of companionship and empowerment requires a genuine reconciliation with our neighbor. Christ brings wholeness in society through our reconciliation with one another.

Following Christ starts with an invitation to practice a way of life that creates personal and social transformation. It is not an irresistible command to sign up and sell a set of beliefs. Christ calls us to a reconciliation that gives birth to a way of companionship and empowerment with others in society. It goes beyond our identities that were previously rooted in our religion, nation, ethnicity, or family ties. This way gives birth to genuine empowerment through community. As W. H. Auden reminds us: "The slogan of Hell: Eat or be eaten. The slogan of Heaven: Eat and be eaten."[13] In saying this he echoes the words of Jesus who offered himself to the world to be eaten: "Whoever eats my flesh and drinks my blood has Life that never dies."[14] The way of Christ is not to consume people into our plan for a big-

13. Auden, *A Certain World*.
14. John 6:54.

ger national church on our way to "occupying the high ground" and remaking a New Christian West. The purpose of those who follow the way is to be consumed as living sacrifices in our neotribal neighborhoods. That is the way society is renewed and "all things are made new."[15] Our substance is to be devoured even as Christ's substance is devoured. This is what it means to practice reconciliation in our churches, neighborhoods, towns, and cities. That is what it means to follow Christ in neotribal society.

A QUESTION OF PURPOSE

In a neotribal society the aims of a Christian missional movement have become impossible:

- Missional language keeps Christianity captive in its mission-misshaped past.
- The missional movement is not moving Western Christianity far enough out of the polarizing and divisive social dominance of modernity.
- It is not moving the mainline churches beyond their default settings of hierarchical and managerial domination, or ideological and cultural supremacy.
- A mission God is eclipsing a G-d of reciprocity.
- Missional living is eclipsing reciprocal living.
- Missional leaders are eclipsing faith-community poets.
- Missional map-making is eclipsing neighborhood cultivation.
- Missional communities are eclipsing reconciliation communities.
- A vision for a New Christian West is eclipsing a Gospel of neotribal peace.

People of faith can rise to the maturity of their birthright as the communities of G-d in our neighborhoods, towns, and cities. Leaving Earth's proud empires behind they can learn to sing a new song with many other different voices in a strange land. Missional Christianity can learn to move beyond the barriers created by its history and agenda of cultural superiority to a new life of neotribal belonging.

15. Revelation 21:5.

PART 3

Recovering Reconciliation

A COMMUNITY OF PARTNERSHIPS

7

Conversation Communities

"Perhaps more accurately our future will come from the individual imagination in conversation with all other imaginations ...A sea formed not from a general's command but from the flow and turn of a thousand creative conversational elements."

—David Whyte[1]

"It is not the answer that enlightens, but the question."

— Eugene Ionesco[2]

POOR LITTLE TALKATIVE CHRISTIANITY

Protestantism has produced at least one listening bank but no listening churches. It has preached people to death and is infamous for its inability to listen. The churches are characterized by an addictive preoccupation with

---

1. Whyte, "Life at the Frontier."
2. Wells, *Choosing the Future*, 15.

preaching and teaching. In modernity Catholicism has not been much better. Even attempts at more contemporary services are made anodyne and saccharine by the overuse of words. This addiction does not emerge from a scriptural picture of G-d or of preaching and teaching. An overconfident Enlightenment, with its emphasis on knowledge as power, has seduced Christianity. The result is a religion of clanging cymbals, ego, pride, and vanity; and many words; a religion of big mouths. Self-aggrandizement is the name of the game. It has nothing to do with the example of Christ the wisdom teacher from Galilee. As the apostle Paul warned Corinth, "We all possess knowledge. But knowledge puffs up while love builds up."[3]

MODERN PREACHING: THE DECEPTIVE "TEACHING"

Over 80 percent of all human communication is non-verbal. We learn by watching and following the example of others. Example and action is the teaching in the ministry of Jesus. "Follow me" was his invitation, not "listen up." Jesus acted and his learners copied. We only learn to pray by being in a group of practitioners and not by listening to weeks of teaching *ad nauseam*. To follow Jesus means to follow his practices. Yet modern Christians actually live as if knowing the words of the Bible is what will transform them. It is the practice of preaching itself that teaches and endorses this belief. Preaching communicates a belief in words as a form of magic. In Western Christianity the example of promotional preacher and passive listener has created religious consumers and education junkies. Modern preaching is deceptive because it demands nothing active or engaging. The preaching encounter is with words and concepts but not real people. Paul the apostle writes of the danger of preaching to others yet being disqualified. The most serious and pervasive fallacy in modern Christianity is to mistake knowledge for personal experience. Information download has its uses but it does not transfer or create potent spiritual experience. The practice of modern preaching sets up a catalog of spiritual errors and difficulties. The map is not the territory. The words alone are never the experience. In modernity we have focussed on the safety of words because it offers a feeling of control and power.

Preaching and passive listening are pseudo-spiritual practices. The preacher practices talking and the congregation practices passive listening. People then feel guilty for their passivity. The spiritual error of the preacher

3. 1 Corinthians 8:1.

is that they believe they have power through specialized knowledge. The error of the consumer is that they need what the preacher has got. It is a spiritualized sales pitch. The preacher acts as though they have all the answers. They may tease, tempt, cajole, punish, baffle, and blind in pursuit of their aims. The preacher is put on a pedestal by, quite literally, standing above all others present. It is knowledge on show. Yet the philosopher Francis Bacon was wrong when he said knowledge is power. It is the ultimate modernist presumption. Knowledge gives power and control over things and people. It does not create power with and through others. In reality, it is our wordless actions that connect us with others and create mutual power. In the West both preacher and people are out of practice with everyday life. They have created a cocooned world. Yet they believe they are practicing because they are either preaching or passively listening. Example is the teaching. The example set by the practice of preaching is one of untouchable, self-righteous, authoritarian monologue. This is what forms the modern disciple of domination Christianity Sunday after Sunday.

PREACHING: THE OPIUM OF THE CHURCH

It was Marx who called religion the opium of the people. In many ways he was right. Religion has been used in the past to pacify and prevent much needed social change and justice. The same can be said of preaching. Preaching has, in fact, become the opium of the church. Preachers speak about topics from the pulpit but then do nothing. Preaching is a pacifier. It conditions passivity. Knowledge retention becomes the name of the game. People enjoy the illusory feelings of power that knowledge consumption and its regurgitation brings. This, in fact, becomes like an addiction to the power and pleasure of words and knowledge. Opium brings decline in social standards and attitudes, and dulls the awareness and motivation. The drug of preaching has acted in a similar manner for its passive consumers. It has become the major factor in the decline of the mainline churches.

Preaching alienates church members from the rest of society. It does this in the way that all drug use alienates. People are drawn together into groups of initiates in a search for special and privileged knowledge or experience. It is like a word hit or a word high. Others are excluded. This shapes a self-righteous and defensive mindset. It also creates guilt. Preaching causes Christians to take on an air of judgment and criticism in the wider society. Through the example of preaching they are taught to judge and reject, rather than question and reflect. This perpetuates a sub-Christian subculture based around knowledge of the Bible. Those who are not conditioned into this approach find it strange and out of touch with society. It creates unrealistic expectations. Christians then become alienated in the wider culture. This is because they have been conditioned by preaching. They think and act in a judgmental and critical manner with ordinary people. This is because preaching teaches a one way method of communication. There is no right of reply in Christian preaching. Of course communities of G-d do have a role in shaping behavior. Yet they shape it through practicing conversation and reconciliation in community.

PREACHING: A SHIBBOLETH OF MODERNITY

The Protestant Reformation used preaching as its primary method of communication. Use of the printed word also accompanied this cultural shift. Protestantism has a strong identity in these modes of communication. Yet, what once made something successful can become its downfall and death. An unthinking overreliance on something that once worked well can create a false sense of security. It has been said of the Welsh revival that it was born in song. Yet it also died there. Chapels that were once full became empty. The same has happened to all the mainline Christian denominations that have unwisely clung to preaching. Methodism and the United Reformed Church in the UK are glaring examples. They have experienced massive decline and will soon be nonviable institutions. They are already socially dysfunctional for the majority of the population.

Preaching has therefore become a shibboleth of modernity. It keeps the twenty-first century church locked in a Victorian subculture. Preaching confuses the rest of society. The general population of Europe find it totally alien. Their communication is in simple soundbites that are visually engaging and well-crafted. TV, the Internet, email, texting and all the tools of i-culture provide instant information. Attention spans cannot cope with sermons and preaching. Contemporary education has employed a range of learning styles that include reflection, pragmatism, and activity. Yet when people come to church on Sunday they find none of these learning methods being used. These changes have presented real difficulties for the churches of institution. They rely on preaching and are addicted to a word culture centered upon a book—the Bible. The word god of Protestantism is dead for the majority of the population in Europe. This reliance on the word also perpetuates social death within Christian institutions. This is because it inculcates values that are not shared by the majority of the population. It used to be said, "God only had one son and he made him a preacher."[4] It might just as easily be said that G-d only had one son and he made him a storyteller or a poet. The tradition of storytelling and poetry is redignifying the communities of G-d in postmodernity.

PREACHING: MONOLOGUE G-D

The preaching of Jesus and the apostle Paul were vastly different from preaching today. The Sermon on the Mount is a series of pithy sayings and short aphorisms of holy wisdom. It is in bite-size chunks for everyday people. Jesus spoke in a strong local dialect and used images and stories. Preaching today uses technical language from psychology, theology, and philosophy. Biblical language itself is a huge hurdle for many. Often it becomes an in-house shorthand. It is used to perpetuate spiritual one-upmanship and pseudo-authority based on knowing the magic Bible words. It is a formidable barrier for the majority of the uninitiated population. What are all these words for? Who is it all for? What's really happening in modern preaching and teaching? Once again, it is insightful to return to the wisdom of Marshall McLuhan. He observed that the medium is message. Preaching as a medium of communication is wordy, technical, and one way. What does that say about the Catholic and Protestant G-d? It is obvious that listening is not on this word god's agenda. Preaching is delivered in rhetorical and theological verbiage for anything from ten minutes up to an hour. Is G-d really that verbose?

The answer for most is, unequivocally, yes. This creates an image of a distant G-d, speaking a stream of strange, difficult, and sometimes accusational words from on high. Christians are saturated in this word god through the practice of modern preaching. Preaching that worships at the footstool of modernist knowledge creates the self-righteous mind found in so many modern Christians. It seeks to dominate through the use of words and knowledge. Like managerialism, preaching is another modernist tool of domination Christianity. It is through this medium that Christian doctrinal and social dominance is maintained. There is no right of reply

---

4. Walker, *The Methodist Preacher*, 5.

in Christian worship. Christians are formed and taught by this example to practice a non-negotiable, put up or shut up religion.

The image of a monologue G-d is perpetuated through the practice of preaching. Passive consumers begin to believe G-d is like this because that is what they experience in church. There was preaching in the New Testament. It was in the form of public proclamation in the streets. It was not technical, long, or knowledge laden. Certainly, the proclamation described in the New Testament did not produce over-analytical, proud, knowledge-overloaded, spiritual passengers. As the apostle Paul reminds us, it is the letter of the word that kills but the Spirit that gives life. Liberation is needed from the idol of the garrulous G-d. This happens through an encounter with the G-d of conversation. G-d is not obsessed with getting it right or dominating others with powerful words. A conversation G-d joins with people on a journey of experience and action. This is exactly what we find Christ doing in the Gospels. His ministry style was characterized by the rabbinic practice of eternal dialogue. There was engagement and right of reply. His listeners were not passive blank slates. They answered back. The energy of modern preaching is static and imposing. The energy in the eternal dialogue of Christ is dynamic, responsive, and engaging.

CONVERSATION G-D

Good talk restores unity to a fragmented world. What if Christianity became generously talkative and changed its verbose domination ways? What if, all over the planet, when people walked into church there was no preaching? What if preachers became obsolete? What if Christians stopped playing the powerful preacher/passive passenger game? What if, instead of the sermon, there was guided conversation in small groups? What if people of all faiths and none helped each other reflect on questions about life and G-d? What would that communicate to the world about G-d? It would send a clear and unambiguous message that G-d actually wants to listen and has become a human being. This is a G-d of whom people can ask questions. They can journey together. It models, and therefore teaches by example, a reciprocal G-d rather than a one-way, preacher-mission G-d.

Through encountering G-d in conversation groups of people learn a trinitarian and perichoretic faith. They experience G-d as interactive, engaging, simple, experiential, and active. It enables people to move beyond being the passive passengers that preaching has created. By example, this has taught people to practice being observational, analytical, judgmental, and controlling of knowledge. People can learn to follow in a different way through the example of the wisdom teacher. He taught as a Rabbi, using questions and open-ended conversation. He focussed on spiritual life skills and introduced people to an eternal dialogue with G-d. He did not offer a corporate, pre-packaged, doctrinal-based, management-directive download. In conversation communities those who are preachers are delivered from the burden of being overly pious minor celebrities with all the answers and all the power. Most importantly, people are liberated to practice a faith of their own instead of being spoon-fed. Through the risk of conversation faith becomes authentic. People become adept at creating their own spiritual food. In a conversation community people are encouraged to ask, seek, and knock for the answers. In the process their spiritual journey becomes real. It is not just drip fed or filtered through the preacher. People no longer have the feeling that they can never get all the spiritual promises that the preacher is selling this Sunday. They learn to talk together and love people of differing beliefs. They become genuine learners of Christ's Way. When churches become conversation communities a pseudo-proxy faith is transformed into an authentic living faith.

MUTUAL CONVERSATION: NOT A COMMAND

The poet David Whyte points to the reason that conversation is so essential in faith communities today. By implication it is also clear why preaching is redundant in postmodern democracies, because it is rooted in the organizational and military power, which is domination Christianity's legacy.

> Even for our parents and our parents' parents, the images of individual identity that formed and made them were drawn from the atmosphere of the Second World War and the organizational power of military might. In North America, Northern Europe, Russia and Japan hardly a single adult of the war generation was untouched by the forming hand of the military, or the necessities of military production. Our corporate identities of the fifties and sixties were made in the image of those military organizations, which having fought the good fight and in the West, finally prevailed. Our organizations and our approach to work has necessarily been a product of military mobilization. But the forces that

are now shaping our future are being mobilized by the individual imagination. Perhaps more accurately our future will come from the individual imagination in conversation with all other imaginations. A mobilization that exists at the edges between things. A sea formed not from a general's command but from the flow and turn of a thousand creative conversational elements.[5]

Another potent fact that demands that preaching should be consigned to the dustbin of Christian history is that it is fundamentally undemocratic. The kingdom of G-d is not a corporation. In the spirit of companionship people do not dictate, direct, preach at, or dominate one another with words. They search for a way forward together. In postmodern democracies this is the most compelling reason why conversation needs to be firmly established as the spiritual practice of revelation. Exposure to the medium of preaching teaches by example an undemocratic approach to life. Christians then act in an undemocratic way toward others. They find themselves unnecessarily at odds with people in the general population who live out of the democratic ethos of postmodernity. The attitudes created by Christian preaching are redundant, anachronistic, and ill-fitting in the democracies of the West.

Since the Enlightenment people have been given the grace and the authority to make up their own minds. Yet mainline Christianity is still living in an age where priests or pastors tell people what to believe and how to live from the pulpit. Stage-managed Christianity endures in the mindset of most people who call themselves Christians. Preaching does not resonate with contemporary education systems either. These have given primacy to individual thought and reasoning as a way to find out truth. Contemporary education methods emphasize a range of learning methods with a bias toward learning through group activity and pragmatic interaction. When people who are used to learning in this way come to a church where preaching is the only form of learning there is a massive disconnect. Hierarchical priest and managerial pastor are unfaithful models to the example and practices of the Rabbi Jesus. He used short statements, stories, and images that made people question their assumptions about G-d and themselves. This provoked people to action in new directions. The way Jesus practiced as wisdom teacher empowered people in their own journey with G-d. It did not tie them to him for quick and easy pre-packaged answers. Nor did it tie people to the prescriptive doctrinal positions of religious institutions.

5. Whyte, "Life at the Frontier."

He set people free to journey with G-d and others in the multi-voiced way of companionship.

THE INSTITUTION ILLUSION

The truth is not located in the doctrinal statements of any one church. Even within churches there is diversity of opinion on basics. Mainline Christianity's great illusion has been to convince people to believe in doctrinal systems created by their institutions. These creations have then been used to perpetuate Christian social dominance through institutional means. However, even though truth cannot be found in institutions it remains vitally important to find and affirm a common way of life. Roots are, without doubt, essential. Postmodern people certainly need them. Yet, where can roots now be found and in what way? In our time it is not in the institution. They are powerless in the face of the democratization of knowledge brought about through globalization and the Internet. Open source knowledge has undermined institutional authority and managerial mind control across the planet.

Tolstoy's *Confession* convincingly describes the bankruptcy of any institution or religious hierarchy to hold an authoritative plumbline or socially binding creed. He recognized that neither Protestant, Catholic nor Orthodox could claim to be the final authority on matters of faith and life. Nor could their preachers or hierarchies. All institutions have held to a "tradition in every age," as Karl Barth described it.[6] The Catholics now doctrinally endorse theistic evolution, and the Anglicans have changed their doctrinal position on divorce and remarriage, and women priests. There are numerous examples of institutional climbdown in the face of societal norms. Ever tightening, institutional, doctrinal orthodoxy has not prevented criminal sexual and financial abuse by priests. In modernity the rivalrous Catholic and Protestant hegemonies have perpetuated fragmentation by polarizing communities and nations. They have maintained a kind of Christian Cold War. A mutual standoff is the result of such intransigent and non-negotiable bids for social dominance. In this way Christianity became the bitch of a dualistic modernity. One Way! is pure modernity; a pseudo-christian, ur-fascist slogan.

Tolstoy reaches the following, obvious, conclusion concerning the institutional truth-packages of Protestantism, Orthodoxy and Catholicism:

---

6. Bromiley, *An Introduction*, 192.

Part 3: Recovering Reconciliation

"I have no doubt there is truth in their teachings, but I have no doubt there is falsehood in them too."[7] Ironically, within any congregation of people, even fundamentalist, there is always a tremendous spread of difference and opinion. People have a variety of views on the atonement, the return of Christ, divorce, or homosexuality. Many cradle Catholics have rejected their church's view of morality in favor of some personalized version. People feel part of the church for other reasons, such as a sense of peace, or great beauty, or common journey. Doctrinal consensus is a myth. It is therefore overwhelmingly problematic to uphold the institution as doctrinally authoritative, and, by implication, as authoritative at all. It is a fiction. This is particularly the case because Catholic, Protestant and Orthodox propose different versions of the truth, which are regarded by their hierarchies as non-negotiable. C. G. Jung saw the situation clearly: "There is only one way and that is your way. You seek the path? I warn you away from my own. It can also be the wrong path for you. May each go his own way. I will be no savior, no lawgiver, no master teacher unto you. You are no longer little children . . . May each seek out his own way. The way leads to mutual love in community. Men will come to see and feel the similarity and commonality of their ways."[8]

People are not made loyal or obedient through outward conformity to an institution or creed. Yet, what does influence people to embrace a common way of life? The information age has birthed a spectrum of guides and diffused authority. Since the Enlightenment authority has rested with the individual. The imposition of any one doctrinal position is a dangerous illusion. It has often been the justification for all kinds of authority abuse by institutional Christianity. Church creeds created by third century Roman politicians have created in groups and out groups. These practices fly directly in the face of the wisdom of Christ, who required no such list of doctrinal requirements from people. He was looking for something much deeper than external doctrinal assent and conformity.

Christ knew that "only with the heart do we see rightly."[9] He came to capture our hearts, but not in a spirit of mind control or bureaucratic and hierarchical conditioning. The wisdom teacher did not manufacture doctrinal consent. Christ invited free enquiry about our common journey and drew people into an enigmatic face-to-face encounter with the awesome

---

7. Tolstoy, *A Confession*, 94.
8. Jung, *The Red Book*, 231.
9. de Saint Exupéry, *The Little Prince*, Ch. XXI.

nature of YHWH in themselves. His purpose was to liberate and never to dominate. He held a mirror but never a gun. His outstretched hand was an offer of genuine partnership. If any kind of doctrinal consensus exists today it can be found primarily in the small communities of courageous people who journey together with Christ. These are people learning to share their experiences in the context of their personal histories and the plurality of their traditions. That is how they are being made whole and saving society.

SMALL COMMUNITY: THE NEW AUTHORITY

In the Catholic age the authority was the church. In the Protestant age the authority became the Bible. In the secular modern age the authority became the individual. In the post-secular and postmodern age the new authority is the community. It is created in the community of G-d as people of all faiths and none submit to one another. Only out of this mutual submission and reconciliation is any kind of socially binding authority created. It is only this unity in diversity that has genuine authority in postmodern neotribal society. What really shapes our lives is created in the mutuality and genuine open source conversation of small communities.

Jesus recognized authority as being vested in, and established through, the companionship of empowerment. In other words, authentic authority emerges out of mutuality in relationship and sacrifice. It is not in a role or position. For Jesus, authority is established through voluntary submission in the community of G-d. It is not conferred or maintained by hierarchy. It is recognized and authorized by the community. Therefore, locating religious authority within an institution is today a dangerous illusion. This is because real community is absent from institutional Christianity. The hierarchical and bureaucratic nature of institutional life destroys mutuality. It therefore lacks authentic authority. The institutional methods of putting people in managerial positions over others ruptures the naturally occurring authority that is only recognized and authorized by the group. The person who has institutional authority never really exercises moral authority in the group. This kind of genuine authority is only born from sacrifice, love, and contribution in the group. Obedience is created through the practice of mutuality, reciprocity, and sacrificial love. These practices create authority that is charismatic and familial.

Part 3: Recovering Reconciliation

Mutual authority is so threatening that hierarchical authority always seeks to undermine and nullify its power. To do this it allows lip service to community. Yet it cancels out mutual authority by exercising and maintaining hierarchical controls and practices. Institutional churches even try to pass themselves off as mission communities or church communities. Whatever titles are used, mainline churches continue to operate as bureaucratic hierarchies in precept and practice. A simple way of testing this is to try and change anything. It is always the church hierarchy that needs to be consulted to grant permission before anything happens. The final yes or no rests with paid professionals. Their decisions are significantly biased toward maintaining institutional authority, and their own roles and stipends. Paid professionals are, in effect, mercenary.

SELF-AUTHENTICATING COMMUNITIES

What primarily forms our behavior and beliefs is the small community. It is not the preacher, church hierarchy or institutional creed. Martin Buber said, "Encounter is the only possible way of learning."[10] People are not shaped primarily by verbal instruction or written statements but through mutual conversation, experiential learning, and the example of others. People gain authority and foster a mutual obedience simply by taking time to be together. A set of beliefs or creed is believed because of the guidance and help of generous people. It is not because the institution holds to a creed. Self-regulating, interconnected communities are now able to act as a new kind of plumbline; a faith generated in neotribal conversation in small communities and in the presence or absence of G-d. Conversation communities are the pivotal practice for the discovery of any such plumbline. In the self-authenticating conversation community residing priests, pastors or organizational staff are only representative. In postmodern democracies the mutually submissive, self-authenticating community is the authority. This reflects the nature of G-d; a trinity in unity and authority in mutually submissive equality.

10. en.wikipedia.org/wiki/Martin_Buber.

THE CONVERSATION REVELATION

People complain about loss of truth. Yet the question must be asked, whose truth is being lost? Is it the truth of the Protestant preachers who all disagree? Is it the truth of the hierarchical institutions that all have a different creed? A community of conversation is a way of getting real about the fact that truth is never held by one preacher, one church, one man, or one woman. People realize it as they submit together in a conversation community. The truth that matters is what is real for the here and now where we live and work. As Rilke says, "do not seek the answers which cannot be given you because you will not be ready to live them."[11] What matters is the revelation that occurs through a community of conversation between whoever is gathered. Whatever teaching is received through conversation, it is important that it can begin to be practiced in society. Example is the teaching. How do I pray? What is prayer? Where is G-d encountered as father or mother? How will reality set me free? What matters is that we are ready to live the questions in family, work, and neighborhood. Religion is pointless if it is just gathering information about the Bible.

Postmodernity has fragmented and atomized our experience of life. Yet, practicing open source and contemplative conversation is a way to gain a sense of perspective in the perplexity of the postmodern journey. It heals fragmentation and brings cohesion and allows people to find their way again. They discover commonality through open and honest connection with other postmodern pilgrims. Missional conversation goes some way to achieving this. Yet its modernist language brings assumptions that are retrograde to its practice. The conversation community has no stated mission, leader or plan, yet in a profound way it fosters a way of life. Common purpose emerges as people of difference connect. They begin to lead together on the basis of their common experiences. This flies directly in the face of modern highly individualistic tendencies that have shaped people in the West. Yet, voluntary mutual submission in our common journey is essential to following Christ's Way of Life in postmodernity.

The missional community is not a genuine approach to conversation. This is because it has a bias toward mission and a covert agenda of Christian social dominance. It seeks to perpetuate ideological supremacy. In genuine conversation people begin with their personal histories and questions. These are in dialogue with one another. Through these very different

11. Rilke, *Letters to a Young Poet*, Letter Four.

Part 3: Recovering Reconciliation

people G-d is made flesh and made present. All people hold in common a G-d experienced as absent and present. The Bible, Christian history, prayer and communion are not common ground for the majority of the population in post-Christendom Europe. Christianity's history of domination and war is also a necessary part of the neighborhood story. This must be acknowledged if honesty is to form the basis of any genuine conversation. Christianity has no community rights over any other stories or histories. G-d's presence and work of salvation in other faiths needs affirmation and inclusion. The result is a patchwork quilt of breathtaking beauty and surprising unity in diversity.

REALITY: A CONVERSATION

The poet David Whyte emphasizes the pressing need for organizations to have courageous conversations with/in their communities. This certainly rings true for institutional Christianity because it has failed to acknowledge the conversation it is involved in with the rest of society. By ignoring the real and changing needs of neotribal society it has ceased to be socially functional or necessary. It has maintained its practice of doctrine-based teaching and created a socially irrelevant and anemic sub-Christian subculture. By refusing to listen to others it has shut itself off from the living G-d. For G-d is only found in and through society. This is because G-d is community. To experience G-d means engaging in the journey found in one another and in our neotribal societies. Where there is no genuine experience of community there is no G-d. G-d is absent from mainline Christianity because bureaucratic hierarchy destroys genuine community. It therefore destroys G-d with/in us. Christianity is still trying to project itself as a monocultural final solution. Society is defiantly shouting back its holy and justified rejection of this pre-packaged, anemic, and fake way of life.

In great contrast to mainline institutional Christianity David Whyte humbly acknowledges that:

> Every creature . . . is in a thousand different conversations with a thousand other elements and dynamics and forms in order to keep itself alive and its environment alive. Every ecosystem in the world is this astonishing meeting, this conversation, between various dynamics which contribute to this central conversation of life . . .

How many edges and conversations are meeting inside me?—or am I a monocultural idea that I am attempting to project on reality ... In order for an organization to live out its life it has to find that edge between its own particular signature and genius and what its being called into by its surrounding world ... Path maker there is no path, you make the path by walking ... You actually change the world by meeting it.[12]

This understanding of life accurately reflects the G-d of conversation to which Jesus, Scripture, tradition and community all testify.

In order to change the world we must be changed by it. This is where the language and ideology of mission is redundant. Modern Christianity is failing to keep itself alive because it is does not recognize its interdependence with/in neotribal culture. It needs to be changed by society. To do that it needs to listen and not preach, and accept criticism, and change its mind. The way to do that is to establish the spiritual practice of open source conversation in faith communities. These groups have to replace the preaching and mission emphasis entirely. Only in this way will postmodern faith communities reflect the conversation G-d revealed in Jesus, Scripture, tradition and community.

YOUR G-D, MY G-D ... OUR G-D

Georges Bataille writes that, "Opening myself to inner experience, I have placed in it all value and authority. Henceforth I can have no other value, no other authority (in the realm of mind). Value and authority imply the discipline of a method, the existence of a community."[13] In a conversation community the starting point is experience: your experience, my experience, and our shared experience. It is about life, G-d, the universe and everything. In the conversation community everything belongs. This is where G-d is also found, either as absent or present. People reflect on their experiences of G-d, listen to the experiences of others, and share what they have in common. Sharing and listening enables people to identify patterns and themes. These emerge from, and can be applied in, our local context and neighborhood. G-d has been lost in the monologue of modernity but is encountered again in our conversation in postmodern community. Very simple questions are asked such as: what is my experience, what is our

---

12. Whyte, "Life at the Frontier."
13. Bataille, *L'Expérience Intérieure*, 7.

Part 3: Recovering Reconciliation

experience, and where can God be found in society? The starting point in the conversation is not the church, the word of the preacher, the Bible or Christian history. These only become authentic in conversation with others who have no such background, yet may have equally deep and profound experiences of G-d. G-d is present and listening and speaking through all people in the conversation. The starting point is the story itself in which Christ is already present. My story and your story then becomes our shared story. Your G-d and my G-d then becomes our shared G-d. "God has no religion."[14]

In the conversation community people of all faiths and none are in open source dialogue. G-d is revealed in an entirely new way for a unique time, place, and group of people. All things are always being made new through reconciliation. This transforms people as they meet Christ in each other. It is unimaginable in the pre-packaged programs of institutional church. The conversation community enables the postmodern pilgrim to become part of the process of spiritual formation. They are giving and receiving, dying and being reborn, again and again. Something totally new and real about G-d is realized. Where our different experiences of G-d are reconciled then a new realization of G-d becomes possible. G-d is made flesh and given skin in a totally new way. We come to realize our G-d is present. This is the G-d we share in society who is revealed in the experiences of our daily lives. It is not a monolithic mission God projected onto our postmodern reality. This G-d remains impotent, deaf, blind, and dumb for the majority of the population. As Nietzsche observed this is a "dead God" of "the letter that kills"[15] and of empty words and blind reason. It is not the kaleidoscopic, perplexing, and invigorating G-d of human experience. This is your G-d, my G-d and our G-d.

THE QUESTIONS AND THE EXPERIENCE

Leonardo da Vinci said, "Although nature commences with reason and ends in experience it is necessary for us to do the opposite, that is to commence with experience and from this to proceed to investigate the reason."[16] Something doesn't become wisdom until it's experienced. Eloquent Biblical teaching, knowledge, and philosophy are useless unless ap-

---

14. Bellows, *Re-statements*, 149.
15. 2 Corinthians 3:6.
16. *en.wikiquote.org/wiki/Talk:Leonardo_da_Vinci*.

plied in daily life. The Jewish people knew this. It was their experience of G-d that shaped their history, community, social practices, and way of life. They encountered G-d as "I will be what I will be," holy, healer, provider, father-mother, deliverer, and a whole host of different ways. They named their G-d on the basis of their experiences. Their knowledge of G-d was experiential. It was not based on words, theory, or books. Their G-d had to transfigure life. The words and the books only came after the experience as communities wrestled with what their experiences meant. This is how the Bible was formed. Experiences of healing, deliverance, and encounter with G-d passed into communal history and were only then recorded. What was true for the pilgrim people of G-d in the writing of the Bible is now true for postmodern pilgrims seeking G-d in our neotribal societies. In our time, experiences can be discerned in communities of journeying pilgrims made up of people of all faiths and none. What is essential is that experience in community is recovered. Gathering around books and words is anemic in comparison to encountering G-d in each other.

A G-d of society can only begin to be experienced in open source conversation communities. People can be encouraged to gather in small groups and interfacing collections of small groups to practice these skills. They can learn the art of listening in mutual contemplation and personal reflection. In effect, these are skills of group contemplation or group spiritual companionship. People learn to reflect on simple questions in the presence, support, and witness of others. Contemplation is not the same as figuring it out. It means to look from all sides. You become the problem you are working on. Once you become it the solution reveals itself. If G-d is to be experienced it requires the creation and maintenance of groups of people who have different experiences. Yet, within this difference there will also be profound and surprising commonality. G-d is discovered afresh in this mutual and supportive reflection and companionship.

Open source G-d talk restores unity in our fragmented world/s. A conversation community enables people to reflect together on one fundamental question, which is then applied to daily life in our neotribal society, what is our experience of G-d in society?

As gift? as freedom? as power? as energy? as suffering? as dead? as secular? as change? as flesh? as homeless? as home? as enigma? as mad? as sad? as shopping? as politics? as loss? as addiction? as absent? as present? as emptiness? as fullness? as transformation? as pattern? as revelation? as time? as community? as death? as rebirth? as betrothal? as wholeness?

as brokenness? as holy? as health? as marriage? as father? as mother? as earth? as sky? as art? as human? as person? as family? as goodness? as man? as woman? as gay? as technology? as dance? as child? as conversation? as king? as creator? as lover? as authority? as equality? as fire? as water? as purpose? as identity? as life? as beginning? as end? as space? as joy? as paradox? as word? as stillness? as now? as here? as birth? as death? as masculine? as feminine? as judge? as law? as mercy? as fun? as direction? as pathmaker? as friend? as enemy? as fear? as sex? as healer? as nothing? as everything? as strong? as weak? as darkness? as light? as society? as world? as food? as money? as learner? as wisdom? as teacher? as divorced? as betrayal? as tragic? as big? as small? as forgiveness? as resurrection? as hell? as heaven? as crucified? as risen? as wonder? as terror? as awe? as bread? as wine? as reborn? as new? as old? as unity in diversity? as closed? as open? as lover? as friend? as all? as me? as all in all?

This one fundamental question leads participants to reflect in four interconnected reflective directions:

- what is my experience of G-d?
- what is your experience of G-d?
- what is our common experience of G-d?
- what is our common experience of G-d in our society?

The starting place for the conversation community is not the Bible, the church, doctrine, the Eucharist or Christianity. The conversation does not focus on discussion of ideas but invites people to explore, reflect and speak with honesty about their experiences. This may be of G-d as absent as well as present. The conversation community is not theoretical or cerebral; it is relational, experiential, emotional, and visceral. The tragedy of modernist Christianity is the flight from experience, emotion, and addiction, to reason and certainty. Leonardo da Vinci knew better. The practice and example of Christ is rooted, first and foremost, in experience and action. G-d is encountered in our guts and in our common life in society. One is nearer G-d's heart in a tube train than anywhere else on earth.

A life in conversation becomes more visceral and less monolithic and mechanical. All people have an experience of prayer. It is universal. In the same way everyone can talk about their experience of G-d. An experience of absence and of G-d as unknown also needs to be strongly affirmed and reflected upon. As commonalities and patterns emerge in our experiences, truths for living become clearer. These will be provisional. It may be a truth of the moment and not necessarily a truth for all eternity. As truths are applied in our geographical, historical, and political contexts a common experience emerges and a common discernment becomes possible. It is not a common discernment that is imposed by the group. Participants realize the answer to their question or the next step of their journey. This is not achieved through argument or a discussion, but only in mutual reflection. Conversation helps us to discover a G-d that is multi-voiced and kaleidoscopic. Ezekiel and Isaiah and the apostle Paul would concur. Their experiences left them speechless. Reflective open source conversation leads us to a place beyond words. We realize together that G-d is through all and in all. G-d becomes all in all.

IDENTITY FORMATION IN NEOTRIBAL COMMUNITIES

A conversation community also leads us to begin to answer the question: Who do you say that I am? Our identity is formed in the context of genuine community. Identity formation is a mixture of what I bring and how I am received and recognized. People hide or become lost behind their roles in institutions and remain fundamentally unsure about their real identity. Maintaining a role as a priest or pastor or youth leader in a corporate structure, and genuine transparency are mutually incompatible. Bureaucratically prescribed church, state and business roles destroy people. Yet conversation communities help people rediscover who they are. Identity cannot genuinely be rooted primarily in Christian history or the Bible. It emerges from our experience of living in our neotribal postmodern post-secular society. That is our location and where we have been formed. Identity is always here and now, and not now and then. People are formed by their society: politics, geography, history, and family or lack of it. Part of identity is religious affiliation—or lack of it—and our national identity. This is the way G-d is revealed and/or obscured. Conversation in community enables us to discern how G-d has been obscured and where G-d is revealed in our particular social context.

The community of G-d can only genuinely be manifested in our specific time and place as we meet together in increasing transparency. Identity is formed as experiences of G-d are shared. Change and growth happen as we are born again into a new social reality, the companionship of empowerment. This means forming an identity as the community of G-d that has a highly localized expression. These communities will be radically different from one another, but also have commonalities that are not dictated by institutional requirements. They arise out of a shared biology; we are made in the image of G-d. How that is expressed in our immediate geographical, historical, religious, political, and social context is something that only the unique set of people who gather can create. It is in this way that G-d is made flesh and contextualized in our time and place. In such communities we give skin to G-d. We can begin to realize with the Franciscan mystics that "I am that which I am seeking."[17]

LISTENING CHURCH: CONFESSIONAL COMMUNITIES

American Indian wisdom says, "Listen or your tongue will make you deaf." Another type of small community is one of confession. This is different from the conversation community because the emphasis is not on our common experience of G-d, but confession with one another. It is deeper than the conversation community because it focuses on the personal things for which I am responsible. Through honesty G-d is present in reconciling love whether as known and/or unknown. Some people have begun to recognize that the church is going to become a movement in the style of Alcoholics Anonymous. Such a community is flat in structure and without paid or clearly defined leadership. It takes an agreed form of questions and reflection based on a commonly held pattern. This is interpreted according to local and group needs. The prerequisite is to come as you are. It requires leaving roles, responsibilities and status at the door. Confessional communities practice, and therefore teach, transparency.

The culture of church, state and business is predicated on presenting a cleverly crafted image in order to be accepted and earn respect, and therefore money. Capitalism runs on prefabricated image consumption. Real and honest emotion has been censured. This is what makes the honesty offered in psychotherapy so popular. Yet what could be a better expression of the companionship of empowerment than a community of mutual confession. These are transparent and honest people on a journey together who are facing themselves with courage and compassion. Addiction is common to us all and takes a myriad of forms. It qualifies us for the journey. The community of confession is a quest toward courageous living. It is a stark contrast to a church culture characterized by the verbose, the anodyne, the

17. Rohr, *Franciscan Mysticism*.

bureaucratic, the deceptive, and the fake. This is institutional church culture no matter how sweetly repackaged and resold. The divine antidote is humble, earthy, dirty people that can be honest about it. In his book, *Life Together*, Dietrich Bonhoeffer recognized listening as an essential expression of our love for one another. He writes, "The first service that one owes others in the fellowship consists of listening to them. Just as love of God begins by listening to his word, so the beginning of love for our brothers and sisters is learning to listen to them."[18] In such a place of vulnerability, open heartedness, and humility G-d is made manifest.

COMPANIONSHIP: PERICHORESIS AND RECIPROCITY

Christ's example teaches us to ask, above everything else, what is in the heart? Is the heart open to G-d and others? What holds our affections? What is chosen first and what is second? What is loved and invested with time, money and energy? What is the treasure of the heart? It is out of the heart that evil, murder, and adultery are manifested, and also faith and love. Belief in the Trinity is of no consequence if there is no experience of the Trinity. It does not matter whether it is believed that G-d was made flesh if we have not experienced G-d in our own bodies and the bodies of others. Modern Christianity has divorced doctrine from experience and life skills. In contrast, conversation communities enable us to get in touch with our experience, or lack of it, and to begin a more earthy and visceral journey together. This is a journey authorized and authenticated by common consent and witness. It is impossible to take alone. The conversation community teaches by example a perichoretic way of life. It expresses and communicates the reciprocal G-d of interface. This is the conversation G-d of Jesus, Scripture, tradition and community. There is a difference between knowing the path and walking the path. The group empowers us to bridge that difference and strip away our powerful illusions and self-deceptions. We can then connect with the underlying reality of our common human experience, "I will be what I will be." Good G-d talk restores wholeness in our fragmented souls and societies.

Rainer Maria Rilke instinctively understood this when he wrote:

---

18. Bonhoeffer, *Life Together*, 97.

> Live the questions now.
> Perhaps you will then gradually, without noticing it,
> live along some distant day into the answer.[19]

EVER SEEN G-D?

There was once a little boy who was very curious. He went around asking people the question: "Have you ever seen God?" He asked his mother who told him it was a silly question and to stop it. Then she sent him out to play.

When he was out playing he met the Minister. He asked the Minister, who said it was much too big a question for a little boy to ask. Then he told him to run along and play. Then he met an old man, with a big long beard and a big friendly dog, sitting in the sun on a fence looking into a field. "Have you ever seen God?" asked the little boy. The old man didn't reply for some time. He looked all around him: at the field; the cows; the rabbits; the sky; and at his dog. They listened to the birds. Then he looked into the little boy's face with a very kind smile, "Sometimes, I thinks I see nothing else."

---

19. Rilke, *Letters to a Young Poet*, 4.

8

Reconciliation Communities

> "First go and be reconciled to them;
> then come and offer your gift."
>
> —Jesus[1]

> "The meeting of two personalities is like the contact of two chemical substances: if there is any reaction, both are transformed."
>
> —C. G. Jung[2]

THE PROTESTANT AND CATHOLIC RECONCILIATION

PROTESTANT AND CATHOLIC MISSIONS have vented their ideological fury upon humanity for the past 1,500 years. It's time to move beyond this impasse. Reconciliation is central in the practice of the way of Jesus. It can also become the central practice in communities and neighborhoods willing to

---

1. Matthew 5:24.
2. Jung, *Modern Man*, 49.

take that journey together. They can learn to say: "Here there is no Gentile or Jew, circumcised or uncircumcised, barbarian, Scythian, slave or free, but Christ is all, and is in all."[3] They can also learn to say there is no Protestant or Catholic, conservative or liberal, no left wing or right wing, no gay or straight, no Christian or Muslim, no atheist or theist, no upper class or lower class, no rich or poor, no able or disabled people, no addicted or clean, no old or young, no sick or healthy, no worker or manager, no employed or unemployed, no secular or church person, no male or female, no priest or laity; but Christ is in all and through all. Social wholeness and integration is the concrete manifestation of salvation in society. It is experienced in and through community because G-d is community. Reconciling our differences is the tipping point where we keep on being born again and again. The practice of reconciliation results in our regeneration and the regeneration of our communities and neighborhoods.

Jesus Christ is not the founder of Christianity in any of its forms. He is the light of the world and the salt of the Earth. It is his willingness to be a person of reconciliation that releases and makes manifest his light. It is through the sacrifice of his body, and our acceptance of it into our bodies, that our humanity is made whole. This is how we are saved. Christ is himself made whole (complete) through his sufferings, says Hebrews 2:10. It is through his suffering as a political pawn and religious scapegoat that Christ made reconciliation possible in a violent, oppressed, and divided Jerusalem. Through suffering, dying, and rising from the dead he became a Messiah. He was crucified by the fear of an elite group of religious leaders, the calculated indifference of imperial Roman authority and the betrayal and weakness of his friends. Yet it is through this experience that Jesus is transformed and resurrected as the Christ of everybody. It is his willingness to be the place of reconciliation in his own neighborhood that transforms it and all others who will follow his example. Reconciliation is the message of his life. It is expressed through the medium of his broken body and blood. His action of reconciliation makes his community whole. The people who follow the way are also called to suffer in their neighborhoods between the fear of secular authorities, the misunderstanding of rigid religion, and the betrayal of friends. Vested political and religious factions will always pursue their own interests to the bitter end. In these circumstances it is taking a stand for the right thing that brings wholeness through reconciliation in our neotribal neighborhoods.

3. Colossians 3:11.

Christ calls those who follow his way to "take up his cross."⁴ It is expressed in the apostle Paul's invitation to "make up the sufferings that are lacking in Christ."⁵ Christ invites us to join him in making our communities whole by bringing reconciliation. This means laying down the substance of our lives and reputations in loving sacrifice. It is through courageous suffering and giving that we become "partakers in the very nature of God."⁶ Through practicing reconciliation with our neighbors we give skin to G-d in our neighborhoods. In the process we become divine humans and are made messianic. We join with Christ in saving the world and making it whole. This happens through the sacrifice of our own flesh as we refuse to bow to unjust and abusive systems and, in consequence, suffer kickback. Jesus is the first born of these divine humans, a new race. The way of divinisation is always to enter into the process of death and resurrection in our communities. Yet this reality has not been emphasized in the religion that has passed for Christianity. Conversely, it has focussed on self-preservation and management of its market share. It has not given its life in order that the world can be reborn. It has instead tried to stake its claim.

Richard Rohr reminds us:

> We share many things with many religions, but no other world religion has the revelation of the cross . . . The mystery of the cross is saying that human existence is neither perfectly consistent (though that's what educated, ideological and control-needy people want), nor is it total chaos (our philosophical words for that are postmodernism, nihilism or even atheism). Human existence, though, is filled with contradictions. To hold the contradictions with God, with Jesus, is to be a Christian and to share and participate in the redemption of the world (Colossians 1:24). It feels like a forgiving of reality for being what it is. If the choices are either perfect consistency or utter chaos, don't go there. The cross is holding the middle. The world is neither particularly consistent nor total chaos; it's a coincidence of opposites, and even geometrically that forms the cross. The price you pay for holding together the contradictions within yourself, others and the world is always some form of crucifixion, but the gift you receive and the gift you offer is that at least in you "everything belongs."⁷

---

4. Matthew 16:24.
5. Colossians 1:24.
6. 2 Peter 1:4.
7. Rohr, *Things Hidden*, Ch 9.

Part 3: Recovering Reconciliation

Communities and neighborhoods can belong but only if we take up our cross. Belonging does not come without generous and sacrificial giving. It is not created through rallying the people to a mission, like the energy that galvanized the unholy Crusades. It comes through making peace and through acts of reconciliation in our communities and neighborhoods.

THE MISSIONAL COMMUNITY: A CLOSER LOOK

It is useful to contrast the ethos and purpose of a reconciliation community with a missional community. Wikipedia describes a missional community in the following way:

> A Missional Community or missional communities (also called Clusters, Go Communities, Mid-Sized Communities, Mission-Shaped Communities, MSCs) are groups of anything from 20 to 50 or more people who are united, through Christian community, around a common service and witness to a particular neighborhood or network of relationships. With a strong value on life together, the group has the expressed intention of seeing those they impact choose to start following Jesus, through this more flexible and locally incarnated expression of the church. The result will often be that the group will grow and ultimately multiply into further Missional Communities. Missional Communities are most often networked within a larger church community (often with many other Missional Communities). These mid-sized communities, led by laity, are "lightweight and low maintenance" and most often meet three to four times a month in their missional context.
>
> A Missional Community is a group of between 20 and 50+ people aimed at either a geographic location (a neighborhood) or an existing network of relationships. Missional Communities are often described as "small enough to care but large enough to dare." Key to the success of Missional Communities are the participants finding their primary identity of "church" within this community, rather than, say, a larger worship service or Small Group. In essence, this group of people becomes a close-knit spiritual family on mission together.
>
> This group usually has 2 or 3 leaders who, through a process of discernment, decide their mission-vision and then invite people to join them in reaching that particular context. The leaders of the MC are held accountable by the leadership of the greater church community, both for what they do and for the way in which they do it (i.e., character as well as task). The tagline that is often used

is "low control/high accountability" to describe relationships between the Missional Community and the church body and leadership. Alex Absalom is one of the early pioneers in the United States with Missional Communities—on average he oversees the start of at least 15 Missional Communities each year—and described in the book co-authored with Mike Breen, "Launching Missional Communities—a Field Guide."

The group balances its energies between an upward movement toward God, an inward movement toward the MC as a place of identity, and an outward movement to represent Christ to their mission context. When they gather, they express this in creative ways that are appropriate to their context. In fact, there will be great diversity between groups in how this looks, with a variety of faces and voices being given room to step forward and contribute what they can. The only "rule" is that they do not try to do a miniature version of a Sunday church service.

Since Missional Communities are meant to be "lightweight and low maintenance" and led by laity, running the community is spread throughout the group so it isn't only 2 or 3 leaders doing all of the work. This is a key ingredient and one of the main benefits of these mid-sized groups. People don't approach it as consumers but as participants. While some MCs meet in homes, it is not uncommon for many of them to meet in the particular mission context they are reaching into. (For instance, a MC reaching out to the homeless would meet on the streets with the homeless rather than trying to bus them to another location).

Missional Communities often have Small Groups within the larger body, with Small Group leaders being held accountable by the Missional Community Leaders. The small groups work as places of support, challenge and closeness, as the wider MC gathering is too large for general sharing of prayer requests and the like. MCs will also gather periodically with the larger church body for what is referred to as a Celebration Service. This usually involves a time for corporate worship, teaching, stories and re-envisioning the wider community. The larger church body determines the frequency of these Celebration Services, ranging from every week to once a month. In an existing church, as opposed to a new church plant, regular Sunday services often perform this function, showcasing and celebrating what is going on across that particular church in their Missional Communities.

More often than not, when Missional Communities reach the size of 30–40 people they begin to intentionally work on starting a new MC. As before, any new MC is driven by the presence of accountable leaders who have sought God for a clear and specific mission-vision. This could mean sending out two leaders to start a new community, maybe a Small Group is sent out en masse, or even half the group stays with the current MC while the other half begins a new community. However the group is multiplied, the essential element is expanding the reach of the church into a new context.

Network and Accountability

If MCs are "low control/high accountability," having a church structure that invests in lay leaders and empowers them while holding them accountable is of paramount importance. Perhaps the most widely used vehicle for this are called Discipleship Huddles, which is a group of 4–10 leaders. The frequency of these groups differs based on each individual church, but generally speaking they meet at least once a month and as often as once a week. Huddles are a place where leaders are actively being discipled in a community of peers, where their Huddle leader holds them accountable for the leadership of their groups. The two central questions of a Huddle are: 1) What is God saying to you? 2) What are you going to do about it? By seeing that leaders follow through on the plans they form from answering both of these questions, a culture is developed of both high support and high challenge. Over a period of time, this allows leaders to cultivate and sustain the character, skills and spiritual depth needed to lead.

As churches with Missional Communities tend to be far more decentralized than most Western churches, the network of these Huddles are essential to the unity and direction of the wider church. Usually the Senior Pastor will Huddle 4–10 leaders, these leaders will in turn Huddle 4–10 leaders, who in turn Huddle the leaders they are responsible for. As the church grows, multiplying Missional Communities and Small Groups, more Huddles are added as necessary. What most churches have found helpful is an agreed upon DNA in the language that all leaders use that filter down to their various groups. Most often this is the language of LifeShapes, a set of 8 Shapes that distill the teachings and principles of the Bible and Jesus, that were fashioned by Mike Breen as Missional Communities first developed and captured in his book "Building a Discipling Culture."

A Typical Missional Community Gathering

There is tremendous flexibility in the forms of Missional Communities, since the intention is that they are highly accessible to the culture into which they are planted. They are anchored around the three core relationships of life—UP to God, IN to family and friends, and OUT to the wider society, in which they seek to be a blessing. In practice MCs do tend to do certain things pretty regularly, albeit in slightly different ways according to their context, including:

- Food—ideally sharing a meal together
- Socializing/laughing/having fun
- Breaking Bread/sharing Communion
- Storytelling (i.e., testimony), especially of things people are grateful to God for
- Bringing praise and worship to God
- Offering prayer for healing and prophetic encouragement to anyone who has particular need
- Studying the Scriptures together, especially from what God has been speaking to the leader (or whoever is leading that portion) about during the past week.
- Praying for the wider community that you are seeking to reach, as well as for the MCs witness there
- Planning practicalities for mission activities.

In addition to providing this list, Alex Absalom comments, "We would summarize this as a 1 Corinthians 11–14 model, which seems the fullest unpacking of how a church *oikos* [extended household] would meet and express its life together. From what Paul writes, it is also clear that those gatherings were led in such a way that people who weren't yet Christians could come in and be welcomed, without it throwing all the plans into confusion."

As well, a Missional Community will go out together in specific missional activities, to serve and witness to their place of calling. Such events need to be regular and rhythmic, so that the group sees this as an integral part of their life together. It should be no more "special" than meeting to eat together or pray together is.[8]

MISSIONAL: FRAGMENTING THE NEIGHBORHOOD

The missional community described above contains a mixture of helpful and unhelpful practices. If compared to the description of the faith community in Colossians 3 it is found wanting in some very important aspects.

8. *en.wikipedia.org/wiki/Missional_community.*

A missional community is too homogenous. The missional task is explicitly stated as "seeing those they impact choose to start following Jesus through this more flexible and locally incarnated expression of the church." The question then becomes how do you start following Jesus? Is following Jesus really about joining the Christian religion, reading the Bible, and breaking bread? Is that what Jesus got his learners to do? Or did they just eat together, gather around his teaching, and begin to learn by practicing the way of reconciliation and empowerment together. What is the ultimate litmus test of being a learner of Christ? Surely it is the practice of reconciliation and love of the neighbor who is different. Faith is expressed in reconciliation with people who are different from us.

What is positive about missional communities is gathering together and sharing conversation. What is problematic may be having bread and wine and Bible reading at the center. These are negotiable but not central. Small communities have to discuss together how to express their common spirituality. For some stakeholders this will not include the Bible and bread and wine. For others it may. There are common concerns that will need to be incorporated and included. If some form of breaking bread or meal of reconciliation is decided upon even this can be done in a way that emerges out of conversation with people of all faiths and none. The Cosmic Mass created by Matthew Fox is one example, as are various forms of inclusive Eucharists. The meal may not even be called a Eucharist. Thanksgiving meal or Thank You! meal would be a contemporary way of expressing it. What is important is that there is a conversation and a way forward together in terms of a shared meal of peace. This celebrates the reality of community reconciliation in a tangible way in the neighborhood.

The missional community positively embraces a simple structure and sharing stories. However, in neighborhoods of all faiths and none community worship necessarily has to be inclusive. It has to emerge out of genuine neotribal conversation. Worship and the reading of texts have to reflect the histories and stories of all those present and their experiences of G-d. Therefore, worship may not be identifiably Christian at all. Reading and study may involve using the Bible, but may include the Qu'ran, the Vedas, poetry, or humanist readings and thoughts. Of necessity the person of Christ must be in conversation with other ways present. This is exactly how we find Christ acting in the Gospels. He is in eternal dialogue with everyone he meets. His abiding question is, what is in the heart?

Groups must be open to the creation of a totally new kind of community that is not primarily Christian but still follows the reconciliation practices of Christ. A community practicing reconciliation is embodying Christ, whether it sings Christian songs and has Bible readings or not. In *Missional: Joining God In The Neighborhood* Alan Roxburgh shifts the emphasis away from Christian beliefs being the central concern of community life. He rightly emphasises the importance of developing community practices such as: speaking peace, going local, practicing hospitality, leaving your baggage at home, being received as a stranger, not moving from house to house, eating what is set before you, listening people into speech, and experimenting around the edges. Whilst all these practices are excellent, reconciliation remains the defining practice of the learner of Christ. Speaking peace is not the same as the practice of making peace with one another. Reconciliation is both the reason for going to others and the way that peace is manifested as a concrete social reality.

REALITY: PREREQUISITE FOR RECONCILIATION

The Truth and Reconciliation Commission of South Africa is one concrete example of the profound impact reconciliation can have upon a divided society. Yet its catalytic effect was complicated and distorted by managerialism, bureaucracy, and legal process. The kind of reconciliation that Christ practiced was without legal guarantees or predetermined consequences. Once this is taken into account, it must be recognized that truth and reconciliation expresses an instinct that is deeply healing for any neighborhood. Healing is manifested through an acknowledgement that wrongs and offenses have been committed. It is not easy and takes time, effort, and determination. Learning happens through practice, repetition, and persistence. There are mistakes on the journey together. Sometimes reconciliation is not possible.

The important thing to take away from the South African experience is that an admission of the truth makes reconciliation possible. No truth, no reconciliation; know truth, know reconciliation. However, in the distances of loneliness and disconnection that plague the West the difficulty is not so much racial and class violence but alienation. This is perpetuated through distance, numbness, confusion, suspicion, individualism, consumerism, and i-culture. These are the sins of omission toward our neighbors; the people not spoken with and not loved because they are not known. To acknowledge this is perhaps the first step in the process of reconciliation. It must also be understood that it may be exactly at the point of conflict that relationships can be either broken or healed. Anger, conflict, or distance between neighbors can be a chink of light in the doorway to reconciliation. This happens not in the formalized necessities of a legalized process but in risk and vulnerability. It is never guaranteed to succeed. The machine society has conditioned people to believe it is their right to have pain-free relationships. Yet all things cannot be made painless. Indeed, anything that is worthwhile seldom is. What is sublime is born through trial, test, and endurance.

Reconciliation is the defining characteristic of the communities of G-d. Tragically, it has not been modeled or practiced by church leadership. For Protestant and Catholic the missing practice is reconciliation. It has been largely anesthetized and formalized into the Communion ritual and private prayer for forgiveness. This does not involve going to our brother or sister and making peace regarding our differences or offenses. When the Holy Spirit moves upon a congregation, or an area, or a nation it is exactly this kind of reconciliation and peacemaking that begin to occur. The walls come tumbling down. Christ is then risen in his people and we are born again from above into a new experience of G-d in community.

RECONCILING THE NEIGHBORHOOD

Miroslav Volf has reflected on the practice of reconciliation in the context of his family's experience of living through war in Croatia. During the Croatian War of Independence Serb-led JNA and rebel militia committed widespread ethnic cleansing on the occupied areas of Croatia (self-proclaimed Republic of Serbian Krajina) from 1991 to 1995. Large numbers of Croats and non-Serbs were removed, either by murder, deportation, or being forced to flee. According to the ICTY indictment against Slobodan Milosevic, there was an expulsion of around 170,000 Croats and other non-Serbs from their homes. Out of this context Miroslav Volf considers the many ways people exclude those who are different by dehumanizing, judging, labeling, and demonizing. People are rendered inferior and less than human by race, culture, economic status, religion, and gender. Injustice and victimization are perpetuated. Volf then shows that the injustices of exclusion cannot be righted by revenge. Victims need to repent of what the perpetrators do to their souls lest they mimic the behavior of their oppressors and let themselves be shaped in the mirror image of the enemy. Neither revenge nor reparation can redress old injustices without creating new ones. The only healing path is forgiveness and reconciliation. He suggests that agreement on justice depends on the will to embrace the other and that justice itself will be unjust as long as it does not become a mutual embrace.

Volf believes that the practice of reconciliation emerges from a recognition of the mutuality of G-d's love; G-d is a Trinity held together in a unity of love. This theology is also understood as a way of increasing peace in the multiple divisions of today's world. These are present in denominations, faiths, ethnic groups, the sacred and the secular, and perpetuated through business, politics, and globalization. Miroslav's father found the G-d of love in a communist labor camp. His mother had a rich and articulate spiritual interior life. His nanny led a life marked by joy and hope. In their own way and under their own unique constraints, each of them lived the kind of life that Volf seeks to make possible for diverse peoples living in today's fragmented and globalized world. The key themes of his work are G-d's unconditional love, justification of the ungodly, love of enemy, forgiveness, and concern for those who suffer. These qualities marked his family as they lived under political oppression and economic deprivation and endured life-shattering personal tragedies.

Volf's book *Exclusion and Embrace* deals with the challenges of reconciliation in contexts of persisting enmity. This is where no clear line can be drawn between victims and perpetrators. Today's victims become tomorrow's perpetrators. These conditions describe the majority of the world's conflicts. However, reconciliation is also needed in neighborhoods where there is alienation. In the distance created through conflict or alienation, embrace is marked by two key practices: acting with generosity toward the perpetrator or neighbor; and maintaining porous boundaries and flexible identities. Identity is porous and flexible when we know we are firstly all human and a brother or a sister, but secondarily English, secondarily Christian, secondarily male or female, and so on.

Embrace does not stand in contrast to justice; it includes justice as a dimension of grace extended toward wrongdoers. Embrace also does not stand in contrast to boundary maintenance. On the contrary, it presumes that it is essential to maintain the self's boundaries and therefore pass judgment. However, these boundaries ought to be porous. This is so the self can make a journey with the other in reconciliation and mutual enrichment.

Part 3: Recovering Reconciliation

Volf cites the father in the story of the prodigal son as an example. By forgiving, the father accepted the change in his own identity as "the father of the prodigal."[9] The best example of embrace is found in the death of Christ on the cross for the ungodly. Christ assumed humanity, forgave, and embraced with open arms. Central to Volf's theology of the cross is Christ's death as an "inclusive substitute" for the ungodly. Christ's dying makes space in God for them as well as for us. Solidarity with victims remains a key aspect of G-d's embrace of humanity.

The practice of embrace is ultimately rooted in G-d's trinitarian nature of mutuality; G-d is love. This love is unconditional because it is the very being of G-d. Embrace is also rooted in an understanding of the mutual indwelling of the divine persons of the Trinity. Their boundaries are porous and flexible and therefore celebrate a joyful exchange and reciprocity. In this Volf echoes the theology of perichoresis of the early Church Fathers. His understanding of G-d is rooted in the Bible and is fundamentally reciprocal and not missional. In *The Trinity is Our Social Program*, Volf argues for a reciprocal correspondence, as in a social interfacing. This is made possible by G-d's indwelling presence. This correspondence occurs between G-d's trinitarian nature and our human relationships. Volf also notes the limitations of such correspondences. Humans are not G-d and are sinful. This requires that humans embrace. Volf also understands that such an embrace has eschatological consequences. The Last Judgment is understood as the final reconciliation and a portal into the world of love.

With awesome prescience on September 11, 2001 Miroslav Volf addressed the Sixteenth Annual International Prayer Breakfast at the United Nations. His theme was: "From Exclusion to Embrace: Reflections on Reconciliation." In it he describes the process of reconciliation:

> The cross of Christ is an act of reconciliation of God with humanity. On the cross of Christ, God is manifested as the God who, though in no way indifferent toward the distinction between good and evil, nonetheless lets the sun shine on both the good and the evil; as the God of infinite and indiscriminate love who died for the ungodly in order to bring them into divine communion. Since the God of Christian belief is the God of unconditional love and the God who died for the ungodly, the will to embrace the other, even the evil other, is a fundamental Christian obligation.
>
> The will to give ourselves to others and "welcome" them, the will to readjust our identities to make space for them, is prior to

---

9. Luke 15:11–52.

any judgment about others, except that of identifying them in their humanity. The will to embrace precedes any "truth" about others and any construction of their "justice." This will is absolutely indiscriminate and strictly immutable; it transcends the moral mapping of the social world into "good" and "evil." This is a scandal when you think about it. But it is qualified by the reality that truth and justice are essential preconditions of actual embrace. A genuine embrace—an embrace that neither play acts acceptance nor crushes the other—cannot take place until the truth has been said and justice established. Hence the will to embrace includes in itself the will to find out what is the case and the will to determine what is just; the will to embrace includes the will to rectify the wrongs that have been done and the will to reshape relationships so as to correspond to truth and justice.

Does this not bring us back to the unacceptable first justice, then reconciliation? Not quite. For, third, the will to embrace is the framework of the search for truth and justice. How do we find what has transpired between people so as to be able to pursue truth and justice in a particular case? Unless you want to embrace and be reconciled to the other, you will not find what truth is and what justice is in any particular circumstance or situation. For you can always interpret somebody's outwardly generous action as a covertly violent action, as a bouquet of flowers in which a dagger is hidden. You have to want to see the other's goodness in order actually to perceive it. Fourth and finally, embrace is the horizon of the struggle for justice. As in many of our activities, so in the struggle for justice: much depends on the telos, on the goal of that struggle. Toward what is it oriented? Is it oriented simply toward ensuring that everyone gets what one deserves? Or is it oriented toward the larger goal of healing relationships? My contention is that it must be oriented precisely toward the latter. The reason is simple. You will have justice only if you strive for something greater than justice, only if you strive after love. I leave you, then, with two things: the will to embrace and an emphasis on creativity, on finding out how one ought to implement that will in particular cases. My time is up and I want to invoke God's wisdom since I don't have time to suggest how you would acquire or implement the will to embrace in concrete situations, whether in your personal or in your more communal lives. I want to leave you with a challenge.[10]

The G-d shaped goal of our human journey is healing through reconciliation.

10. Volf, "From Exclusion to Embrace."

Part 3: Recovering Reconciliation

BEING RECONCILED: AN EXCHANGE OF OUR GIFTS

The missional movement encourages the announcement of peace or the kingdom as practitioners go into the neighborhood. Yet the announcement has to be embodied. It happens in flesh and blood communities and in the practice of reconciliation with neighbors. The failure of Christianity is that it has not practiced reconciliation in society. Christianity has largely relegated forgiveness to the act of private prayer. In *Being Reconciled: Ontology and Pardon* John Milbank has drawn attention to this gap. Milbank is seeking to practice Christian redemption through a rediscovery of life as an exchange of gifts. A gift way of life enables people following Christ's pattern to create a gift society. The gift way of life can overcome a society based on competitive domination. Such a society is enslaved by requiring threatening and submissive behavior between competitors who are fighting each other for access to the same resources. In such a narcissistic and fragmented world it is gift giving that can create cycles of gratitude and obligation. Milbank also cites "Gift" as the name for the Holy Spirit in Augustine's *De Trinitate*. He extends Augustine's account of the Trinity and its corresponding ethic of love in distinctively gift-giving terms; through the Spirit persons are brought into the trinitarian "exchange." Through gift giving people participate in G-d's abundant nature, and humanity can in this way "partake in the divine nature."[11]

Milbank's understanding of reconciliation is rooted in an understanding of G-d's perichoretic nature. He also recognizes that all humanity participates. G-d gives to humanity through the acts of creation and redemption. This draws humanity into G-d's being; a gift exchange is made possible with/in the life of a trinitarian G-d of love. People share the love they experience through G-d with their neighbors. It is impossible to receive G-d's gift while refusing to love our neighbor. The gift is experienced on both horizontal and vertical planes through human interactions. G-d is made present and manifested through reconciliation and cycles of giving and receiving. Such reciprocity is characterized by the giving and receiving of gifts through which humanity is transformed and divinized. Through this practice we give skin to G-d in our neighborhoods. The Prayer of St Francis is exactly right when it says, it is in giving that we receive, and in dying that we are born to eternal life.

---

11. 2 Peter 1:4.

AN ECONOMY OF EXCHANGING GIFTS

Edo writes: "We have all been given a gift, the gift of life. What we do with our lives is our gift back."[12] Charles Eisenstein's book *Sacred Economics: Money, Gift and Society in the Age of Transition* arguably applies Milbank's social theology to economics. The end effect of the gift society is that a monetized society is undermined, along with its bureaucracies of domination and institution. A gift society births community. Sacred economics is rightly described as a pathway of truth and reconciliation. Eisenstein writes: "What is this truth that has always existed? It is the truth of the unity of connectedness of all things, and the feeling of participating in something greater than yourself, yet which also is oneself."[13] This is arguably one description of what Milbank and the early Church Fathers understand as a theology of participation in the life of G-d. This trinitarian G-d is always in a dancing exchange of gifts with/in the multiverse. To enter into the life of G-d is to enter into that dancing exchange. Eisenstein shows that the money economy and its bureaucratic practices militate powerfully against gift relationships. Gift relationships have become commodified in the money economy and sold as services. The money economy demands that people take something that people once got for free, or did for themselves or for each other, and sell it back to them. By turning free things into commodities and services people become cut off from nature. In the same way people are also cut off from real community and one another. This creates a great loneliness and desperation and many basic human needs go unmet.

To survive in the money economy people are forced to look at the world and others in a utilitarian way. They have to calculate how food, persons, and materials can be utilized and capitalized. As society and church have become monetized and bureaucratized real community has evaporated. This is because community is not possible as an add-on to a monetized life. It requires social and economic interdependence. Community is not an add-on to a monetized and bureaucratized church either. Such a church destroys the life of G-d and community. The gift society values the gifts of the whole people of G-d and not only those of paid professionals. In a gift society everyone is not in competition with everybody else. Status is achieved by gift giving and not selfish taking. A gift society is actually a stewardship economy because gifts are constantly in motion. The brief time

---

12. Eisenstein, "Sacred Economics . . . A Short Film."
13. Eisenstein, *Sacred Economics*, Introduction.

that people have gifts in hand before passing them on can be considered a time of stewardship. St. Francis connected to something fundamental about life with/in G-d when he prayed that it is in giving that we receive. If there is no reciprocal gift giving there is no mutuality, reciprocity, or community. If there is no community there is no experience of G-d. For G-d is community.

SEEKING AND FINDING PEACE WITH/IN MY NEIGHBOR

Seek and you will find. Communities of G-d are called to take up their cross and practice reconciliation in their neighborhoods. The center of G-d's neo-tribal postmodern story is now. It is in our communal and contemporary stories that G-d is to be found and already present with/in the collection of people gathered. In conversation all our histories and stories weave into a new pattern of meaning. This is shaped by the concerns of our time and place and our neighborhood. In a post-secular and multi-cultural society that will mean Muslim, secular and Christian stories in mutual conversation creating a people of all faiths and none. We do not bring Christ with us to others but seek Christ who is already present in others. The catalyst for this discovery is reconciliation. It is not doctrine, knowledge, prayer, meditation, church attendance, mission/al work, community involvement, social work, political action, or reform. Only in the practice of face-to-face reconciliation with our neighbor do we discover what it means to be a learner of Christ.

Jesus Christ invites us to be born again into a new and different social reality. It is a companionship of empowerment. This is a non-hierarchical way of being and relating with others. The access point is reconciliation. This new birth enables us to see and walk toward a different horizon. It takes people beyond preoccupations with self, family, tribe, church, denominational propagation, and national identity. Jesus invites us to co-create communities where everyone belongs. As St. Francis embraced and kissed the leper he also embraced and kissed the leper within himself. At that moment joy transfigured them both. Christ is made tangible and given skin through their reconciliation. They are born again as they embrace and reconcile their differences and face their own fears. One of them is a leper. One of them is clean. As they embrace a new kind of society is created. It

Reconciliation Communities

is one in which both lepers and clean belong. As they embrace they are transformed. We are also born again into a different kind of society as we face and reconcile our differences. As we do so our society is turned upside down and we are made whole by the exchange of our gifts. Only together are we made whole and saved. C. G. Jung reminds us: "The meeting of two personalities is like the contact of two chemical substances: if there is any reaction, both are transformed."[14] Anais Nin also saw that: "Each friend represents a world in us, a world not born until they arrive, and it is only by this meeting that a new world is born."[15]

No reconciliation: no transformation.

Know reconciliation: know transformation.

Viva la Reconciliación!

---

14. Jung, *Modern Man*, 49.
15. Nin, "March 1937." *The Diary of Anais Nin Volume Two*.

9

Empowerment Communities

> "Egalité, fraternité and liberté . . . they stood for the things Buddha and Jesus stood for . . . and Buddha and Jesus realized this through small communities. So I think it can only be lived in a small community, in a non-violent sharing, caring community . . . it is a non-violent revolution against that power structure."
> —Brother David Steindl-Rast[1]

> "Here there is no Gentile or Jew, circumcised or uncircumcised, barbarian, Scythian, slave or free, but Christ is all, and is in all. Therefore, as God's chosen people, holy and dearly loved, clothe yourselves with compassion, kindness, humility, gentleness and patience."[2]

---

1. Steindl-Rast, "Beyond Religion."
2. Colossians 3:11–13.

FRIENDSHIP MEALS AND OPEN TABLES

WHAT DID JESUS MEAN when he said, "Go beyond/change your mind, because the companionship of empowerment is within your grasp."[3] Diarmuid O'Murchu describes the practice of the open table that characterizes the companionship of empowerment: "Now we are beginning to glimpse the political, cultural, economic, and subversive characteristics of the early Christian meals—probably going back to the time of Jesus himself. The meals may also have provided the occasion for healing empowerment to take place. People began to dream of a new and more hope filled future. This would have encouraged them to become pro-active in their resistance, not merely to foreign imperialism (Rome) but to the oppressive nature of many of their own Jewish laws and regulations (e.g., Sabbath observance). The commensality pioneered by Jesus was a ritual loaded with pioneering intent."[4] Jesus ate with others in a non-discriminate way in friendship meals and in banquets. These were the popular ways that people gathered together socially in his day. People ate in each other's homes in a more informal way. Pagola[5] suggests that the Last Supper may have been just such a meal. Banquets were more formal and an influence of Greek culture in Israel, usually for the elite. The banquets included formal reading, discussion, and a range of recreational activities, as well as food, drink, and conversation. There were libations or toasts to gods or emperors in the banquets. Early Christians subverted these libations by toasting Christ as the upside down king of the companionship of empowerment.

Mike Morrell also describes the impact of open table practices in his blog:

> Jesus, by contrast, ate indiscriminately. Scholar Bruce Chilton suggests that Jesus, like many tradesmen of his day, was often paid in meals. At these meals, he could invite whomever he wished and his client had no choice but respect his table arrangements. It is here, Chilton believes, that Jesus honed his conviction that God was near when a table was full—of good food and "whosoever." So Jesus invited sex workers and religious leaders, government stooges and terrorists alike to share a common meal around a common table. In so doing, he enacted Isaiah and Ezekiel's eschatological vision of a heavenly banquet come to earth, where God lays a

---

3. Matthew 3:2.
4. O'Murchu, *Christianity's Dangerous Memory*, 98.
5. Pagola, *Jesus: A Historical Approximation*, 345–46.

spread of the finest foods and aged wines to all humanity. How inclusively does Jesus mirror this image of God's all-encompassing shalom? Even at his final meal before execution Jesus invites his betrayer to dine with him.[6]

ALL GROUND IS HOLY GROUND

Much has been made of the sacramental nature of bread and wine as the way Christ is encountered in Christian worship. In Roman Catholic, Orthodox and some Protestant churches this belief is used to exclude people from the open table. People are forbidden to receive communion unless they are part of the church. They must nominally conform to an institutionally prescribed doctrinal initiation program. Communion can only be received from ordained clergy, which in turn reinforces exclusivity and difference. This sends the message that holy things, like bread and wine, must only be given through holy representatives. In this way the simple sacred meal of reconciliation that Christ shared with his learners has been made hierarchical and ritualized beyond all recognition. This is a tragic distortion of the open table practices of Christ. What was a meal of empowerment has become a ritual of disempowerment. Inclusivity is empowering precisely because it overcomes separation and distance between people of all faiths and none. It creates peace. This is the nature of the open table. It is not to enact a memorial of the peace attained by Christ. It is to experience that peace through a tangible encounter with G-d in food, drink, and others. Following Christ's table and fellowship practices makes this possible.

The Roman Catholic tradition has been strongly associated with exclusivity and ritualization of the open table and the meal of reconciliation. Yet some Catholics have managed to go beyond church hierarchy and law and see the inherent sacramentality of all creation. Pierre Teilhard de Chardin recognized Christ as the beginning and the end point of creation. Therefore nothing is profane and everything is sacred because Christ is transparent throughout the created world. The work of humans might seem quite insignificant, but their endeavors are epiphanies of the reality of G-d's presence. In his *Mass for the World* Pierre accessed the deeper reality of Christ in all and through all:

---

6. Morrell, "God in the Material World."

> I have neither bread, nor wine, nor altar, I will raise myself beyond these symbols, up to the pure majesty of the real itself; I, your priest, will make the whole earth my altar and on it will offer you all the labours and sufferings of the world. Over there, on the horizon, the sun has just touched with light the outermost fringe of the eastern sky. Once again, beneath this moving sheet of fire, the living surface of the earth wakes and trembles, and once again begins its fearful travail. I will place on my paten, O God, the harvest to be won by this renewal of labour. Into my chalice I shall pour all the sap which is to be pressed out this day from the earth's fruits. My paten and my chalice are the depths of a soul laid widely open to all the forces which in a moment will rise up from every corner of the earth and converge upon the Spirit. Grant me the remembrance and the mystic presence of all those whom the light is now awakening to the new day.[7]

It may be argued that what gave Pierre authority was his priesthood. The reality is that priesthood is a socially constructed role reflecting Roman hierarchical values rather than the open table of Christ. What is notable is that through his communion with YHWH in creation and humanity he was able to go beyond the separations created by doctrinal hegemony, church hierarchy, and distorted tradition. All life is now sacramental for him. This set him free to experience all ground as holy ground.

COMMUNITY MEALS: RECONCILING NEIGHBORS

Toasting at meals is practiced in many cultures in one form or another. In early Christian meals they subverted the toast to gods or imperial masters by toasting Jesus as YHWH. What is the significance? These libations honored a way of life that went beyond the oppressive demands of all political and religious domination systems. They are rooted in the recognition of the person and work of Christ. He epitomizes and reflects back to all humanity our essential and inherent freedom as YHWH. Toasting or offering libation to him affirms a dignity beyond the conditional approval or acceptance sought through self-interested obedience to corporate religious or political domination systems. Structures that perpetuate power differences on the basis of religion, politics, class, race, gender, or caste were transcended by following the way of Christ. Toasting Christ therefore meant toasting an inherent and essential human freedom and dignity found in all people and

---

7. de Chardin, *Hymn of the Universe*.

through all people. Christ is YHWH in our humanity. Today the toast is still a culturally acceptable way of honoring Jesus as YHWH; the human G-d reflected in all of us. In this way the hierarchical forms of Eucharist are transcended. A toast or libation to Christ liberates those bound in any kind of highly bureaucratized domination system. It celebrates the reality of our social empowerment through the mutuality of the way. What has been called the Mass or Communion is better expressed as a Meal of Reconciliation in the neighborhood. This is how the peacemaking of Christ is manifested in neotribal societies.

MODERN CHURCH PRACTICES

Most modern Catholics and Protestants do not encounter the G-d of reciprocity to which Scripture and tradition testify in their worship. A skewed understanding of G-d as mission and Gospel as domination has led modern Christians to fundamentally misunderstand the ethos of the communities of G-d found in the New Testament. This has created an unhealthy preoccupation with church leadership and hierarchy, church buildings, church attendance, church worship, church preaching, and conversion to church subculture. The result has been Christian disciples of domination who believe that their role in society is to try to convert others to this subculture. "The modern congregation is not a coherent context which can teach us how the abstracted aspects of our lives fit together to create a unified reality. It is itself an abstraction, that institution which has the function of servicing the 'spiritual' aspect of life. Because an individualist society is a mobile society, the congregation loses the power to superintend the lengthy rhythms of the creation of a self. Indeed, the sense that life is related to larger natural and social and spiritual rhythms—or that it is itself such a rhythm in time—is gradually lost."[8] This misunderstanding has led the church to model and reinforce socially impotent practices.

A pastor was once tasked to teach a group about church leadership. He went to an older leader in the movement and asked: "What shall I tell them?" The reply was, "Tell them what you like. They will forget it all anyway ... but be with them and you will mark them for life." Current practices within contemporary European and American Christianity emphasize a religion of education and piety that is weakly connected to devotional life and engagement with/in society. Modern Western Christianity has a big

8. Wiens, "Mennonite Brethren."

brain and talks a lot, but has a small heart and weak hands. It is good on theology but weak on practice. This is the result of the way that Christian formation has been conducted with a gross and misplaced over-emphasis on education. In contrast, it has had an almost non-existent emphasis on example and the development of spiritual skills. Modern Western Christians can tell people how to live but not show them. Example is overlooked and precept is emphasized out of all proportion. The focus is still very much on corporate practices, such as public attendance and passive learning with some emphasis on private devotion. The church is perceived and experienced largely as a school. The social application of how to actually live a Gospel of companionship and empowerment in is almost entirely missing. There is a massive disconnect between what disciples of the modern church know and what they actually do.

Many acknowledge this to be the case and bemoan the situation. Yet virtually nobody acknowledges the problem as structural. It is the way Christianity is hierarchically structured and modeled that produces this malaise. Marshall McLuhan reminds us that the medium is the message. Preaching and management in church produces preachers and managers in society. Social practices in communities produce people who will do those activities and practices in society. Conversation, reconciliation, and empowerment will produce a people with these skills. It is in this way that the G-d of reciprocity will be encountered and is manifested.

PUBLIC ATTENDANCE AND LEARNING PASSIVITY

With this clarification in mind it is wise to examine the current practices that are emphasized in the Christianity of the West. They fall into three main areas. Corporate practice is strongest. Some action-orientated people throw themselves into good deeds. The weakest is private practice, which seems almost entirely squeezed out of a highly extroverted and time-poor culture.

Corporate

- Management
- Bureaucracy
- Strategic leadership

Part 3: Recovering Reconciliation

- Church attendance: Eucharist/Communion/Mass
- Passive listening to preachers/verbal teachers
- Attending stage-managed public worship
- House groups: centered on bible, piety, church.

Public

- Preaching/speaking to other about Christ
- Giving Money: for missions and poverty relief
- Social involvement: co-dependent help to others as benefactors, not companions, with those in need, i.e., homeless people, those in poverty.

Private

- Prayer
- Bible study
- Confession.

These practices are compartmentalized and socially disconnected. They reflect a gospel of the educated and pietistic benefactor not the companion of empowerment. Religious consumerism and institutional co-dependency is reinforced. This is because they actively affirm just turning up and passively feeding off the menu offered by the corporate church. A good example of the impact of this is a man who took someone who was homeless into his house for the night. He went to his vicar the following day and said: "Why isn't the church doing anything to help the homeless?" His vicar replied "The church is doing something. You took in this man and gave him somewhere to stay last night." The story highlights the trap of institutionalized religion. People fail to take responsibility for their own spirituality and personal action and expect these services to be provided through institutional means. This requires little personal risk, involvement, or effort except putting money in the collection. It is the very structure of institutional religion and its centralized bureaucracies that perpetuate this mixed message and create such co-dependency and spiritual infantilism.

SOCIAL PRACTICES

Alan Roxburgh rightly challenges modern church practices in his article "Practices of Christian Life—Forming and Performing a Culture":

> What is called for in this missionary context is a re-engagement with quite specific social practices. Luke 10, again, helps us to think through what might be involved. It is framed around Jesus sending the seventy "home." They return to the places where they had, mostly, been raised, namely, Galilee of the Gentiles. They are sent to dwell (stay in the same house; enter into the whole social and economic life of the household) in the neighborhoods and communities in a very specific way—not in control, not with a new tactic called "entering the neighborhood"—but as those who were in need of receiving hospitality from the other (the household in the community).
>
> Practices are about the formation of a society. They are about the making a world; the formation of a culture that assumes and lives as if God is the active agent in the midst of a people. All other framing of Christian practices are accommodations to other narratives. When the seventy in Luke 10 are told to practice speaking shalom in the households and towns they entered, it was the practical announcement of an alternative story that stood in contradistinction to the PAX of that other empire that promised economic, political and social peace to all who lived under the requirements (practices) of that PAX. The speaking of shalom was the announcement of practices cutting across the claims of PAX. Sitting at table, joining the social and economic life of the household with the open hands of the stranger were practices radically counter to the regnant Pax of that empire.
>
> What is at stake in a missionary encounter with the West is the re-forming of Christian life in terms of social practices. Without this movement away from the expressive and inward to social praxis Christianity will remain stultified and impoverished. What might such social practices involve?

MISSIONAL PRACTICES

In the *Journal of Missional Practice* Alan Roxburgh outlines the context and content of missional practice in the following way:

Part 3: Recovering Reconciliation

The Missional Network's convictions are formed out of an ongoing engagement with a question posited by Lesslie Newbigin over thirty years ago: What is the nature of a missionary encounter with the late modern culture that shapes the West? These convictions are as follows:

1. Because the missionary God is at work in the shifting, turbulent contexts of western societies—the churches are called to enter a new imagination for being God's people. 2. This requires disciples of Jesus to be shaped by disciplines and practices. 3. Local contexts are where God's ordinary people discern the activity of God. 4. The Spirit is leading us on a journey of mutuality and respect toward our neighbourhoods and communities. 5. There are no preferred solutions or formulas.

Experimentation and innovation are important gifts for this journey. Each of these five convictions invites fuller exploration in terms of what they mean as well as their indissoluble connectedness. The way they are framed presupposes a set of practices (ways of acting and, hence, thinking) that have become quite alien to the churches of the West. An underlying conviction resourcing them is that the local, everyday, and ordinary are the location where God's future is experienced and discerned. This, itself, is a massive turn from a long period wherein experts and professionals (that is the ordained and degreed) were empowered to work through abstract ideals that were then standardized, programmed, packaged and transferred down from some supposed centre to the local.

Luke 10: 1–12 continues to provide guidance. Three key elements of this text are important for our discussion:

1. It re-orients the focus of the church's activities from within and among themselves into the communities where they dwell.

2. It reframes the location of the questions—from an ecclesiocentric: How do we fix the church, to theocentric: How do we discern what God is up to ahead of us in our communities? How do we join with what God is already doing ahead of us in our communities?

3. It is shaped around practices. The seventy receive instructions, a set of practices that shape their journey and little more: In pairs (social construction rather than individual heroes).

Dependent on the hospitality of the neighbor (no bag . . .). Speaking the shalom of God (this was not a polite, formal greeting; they went where empire proposed Pax, if loyalty were given the Pax Romana then the good things in life would come to people. These disciples announced a counter-narrative.). Entering the socio-economic life of the people ("eat what is set before you," "the laborer deserves to be paid," "stay in the same place"), healing the sick, announce the kingdom of God.

At the base of their mission was a set of practices shaping their encounters. In the midst of huge social upheaval, when the narratives and roadmaps of a culture are changing and the church finds its accommodations within the culture unravelling, it will be the re-appropriation of such practices that shape a new missionary encounter. Troeltsch sensed this, the early church exemplified it and those of us faced with the end of the detente between Christianity and the modern form of the Western narrative are in a similar situation. What might such practices involve? There are no easy answers. We have to address the issues of missional practices from within the still dominant narratives of the modern Western imagination.

In the UK one is struck by the way many have been influenced by the Northumbria Community. What enlivens this dispersed community is not primarily a list of practices (as important as they are and built around the Daily Office), but its Rule of Life: Availability and Vulnerability. This is a fundamentally social understanding of practices because, at the core, it involves the recognition that the most critical space where we encounter and know God is in our engagement with the other. This, of course, lies at the core of the Luke 10:1–12 text—the practices of becoming and welcoming the other in the name of Christ.[9]

MISSIONAL COMMUNITIES: OPEN TABLES?

There is much that is good in the above article. An emphasis on social practices is vital for the rediscovery of G-d in society. Yet a missional emphasis maintains a Christian hegemony. It perpetuates ideological and cultural dominance through an emphasis on creed and Bible. It is a hegemony of the word and idea. This emphasis is overshadowed by the central Gospel emphasis of reconciliation. Missional has rightly challenged Western Christianity to enter the neighborhood as strangers and practice in a more conversational way. There is a clear recognition that "The Spirit is leading us on a journey of mutuality and respect toward our neighborhoods and communities."[10] Yet the kinds of communities that will be created through

---

9. Roxburgh, "Practices of Christian Life."
10. Ibid.

engagement with people of all faiths and none is not fully acknowledged or recognized or addressed in the missional approach.

Whilst positive, these practices fall short of the full social impact of Christ's practices of reconciliation, companionship, and empowerment. Missional communities incorporate some of the very positive qualities of friendship meals and open tables. Yet how open can the table really be if Christendom-based practices of Christian prayer, Bible reading, or Communion are at the center? How open is the table if, behind the scenes, the modernist language of Misseo Dei, leader, planning, and map-making is informing and guiding the process? Missional communities often dovetail with centralized institutions that are, in practice, doctrinally policed and managerialized mission-visions of Christian hegemony. All centralized institutions are not open tables but are systems of bureaucratic domination through knowledge. Yet Jesus' simple practice of the open table was a meal of reconciliation and a shared way of life.

OUR ESSENTIAL HUMAN UNITY: IN SPIRIT AND TRUTH

The open table is also not focussed on the worship of Jesus as ruler, but celebrates worshipping YHWH in all things and through all peoples. Jesus in fact challenges us to begin to worship YHWH in a new way beyond our tribal or religious identities. Worship in spirit and truth recognizes YHWH as inherent and common in all humanity. Jesus' encounter with the Samaritan woman reveals this possibility. Worship is not based on a location, tribal belonging, religious doctrine, or national identity. Instead, it is rooted in a reconciled spirit of honesty and transparency with all humanity, and seeks to go beyond all differences.

> "Sir," the woman said, "I can see that you are a prophet. Our ancestors worshipped on this mountain, but you Jews claim that the place where we must worship is in Jerusalem." "Woman," Jesus replied, "believe me, a time is coming when you will worship the Father neither on this mountain nor in Jerusalem. You Samaritans worship what you do not know; we worship what we do know, for salvation is from the Jews. Yet a time is coming and has now come when the true worshippers will worship the Father in the Spirit

and in truth, for they are the kind of worshippers the Father seeks. God is spirit, and his worshippers must worship in the Spirit and in truth."[11]

Worship in spirit and truth is not tied to a place: Samaria, Jerusalem, Rome, Mecca, a church, a cathedral or a temple. It is about being in a state of reconciliation and grace with peoples of all faiths and none. This is because, as Jesus said, G-d is spirit and all true worshippers must worship him in spirit and in truth.

THE JESUS WAY: VOLUNTARY MUTUAL SUBMISSION

A key factor in the formation of empowerment communities is developing a style of leadership that expresses mutuality and reciprocity. What undermines empowerment is hierarchical managerialism. Church leadership practices today mirror our capitalist managerialized society. In great contrast what Jesus practiced was an exchange of gifts in a community life in which all lead and all are led. Leadership is exercised according to the measure of faith and gifts in all. Parker J. Palmer (2000) has been able to see past the overreliance on management to a more cooperative and egalitarian leadership that expresses the vision of Jesus; leadership is a concept we often resist. It seems immodest, even self-aggrandizing, to think of ourselves as leaders. But if it is true that we are made for community, then leadership is everyone's vocation, and it can be an evasion to insist that it is not. When we live in the close-knit ecosystem called community, everyone follows and everyone leads.[12] . Seth Godin also reminds us that: "For the first time ever, everyone in an organization—not just the boss—is expected to lead."[13]

THE NON-HIERARCHICAL ROMAN CENTURION

The Roman centurion of Luke 7 is often cited as a proof text for hierarchical forms of authority. Just the opposite is the case. He was repenting of hierarchical domination by refusing to order Jesus to heal his servant. This man recognized that the authority of Jesus came from his life of companionship and empowerment. Jesus praises the centurion for his faith because he was

---

11. John 4:23–24.
12. Palmer, *Let your Life Speak*.
13. Godin, *Tribes*, 20.

Part 3: Recovering Reconciliation

willing to submit to a way of life in companionship rather than hold on to the false power of hierarchy. He did so even though he was part of a brutal hierarchical killing machine. The centurion was saying, in effect, that his hierarchical authority depended on the world system yet Christ's authority arose from a mutuality of companionship and empowerment. He recognized the weakness, deficiency and brutality of his own authority. He also acknowledged the liberating and healing authority of Christ. The centurion refused to treat Jesus like a subjugated Jew. He recognized that it is not on these terms that Jesus is coming to heal his servant. Christ is beyond orders and comes to him in freedom and mercy. Mercy triumphs over judgment.

AUTHORITY: NON-HIERARCHICAL WISDOM

Christ does not affirm or practice hierarchical leadership at any point in the Gospels. He is a master. Yet this arises from his charism, or gift, of wisdom-teaching and healing. His gift gives him authority and not his position as Rabbi. Christ's authority is not rooted in his traditional, organizational, or bureaucratic status. Even his Jewish tradition recognized he taught as one having authority in contrast to other Rabbis.

Authority is created when gifts are shared in a mutual and reciprocal way of life that refuses to lord it. In this way each brings their gifts in voluntary mutual submission alongside all others. Each group member leads with their gift in the service of others and they are led by others. Some coordinate as an expression of their gift, but administration must never become dominant. Some have more wisdom and natural authority due to their depth of experience. It is the level of faith and maturity of gift that creates authority, regardless of any position held in the organization. "One man with no authority suddenly becomes a key figure. Tribes give each of us the very same opportunity. Skill and attitude are essential. Authority is not. In fact, authority can get in the way" says Seth Godin.[14]

This kind of authority "needs no bureaucratical protection, it is its own perpetual resurrection" as Betjeman put it.[15] To regard the authority of the gift as in any way hierarchical is to rob it of its power. As in the Trinity, the authority for leadership within the community of G-d passes back and forth in a mutual exchange of gifts. Organizational and managerial attempts at leadership kill this naturally occurring authority by putting

14. Ibid.
15. Ware, *The Orthodox Way*, 9.

people in positions. The whole community is then robbed of many gifts and talents. Everyone abdicates their own G-d-given authority in a false submission to the person in structurally imposed leadership. Contemporary capitalist culture has authorized and sought to vindicate bureaucratic management as the only sensible and therefore acceptable way of organizing life. In practice this means that naturally occurring gift-based authority has been commodified. Bureaucratized hierarchy in church, state and business has choked it to death.

Hierarchy that is legal-rational, bureaucratic and positional is very different from authority that is familial and charismatic. The former dominates and controls. The latter empowers and sets free, because it is relational and based on an exchange of gifts. A belief in hierarchy and its teachings are often used to exclude, excommunicate, or legalize. Hierarchy is contrived, artificial, and illusory; a fiction designed to impose false and imaginary order. Recently, in the USA, hierarchical domination has been used by the Roman Catholic Church to bring nuns into submission to "sound doctrine." Yet we live in a time when such attempts at dominance through doctrinal means are no longer enforceable. In postmodernity the local community of G-d is self-authenticating and has authority. Priests, ministers, and leaders of any kind are only representative. The attempt to bring doctrinal hegemony through hierarchical means is also significantly undermined by ecumenism and access to knowledge for all. Seeking and finding truth is now increasingly practiced as an ecumenical and interfaith endeavor. It is far from being in the control of any one church. People accepted Christ because they recognized his authority as it emerged from his gift as wisdom teacher and not as bureaucrat or minister. It is not based on legal status or position of invulnerable power, but on sacrificial love. With generosity and vulnerability he gave his gifts and graciously received back in kind from others who were from very different political and religious groups.

LEGAL-RATIONAL, TRADITIONAL OR CHARISMATIC?

Max Weber outlined three different types of authority: legal-rational, traditional, and charismatic. Using his analysis it is vital to answer the questions:

- What kind of authority did Jesus and his learners have?
- What kind of authority has characterized the Church?

Part 3: Recovering Reconciliation

Wikipedia provides the following summary of the different types of authority Weber recognized:

> Authority is the legitimate or socially approved use of power. It is the legitimate power which one person or a group holds over another. The element of legitimacy is vital to the notion of authority and is the main means by which authority is distinguished from the more general concept of power. Power can be exerted by the use of force or violence. Authority, by contrast, depends on the acceptance by subordinates of the right of those above them to give them orders or directives.
>
> Types of Authorities:
>
> - Traditional Authority: Power legitimized by respect for long-established cultural patterns
> - Charismatic Authority: Power legitimized by extraordinary personal abilities that inspire devotion and obedience
> - Legal-rational Authority: Also known as bureaucratic authority, is when power is legitimized by legally enacted rules and regulations such as governments.
>
> Max Weber on authority.
>
> Weber defined domination (authority) as the chance of commands being obeyed by a specifiable group of people. Legitimate authority is that which is recognized as legitimate and justified by both the ruler and the ruled.
>
> Weber divided legitimate authority into three types:
>
> The first type discussed by Weber is legal-rational authority. It is that form of authority that depends for its legitimacy on formal rules and established laws of the state, which are usually written down and are often very complex. The power of the rational legal authority is mentioned in the constitution. Modern societies depend on legal-rational authority. Government officials are the best example of this form of authority, which is prevalent all over the world.
>
> The second type of authority is Traditional authority, which derives from long-established customs, habits and social structures. When power passes from one generation to another, then it is known as traditional authority. The right of hereditary monarchs to rule furnishes an obvious example. The Tudor dynasty in England and the ruling families of Mewar, in Rajasthan (India) are some examples of traditional authority.

The third form of authority is Charismatic authority. Here, the charisma of the individual or the leader plays an important role. Charismatic authority is that authority which is derived from "the gift of grace" or when the leader claims that his authority is derived from a "higher power" (e.g., God or natural law or rights) or "inspiration," that is superior to both the validity of traditional and legal-rational authority and followers accept this and are willing to follow this higher or inspired authority, in the place of the authority that they have hitherto been following.

History has witnessed several social movements or revolutions, against a system of traditional or legal-rational authority, which are usually started by Charismatic authorities.[16]

AUTHORITY: THE DANCE OF G-D

In identifying the different types of authority Weber enables a distinction to be made between the authority of the church and the authority of Jesus. The church today has become increasingly legal-rational. In its history and social role it has been entrenched in oppressive and violent forms of traditional authority. The authority of Christ and his learners was, without doubt, characterized by charismatic and familial authority. By now it must be clear that the church has traded its charismatic birthright for a mess of legal-rational pottage. The authority that Jesus practiced was undeniably charismatic and familial in nature. His challenge of a rigid and abusive use of traditional authority was stinging and vociferous. His disdain and disregard for imposed and oppressive legal-rational authority is clearly displayed in the Gospel accounts. He ate and healed on the Sabbath, spoke with women of other faiths, praised occupying Romans for faith, called the Pharisees vipers, angrily kicked over tables, and threw people out of the Temple.

George Bernard Shaw paints a clear picture of the charismatic authority of Christ and the strong reaction it provoked:

> Take the case of the extermination of Jesus Christ. No doubt there was a strong case for it. Jesus was from the point of view of the High Priest a heretic and an impostor. From the point of view of the merchants he was a rioter and a communist. From the Roman Imperialist point of view he was a traitor. From the commonsense point of view he was a dangerous madman. From the snobbish

16. en.wikipedia.org/wiki/Authority_(sociology).

point of view, always a very influential one, he was a penniless vagrant. From the police point of view he was an obstructor of thoroughfares, a beggar, an associate of prostitutes, an apologist of sinners, and a disparager of judges; and his daily companions were tramps whom he had seduced into vagabondage from their regular trades. From the point of view of the pious he was a Sabbath breaker, a denier of the efficacy of circumcision and the advocate of a strange rite of baptism, a gluttonous man and a winebibber. He was abhorrent to the medical profession as an unqualified practitioner who healed people by quackery and charged nothing for the treatment. He was not anti-Christ: nobody had heard of such a power of darkness then; but he was startlingly anti-Moses. He was against the priests, against the judiciary, against the military, against the city (he declared that it was impossible for a rich man to enter the kingdom of heaven), against all the interests, classes, principalities and powers, inviting everybody to abandon all these and follow him. By every argument, legal, political, religious, customary, and polite, he was the most complete enemy of the society of his time ever brought to the bar. He was guilty on every count of the indictment, and on many more that his accusers had not the wit to frame. If he was innocent then the whole world was guilty. To acquit him was to throw over civilization and all its institutions. History has borne out the case against him; for no state has ever constituted itself on his principles or made it possible to live according to his commandments: those states who have taken his name have taken it as an alias to enable them to persecute his followers more plausibly. It is not surprising that under these circumstances, and in the absence of any defence, the Jerusalem community and the Roman government decided to exterminate Jesus. They had just as much right to do so as to exterminate the two thieves who perished with him.[17]

Charismatic authority is the authority of the gift. People obey voluntarily. They have discovered that real authority is rooted in love that fulfills all the requirements of law. It is only love that gives birth to honest and heartfelt obedience. Christ said, "If you love me, you will obey me."[18] Love creates faithfulness and out of faithfulness is born obedience. This is the authority of Jesus. Christ does not take the quick lazy shortcut and use exacting laws or oppressive and suffocating traditional requirements to change people or the way they act. Jesus knows that it is only mercy that triumphs

17. Shaw, "Leading Case of Jesus Christ," *On the Rocks*.
18. John 14:15.

over judgment. It captivates the heart and obedience of men and women in a way that externalized law and tradition only dream of. The authority of companionship and empowerment is manifested in the exchange of our gifts. There is no other kind of authority which is G-d breathed. Law has a legitimate place when used properly but it is always incomplete unless balanced by the charismata of the prophetic. It is the Law and the Prophets together that find fulfillment in the mutual authority of Jesus Christ.

AUTHORITY IN MUTUAL SUBMISSION

Black Elk said that the centre of the universe is everywhere,[19] and his understanding of reality echoes a perceptive insight about the trinitarian nature of G-d. If the center is everywhere then the authority of the center is in fact everywhere. In G-d as Trinity there is an authority in each of the three persons. The Father has authority, and so does the Son, and so does the Holy Spirit. There is also equality between the three persons. Although equal they all voluntarily submit to one another in a dance of exchanging gifts. This dance creates their centrifugal love. The authority of G-d arises from their mutual submission in the dance. The Trinity is paradoxically authority in equality: one G-d. Without mutual submission authority is distorted. This is because what creates the authority of G-d is only love. This love is created by the dance of mutual submission in which they are continually exchanging gifts. This creates a never-ending, generative, self-replenishing, all consuming, centrifugal love. In this love all life in the multiverse is also dancing.

This picture of the Trinity also provides us with a powerful and egalitarian image of authority in the communities of G-d. Within the dance of the Trinity all lead and all are led. The Trinity is also the origin and centrifugal center of the companionship of empowerment. It is the expression of the Father, the Son, and the Holy Spirit in society. As Father, Son, and Holy Spirit submit to one another in love so do people in the community of G-d submit to one another. All are leading and gifting others; all are being led and gifted by others. Authority in equality is the expression of the companionship of empowerment on Earth even as it is in Heaven. The way of the companionship of empowerment is the doorway to/from the transforming heart of the G-d of reciprocal love.

19. http://en.wikiquote.org/wiki/Black_Elk

Part 3: Recovering Reconciliation

Love can only be expressed in relationships of voluntary mutual submission. A good marriage is a potent example. The practice of Jesus and his learners is unequivocally one of voluntary mutual submission. It is also reflected in the *koinonia* life of the communities of G-d in the Epistles. This practice is based on difference in giftedness and maturity of character and faith. There is certainly genuine authority in that. Jesus practiced the authority of the open table. It is a mutual authority that is genuinely manifested in the communities of G-d.

THE SOCIAL PRACTICES OF THE COMMUNITIES OF G-D

The task facing the peoples of G-d in neotribal societies is not the formation of missional communities. Nor is it to reboot and refinance institutional churches. Neither is it an attempt to remake a New Christian West. What is needed is an encounter with the G-d of reciprocity and the Gospel of reconciliation in small communities. This reorientates the communities of G-d toward practices of conversation, reconciliation and empowerment. It creates an environment where all people lead and all people are led in mutual submission. This will bring healing and motivation to our fragmented neighborhoods.

Alan Roxburgh rightly draws attention to the current paucity of social practices in Western Christianity. He cogently cites Christian professionalism as having commodified and thereby destroyed the essentially gifted and gift giving nature of the communities of G-d. Vulnerability and availability are a huge improvement on the attendance and preaching practices of mainline Christianity. Yet they still do not grasp fully the dynamic contained in an encounter with the G-d of reciprocity and the Gospel of reconciliation. Availability and vulnerability enable a more open and reflexive relationship with others. Yet they do not fulfill the promise of reconciliation. This essential practice is what enables belonging with/in the communities of G-d. It is reconciliation that saves us and makes society whole. Alan Roxburgh is right to emphasize that different areas will create the need for the development of particular social practices. They are shaped and determined by the culture. Yet there are certain practices intrinsic in the example of Christ, which are non-negotiable essentials. Conversation, reconciliation and empowerment remain fundamental in expressing the very nature of G-d in society.

SEEKING AND FINDING G-D IN SOCIETY

How do we discover G-d in society? The practice of open source conversation is central. Common neighborhood concerns are held between people of all faiths and none. Yet, in order to be genuine, the conversation cannot have a bias toward Christianity. Open source spirituality is realized through the practice of conversation. It makes way for reconciliation with one another. This occurs when people of all faiths and none make peace with one another. It is different from the missional practice of announcing a peace that is gained through accepting Jesus as Lord. Jesus is only manifested as YHWH (Lord) when people reconcile. As people of all faiths and none make peace with one another then Shalom is made tangible in relationships. Shalom, or social wholeness, is manifested in the neighborhood through mutual reconciliation. Wholeness and well-being in society comes through practicing the way of companionship and empowerment. It is at this point that G-d's will is done on Earth as in Heaven. Reconciliation and reciprocity are the dwelling place of G-d. It is only as this happens that we really begin to join G-d in our neighborhood.

Community meals of reconciliation and open tables of friendship energize an alternative way of life and social empowerment. Out of genuine open source conversation emerges reconciliation. From this emerges a companionship that empowers communities and neighborhoods. Communities of G-d emerge that challenge oppressive religious, financial, and social structures. People learn to live together through a mutual exchange of gifts. They are empowered to live a life beyond legalized contracts administered through oppressive bureaucratic systems. In the open table people encounter G-d in one another. They find grace to live freely beyond the walls created by religion, suspicion, competition, aggressive narcissism, class, i-culture, and financial slavery. Through reconciliation people are born again into an entirely new and different social reality. G-d is not revealed in Scripture, tradition and community as monastic (Catholic tendency) or missional (Protestant tendency), but beyond both. G-d is reciprocal reconciling love. Conversation, reconciliation and empowerment are more congruent with this image of G-d. They are also more socially dynamic and transformative. Jesus was clear, "Truly, truly, I say to you, unless one is born again he cannot see the companionship of empowerment."[20]

---

20. John 3:3.

PART 4

Our Un/Known G-d

A NEOTRIBAL SPIRITUALITY

10

Home Truths

"There is no self that will survive a real conversation. There is no self that will survive a meeting with something other than itself. There is no organization that will keep its original identity if it's in the conversation."

—David Whyte[1]

"Pathmaker, your footsteps
are the path and nothing more;
pathmaker, there is no path,
you make the path by walking."

—Antonio Machado[2]

---

1. Whyte "Life at the Frontier."
2. Machado, "Proverbs and Songs XXIX," *Selected Poems*.

Part 4: Our Un/Known G-d

LOSING MY RELIGION: EMBRACING OUR RELIGION

THE MODERNIST SKY HAS fallen. The modernist church is dying.

The G-d that was found in this church has left the building. The faithful feel adrift in the bewildering sea of a postmodern plurality of faiths. Yet are we really lost? Imagine someone built a model of a Google map of planet Earth containing all the streets. It was kept in the Tate Modern in London filling the whole of the top floor. Then imagine that there was a bomb that destroyed St. Paul's Cathedral nearby. The shock threw the model up in the air. The bits and pieces landed. Nothing is where it was. Everything is in a perplexing, intriguing, infuriating, sublime mix. The doorways are not where they were. The way is now different. The key holders come and go in confusion and perplexity.

Trust, authority, and power are very different in the mixed up jigsaw of the landscape of the twenty-first century. Seismic events like atom bombs, attacks on World Trade Centres, and Iraq Wars do that. They have massive social aftershocks that reverberate down the decades. These events have been formative in the creation of world in which we live. The old maps and the old journeys no longer work. The global panic these events engendered have prompted the West to ratchet up suffocating levels of security, micromanagement, stratification, demarcation, regulation, and control. Yet simultaneously G-d is also rending asunder this dysfunctional, overregulated, and machinated world. This is a G-d who cannot be contained and controlled by capitalist money, communist ideology, or bureaucratized Christian social dominance. Transparency is G-d's truth weapon against these opaque illusions of modernity.

In such a world we can also begin to see more clearly the christianities we have inherited: Catholic, Orthodox and Protestant. These christianities have, to a large extent, been socially constructed. Men and women shaped expressions of faith that dovetailed with their regional geography, history, and politics. Prophetic men and women kept alive an immediate faith in fresh movements of G-d. Buddhism and other religions have been similarly flexible and adaptable in transmission. It is now possible for all of us to make connections and comparisons and recognize underlying religious similarities and differences. The one-way grip of monolithic modernity is loosening. Yet the questions remain. How do we find our way in such a world where all the street signs are mixed up and all the roads no longer lead where they once did? How do we become whole? How do we find our way home? How will we know it when we get there? When all the pathways have become confused we need to discover again that the ground is still there beneath our feet. It is in our connection with the earth beneath the broken pathways and in conversation with reality that we will find our way. Underneath the street rubble of our atomized religion and society is a deep and abiding neotribal kinship. It is found in the G-d of reciprocal and reconciling love: YHWH in all humanity.

Those who have wandered in the postmodern wilderness are searching for home. They look in vain among the rubble of the broken streets and broken pathways of corporate church, state, and business. There are others who refuse to admit they are, in fact, lost. They look to re-establish the certainties of a bureaucratically ordered modernity for reassurance. This perpetuates comforting illusions of security and stability. Those who have journeyed on the missional way are as far away from finding home as everyone else. This is because missional ideology has really been an attempt to put a sticking plaster on the very disturbing fragmentation of society brought about by postmodernity and globalization. It has tried to do this by doing something socially useful and practical. Yet reliable map-making is not really possible in an atomized world. The sticking plaster is inadequate to heal a church and a society that needs major surgery. It may even need to die in order to be reborn. To find our way again means following Christ in his way of death and rebirth. It is this way that will lead to social wholeness and well-being. For only in dying are we are born to eternal life. There is only one way to die. It means that the way things were will cease to exist in any meaningful or practical way. The church as domination system, and the bureaucratic apparatus that maintains it, will cease to exist.

Ricoeur's process of orientation-disorientation-reorientation is a way forward for the church. It is a way of death and resurrection. It requires honesty and integrity and resisting the temptation of a modernist managerial quick fix. What the missional solution does not do is to help us express our loss and grief at modernity's social failures and dysfunctions: money and power fetishism, lost and broken communities and families, rampant addiction and individualistic narcissism. It offers a premature solution by doing something practical to avoid what is happening to the church and society. To come to a genuinely new place means facing the inconsistencies and pain in our fragmented souls and societies. These have been generated by the dualism inherent in the Enlightenment and the Reformation. These changes regurgitated the vain and illusory idealism of a violent Greek perfection. It is these splits and illusions in our way of seeing and being in the world that have ultimately divorced us from each other.

At the same time they have also divorced us from being able to encounter G-d in society. G-d is community. When we lost touch with each other we lost touch with G-d. This is how the church lost its purpose and function in society. Church language, tradition, custom and bigotry have disconnected us from our secular brothers and sisters. It is not possible to love yourself if you have no neighbor to love anymore. This social disconnection is the root of an inner disorientation. At the heart of this rift is modernity and modern religion in all its forms: Christian, Jewish and Muslim. This is because modern religions have emphasized words and knowledge as the way to G-d rather than a way of life rooted in practices in small learning communities. Most people have yet to encounter the dancing G-d of conversation, community and gift.

The failure of the Catholic and Protestant Churches to affirm and bless society as the dwelling place of G-d has cut off their air supply. An inability to listen to the trauma of the secular as the prophetic voice of G-d has left the church in a state of pseudo-spiritual splendid isolation. It is withering off the vine. In this situation 95 percent of the UK population regard church as a pleasant cake decoration, 5 percent remain enamored. Eddie Izzard humorously reminds us, however, that the stark choice confronting us is always "cake or death?"[3] It is not possible to hold onto a decorative, hierarchical, disempowering institutional church and still sit down to eat at the simple, empowering open table of Jesus. The church has to let go of its ideology of Christian social dominance and the bureaucratic apparatus that maintains it. To play fair and make genuine friends the church needs to acknowledge that, "There is no self that will survive a real conversation. There is no organization that will keep its original identity if it's in the conversation."[4] The church needs to witness, discern, and bless the gifts of G-d in secular society. Disenfranchised church and rootless society are in it together. They are not in it to win it.

---

3. Izzard, "Cake or Death."
4. Whyte "Life at the Frontier."

MISSIONAL MONOCULTURE: REBOOTING CHRISTIANITY?

Missional is a modernist attempt to reboot Christianity. Sim has defined modernism as "an attempt to defend one Universalist culture, often forced to attack regionalism as parochialism [and] the postmodern alternative is to accept that we are living in an age of cultural relativism."[5] The idea of remaking the New Christian West is without doubt "an attempt to defend one Universalist culture."

Wikipedia describes a monoculture as "the practice of planting crops with the same patterns of growth resulting from genetic similarity. Examples include wheat fields or apple orchards or grape vineyards. These cultivars have uniform growing requirements and habits resulting in greater yields on less land because planting, maintenance (including pest control) and harvesting can be standardized. This standardization results in less waste and loss from inefficient harvesting and planting. It also is beneficial because a crop can be tailor planted for a location that has special problems—like soil salt or drought or a short growing season. Monoculture produces great yields by utilizing plants' abilities to maximize growth under less pressure from other species and more uniform plant structure."[6]

Missional ideology cannot heal our souls and societies because it seeks to propagate a monocultural final solution; the remaking of a New Christian West. This has short-circuited the community healing process. It has cut the transformative power from the neotribal conversation in the neighborhood. The missional practices of mission, leadership, map-making, and planning have tended to create a movement with monocultural features. There is a common missional DNA that is reinforced through its modernist language and missional leadership practices. Missional practitioners communicate using missional language and value the use of the Bible and/or Christian Eucharist and Christian history as central in the neighborhood conversation. When dovetailed with the bureaucratized Christian hegemony of the mainline churches, missional churches become even more monocultural. The management and bureaucracy inherent in the centralized institutions of mainline Christianity dictate a monocultural outcome. The denominational HQ's of Anglicanism, Methodism, Catholicism, and so on are steering the resources and determining the agenda. Their intention is

---

5. Scott, 'Postmodernism and Music' in Sim, *The Routledge Companion*, 139.
6. *en.wikipedia.org/wiki/Monoculture.*

the survival or perpetuation of their own brands and market share. What is produced is a centralized monocultural corporation Christianity.

A NEOTRIBAL POLYCULTURE: DIVERSE COMMUNITIES OF G-D

Wikipedia describes polyculture as, "agriculture using multiple crops in the same space, in imitation of the diversity of natural ecosystems, and avoiding large stands of single crops, or monoculture. Polyculture, though it often requires more labor, has several advantages over monoculture: The diversity of crops avoids the susceptibility of monocultures to disease. The greater variety of crops provides habitat for more species, increasing local biodiversity. This is one example of reconciliation ecology, or accommodating biodiversity within human landscapes."[7]

Parish and other church organizational boundaries have enabled order and control of people and resources within borders. Yet this approach is, in essence, a form of religious enclosure. It is an attempt to curtail the religious commons and freedom of citizens through management. As such it perpetuates an injustice inherent in the way Western society is structured by property and land rights. In contrast the way of Christ is characterized by going beyond the attempts of ruling hierarchies to impose arbitrary and artificial boundaries. He lived in a way that recognized that everything belongs. Jesus defended his disciples picking corn on the Sabbath. He borrowed someone's donkey. He used someone's upper room for his banquet. He worshipped neither in Jerusalem nor Samaria, but in spirit and truth. He gave the children of Israel's bread of healing to the Syro-Phoenician dogs. He spoke in public with women of other religions when not the accepted custom. He ate with prostitutes, bad businessmen, and corrupt bureaucrats. He healed the child of an army officer who was oppressively occupying his country. He frequently crossed the borders of ethnicity, religion, and gender. These borders became tipping points. They were places of interface where reconciliation, healing, and transformation took place. Jesus saw the world as a common space of free grace. This was a way of common produce and communal gifts. It was rooted in the practice of communal consent and not individualized capital, robbery, or piracy. There was a freedom inherent in this mutual way of life. It created a spiritual biodiversity.

Many kinds of communities can emerge in neotribal neighborhoods through mutual conversation, reconciliation and empowerment. Naturally

7. *en.wikipedia.org/wiki/Polyculture.*

occurring communities of G-d can emerge without the demands of denominational corporations dominating the agenda with a prescriptive plan. Whilst a missional approach sets out to try and foster polyculture it short-circuits this process. It insists on a Biblical narrative as dominant. In contrast conversation, reconciliation and empowerment are empowering and liberating. They enable a G-d breathed polyculture of the communities of G-d to arise from the work of the peoples of G-d. These communities meet the needs of the neotribal population and not the needs of denominational corporations for their own survival or expansion.

RECONCILING CHURCH AND SOCIETY: G-D IN THE GAP

There is an artificial sacred–secular split between society and church, created by the Enlightenment. It is a rift that needs to be healed in order to bring wholeness to both church and society. Both are in common quest to rediscover the reality of G-d that has been lost in the modernist cultures of the West. The pathways will come from people of all faiths and none. To find our way home we need to begin to make our way across unknown seas. The call is to go as strangers into unfamiliar spaces and discover the G-d who is already there. As we courageously journey together in conversation your G-d and my G-d can become our G-d. In crossing these unknown seas individual fragmented religion can become integrated and whole. Entirely new pathways can be created; meeting G-d in the future tense. Yet it is also a revitalization of the ancient of days. This rediscovery leads to the G-d who is known by many in postmodernity as unknown. It is our un/known G-d. This is the G-d that those who doubt and those who believe have in common. It is this un/known G-d who can be discovered in a new and living way in our society.

The church has rejected the G-d breathed spirituality of 95 percent of the UK population. Reconciliation requires a naming of the truth of the situation that separates people. In particular it requires that a falsity or illusion be acknowledged. In *Being Reconciled*, John Milbank reminds us of the causes of our modern and postmodern fragmented world. The Enlightenment gave birth to a split between religious and secular worlds. Scott Russell says, "The invention of the split, and hence the 'secular,' was a major event that created a new reality—the duality that a lot of people these days are questioning, even in psychology, psychiatry and neurology."[8]

---

8. personal quote from a Facebook conversation.

People therefore behave one way in church or their private religion and another way in society. Church and society have different languages. Different sets of behaviors are reinforced through conformity in these separate spheres. Splitting and fragmentation of a body and soul designed for social wholeness is the result.

The way that society and church are ordered causes us to function in these compartmentalized ways. This is a great conflict underneath our modern psyches. One example is the way we approach doubt. Since the Enlightenment doubt and skepticism has become part of the air we breathe in the West. At the same time doubt is seen as anti-faith. It has become divorced from the development of a real and living faith. Doubt is seen as secular while faith is seen as the domain of the church. In reality all people have degrees of doubt and faith. No clear demarcation really exists in our minds. There are only questions of faith and doubt along the pathways we have taken that inform our questioning at whatever place we find ourselves on our pathway. We are all searching for the next step and trying to get a fuller picture that will help us make sense of the world and our place in it.

Tragically, the Reformation furthered the split in Western society. The Catholic and Protestant Churches annexed different bits of what had been an integrated and whole spirituality of everyday life. The Catholics took Mass and Monasticism and the Protestants took Bible and Family. These artificial separations had pervasive social consequences for people in Western civilization. They have perpetuated separate denominational structures and hierarchies. Factionalism in politics, business, and daily life are all rooted in these splits. After the Reformation, as kingdoms became nation states their new kings delegated the church to fulfill a purely spiritual function in society. This distanced church from everyday life. Before this the role of the church had been a spirituality of the whole of material life, not only the soul. The secular split was a major rupturing of the social fabric and daily life. It created a new inner and outer reality. This has perpetuated a dualistic and split way of living. Ultimately, such splitting has resulted in the atomization of all daily life in Western societies.

As a result, today people survive better without reference to G-d and the church. The survival skills that people need are connected primarily with functioning like cogs in institutional machines of work, money, media, education, health, sports, and recreation. Meditation is filling the gap left by the decline of religious institutional life. This is mostly private and

Buddhist. G-d is a distant memory for most. This is the case even for those who are involved in outward conformity to the church. It is what makes the USA a deeply secular nation despite all its churchgoing. G-d is not needed to function or survive. People rely on a mixture of money and Prozac. Prozac is needed as a palliative to the destructive effects of the money god. Europe is the same but has mostly dropped the religious pretense. Gods, by definition, are what people look to for power, and survival, and salvation. In modern societies the need for G-d in daily life has been eradicated. The church has no obvious function for the 95 percent. Yet this is the effect of a dualistic approach to life created by political and social changes in the way society became ordered after the Enlightenment.

MASS CULTURE FRAGMENTS: NEOTRIBALISM EMERGES

Nothing stands still. Even monolithic modernity shifts and changes. Modernity produced mass culture. Yet now mass culture is disintegrating. Sociologist Michel Maffesoli has argued that conventional approaches to understanding solidarity and society are deeply flawed. Therefore organizational attempts to maintain mass uniformity through harmonization, and an emphasis on contrived stability and order, are problematic and counterproductive. Today, social existence is conducted through fragmented tribal groupings. These are organized around catchwords, brand names and soundbites of consumer culture, identity politics, and the proliferation of lifestyle cultures. Wikipedia defines neotribalism or modern tribalism as:

> an insight that human beings have evolved to live in tribal society, as opposed to mass society, and thus will naturally form social networks constituting new "tribes." Michel Maffesoli predicted that as the culture and institutions of modernism declined, societies would embrace nostalgia and look to the organizational principles of the distant past for guidance, and that therefore the postmodern era would be the era of neotribalism. Work by political scientist Robert D. Putnam has provided data that has pointed to a general breakdown in the social structure of modern civilization due to more frequent moves for economic reasons, longer commutes and a lack of emphasis in the media narrative on the desirability of strong friendships and community bonds.[9]

9. en.wikipedia.org/wiki/Neotribalism.

Part 4: Our Un/Known G-d

Neotribalism in postmodernity is different from ancient tribalism. The Internet and globalization have resulted in greater democratization of information. In consequence, our neotribal identities are more permeable and capable of mutuality, interface, and understanding. Neotribalism offers the opportunity to be rooted in a tribe while connected to/permeable with other tribes who may be very different. Without demanding total assimilation, or the adoption of franchise, branding, or ownership, different tribes can offer their benefits to one another. When this insight is applied to the development of faith communities it brings understanding. The emergence of a polyculture of the people of G-d and the demise of the denominational monoculture begin to make sense. Small faith communities can develop their own particular identities that emerge from their particular local needs and remain rooted and connected.

A recognition of neotribal society allows pilgrims on the journey to see that assimilation into prescriptive institutions is counterproductive. It fails to meet highly localized spiritual and cultural needs. These neotribal communities can also benefit from a mutual exchange with communities who may offer different gifts and emphases. Yet it should be borne in mind that institutions will try to, quite literally, cash in on the life of G-d in these communities. The only way to deal with denominational freeloaders is to strengthen roots with other communities. To not do so is to become isolated and vulnerable. With the development of stronger neotribal cooperation across G-d's developing polyculture the ability of corporate freeloaders to dominate and monopolize is significantly undermined.

OUR NEW NEOTRIBAL HOME

G-d is always making all things new. Open source G-d talk restores wholeness in a fragmented and atomized society. The Protestant and Catholic Christian Empires are over. Rather than harking back to the domination narratives of Christian history Christ offers a new time in an entirely new place. It is in freedom from the oppressive language and attitudes of a mission-centered and polarized Catholic and Protestant legacy. The door and the way are now found through practicing reconciliation as the communities of G-d. Like the Israelites in exile the mainline Christian churches need to weep for the loss of their little modernist empires and let them go. Resurrection will take the communities of G-d beyond their tribal pasts to a new time and place. This will be a world being made whole by the reconciling acts of the communities of G-d. Their prototype is Jesus the Son of Man who became Christ through reconciling the world. He did this by entering a violent and divided society and transforming its suffering. Coming home is only made possible by grieving what was lost and leaving it in the place of exile. The Israelites discovered this when they lost their homeland. It was their grief and complaint that enabled them to live again. They found their G-d and their identity in a new time and place and in a different way. As a result they became a blessing to all peoples and the whole Earth.

Yet before their days of liberation they sang:

> By the rivers of Babylon,
> There we wept.
> When we remembered Zion,
> There we hung up our harps.[10]

---

10. Psalm 137:1.

11

Our Un/Known G-d

"God is not a Christian."
—Desmond Tutu[1]

"God has no religion."
—Henry Bellows[2]

"Secular means respect all religions, including no religions."
—Dalai Lama[3]

---

1. Tutu, *God is not a Christian.*
2. Bellows, *Re-Statements*, 149.
3. Dalai Lama, "Secularism," line 2.

THE BIG CONVERSATION: YOUR G-D, MY G-D, OUR G-D

The greatest contribution of conversation communities will be to heal the rift between a disenfranchised church and a rootless neotribal society. A real and living G-d will be rediscovered in this reconciliation. There is a G-d of the gaps. It is not a G-d in the gaps of the fossil record. It is a G-d who is present in the gap between the church subculture and the wider society. It is the G-d of reconciliation and reciprocity who is our future and our hope. As Chief Rabbi Jonathan Sacks says, God is our future tense. The Christian church no longer has a language or identity that resonates with people in postmodern democracies. It no longer functionally serves the spiritual needs of the population. Church and society need to seek a genuine and transparent reconciliation. This needs to be done without the liability of a missional agenda. Society has plenty to say about the church. It also needs to hear what the church has to say. This begins when the mainline churches affirm the presence and activity of G-d in society.

To do this means listening and accepting the life experiences of ordinary citizens. It also means the church needs to listen to its own people instead of trying to manage them into a missional task. This process is reciprocal. Church and society are always in conversation, yet this eternal dialogue needs to be far more explicit. Both sides are hampered by rigid language and concepts. They are often describing the same reality. What is inexcusable is to try and avoid the conversation by shutting people out. G-d is living, moving, being, and speaking through their voices. In this process we need to beware the leaven of modernist church leadership. They will always seek to perpetuate their denominational structures, pseudo doctrinal authority, and spurious national identity.

THE BIG RECONCILIATION: BEYOND "RIGHTEOUS MIND"

One of the pernicious barriers to conversation and reconciliation is what social and cultural psychologist Jonathan Haidt has termed "the righteous mind."[4] Haidt examines why we are predisposed to believe certain things. He recognizes that our surroundings shape our morality. We are formed by a variety of factors: moral psychology, ancient philosophy, modern politics, advertising, and even the semantics of bumper stickers. He identifies moral values as being not just about justice and fairness, but also that for

---

4. Haidt, *The Righteous Mind*.

some they are about authority, sanctity, and loyalty. The left have identified strongly with justice and fairness and the right with authority, sanctity and loyalty. His research concludes that people and societies are divided by different moral codes, which can make us self-righteous and judgmental. The reason we find it so hard to get along is because we are biologically determined to be moralistic, judgmental, and self-righteous. Our inherent morality is what has helped human beings to form communities and create civilization. This is a key to understanding political and religious divisions. His research explains why some of us are liberal, others conservative. It is also explains why humans are the only species that will kill for an ideal.

With insight and experience people can learn to live together by acknowledging the moral codes of others as valid. People can learn that it is socially beneficial to seek common ground. They can practice listening before responding immediately with their own absolute views. This has great application for politics, religion, and the welfare of society. Haidt gives plenty of evidence of the ways in which morality itself becomes problematic as it binds and blinds people into intransigent positions and conflicts. New evidence from his empirical research highlights that people have a biological predisposition to defend their worldview. Despite this, it is possible to cooperate with those whose morals differ from our own. Groups within society, such as churches, are strengthened by the shared ethical values of their members. Yet those shared values can often blind them to the merits of alternative values shared by other groups. Haidt concludes that the best kind of society is not a centrally-directed one. Neither is it a highly individualistic one with little real trust between its members. A better society is one that consists of groups that trust each other. They can build trust together while also understanding the different emphases of other groups, such as other churches or political parties. This is where postmodern neo-tribalism and overcoming the righteous mind converge. It is also where the practices of conversation, reconciliation and empowerment become socially transformative. By following this way of life the communities of G-d can regain a cohesive function as oil and wine that restores the soul in pluralistic postmodern democracies. This is our true home.

THE BIG EMPOWERMENT: AN EMPATHIC CIVILIZATION

In his book *The Empathic Civilization* Jeremy Rifkin shows that human beings have always formed identities by belonging to groups. However, he also shows that these groupings and identities changed as societies developed and became more complex. We have been able to move from defining our sense of belonging by family, blood ties, and tribes to identifying ourselves as belonging to religions: Jews, Christians, Muslims, etc. From religions we were then able to move to identifying ourselves as belonging to nations. From belonging to nations we have begun to see ourselves as belonging to a single biosphere and a single human community. Postmodernity, globalization, media, and internetization are increasing our ability to see ourselves as belonging with/in the rest of the planet. Our sense of belonging has moved from blood ties, to religious ties, to national ties, and now to the human race in a single biosphere and human community. We can broaden our sense of identity without losing our other identities. If we don't do this Rifkin predicts that narcissism and violence will escalate. On the positive side, people who communicate around the planet via Facebook, email and Skype are going to find it increasingly more difficult to get involved in, or allow, bombing each other into oblivion. Once again, in such a world what followers of Christ need more than anything else is to practice reconciliation rather than mission.

Jeremy Rifkin has worked as an advisor to the European Union and the USA concerning issues relating to the economy, climate change, and energy security. Rifkin argues that the global crisis of 2008 and 2011 marked the end of a fossil fuel energy regime. He thinks that the new global economy will be based upon renewable energy, like wind power, solar energy, natural gas, etc. He calls this distributed capitalism because these energy sources are dispersed rather than centralized. They are best controlled by individuals or small communities. This will entail a very different power structure from fossil fuel financial capitalism. Changes in communication have proliferated mobile personal communication that allows people to be constantly connected to others, regardless of distance, language, or other barriers. This is evolving people's sense of empathy. It is creating a biosphere-wide consciousness and a mode of production; a distributed capitalism. Rifkin believes this new system will allow people to solve more complex issues such as climate change and pathogenic pandemics. It will also enable a focus on quality of life rather than materialistic issues. Collaboration will become a necessity. Competition will become increasingly counterproductive and less important. This new structure is networked and decentralized. It is an inherently more democratic form of globalization.

To enable this shift Rifkin identifies the essential need for civilization to become more empathic. Civilization does not have a future if we do not become more empathic. In order to make this shift we have to move outside our comfort zones and embrace our neighbor and actualize our inherent connectedness.

It is increasingly possible for people to feel a sense of connection in a world of permeable tribes. However, the task of developing empathy in neotribal societies is blocked by institutions rooted in modernist concerns and priorities. This includes institutional religion and its promotion of modernist Christian social dominance. The missional approach is a subset of this. In contrast to the missional goal of remaking a New Christian West, the development of empathy requires going beyond our ties of blood, tribe, religion, and nation. Empathy development in the twenty-first century relates directly to the message of Christ. He practiced reconciliation, companionship, and love of neighbor as self in order to bring freedom and empowerment to rich and poor. However, Rifkin recognizes that for empathy to really begin to affect Western societies it will require us to, "Rethink the institutions of our society and prepare the groundwork for an empathic civilization."[5]

RELIGION FOR ATHEISTS: SOCIAL GLUE AND YOU

One of the fundamental barriers that divides sacred from secular and church from society is the way G-d has been compartmentalized. A reconnection is needed. This will require the development of communities of conversation and reconciliation. *Religion for Atheists* is the enigmatic title of Alain de Botton's recent book. Alain feels unable to believe in a G-d but values religion as socially useful because it adds pleasure, order, and purpose to life. It provides a sense of community, social cohesion, identity, education, and personal and spiritual discipline. Religion has also created structure and order and so maintains authority and safety. Alain also advocates a pick and mix attitude toward religions. One can take the best bits and customize. His approach identifies the way in which it is possible to use the wisdom in religions to develop practices for skilful living.

Alain de Botton's intuition regarding religion resonates with the experience of the majority of people in Western society. People have a need for religion but it must be customized and personalized. This is very positive.

5. Jeremy Rifkin, *The Empathic Civilisation*.

Our Un/Known G-d

The downside of pick and mix religion is it can perpetuate an individualistic, narcissistic, and consumerist approach to life. If the smorgasbord spiritual journey is not shared with anyone else then the very cohesive nature of religion is in fact lost. Points of connection and challenge with others need to be formed in order to create meaning. It is this social cohesion that people are actually seeking in mining the gold of religious traditions. Pick and mix religion is good when rooted and connected with generous open people with whom our gifts can be shared. Out of such exchange emerges personal and communal action. Exchanging our gifts in companionship and community is making a fundamental connection to life. Consumerism, capitalism, and bureaucracy have attempted to distort this life out of all recognition but beginning to love self and neighbor is the way home. The roots of social empowerment can be found primarily in Christ's practices of conversation, companionship and empowerment in small communities.

THE FAITH IN DOUBT: THE DOUBT IN FAITH

Faith and doubt are not mutually exclusive. The recent Pope Benedict XVI has recognized "both the believer and the unbeliever share, each in his own way, doubt and belief, if they do not hide from themselves and each other the truth of their being. Neither can quite escape either doubt or belief."[6] Also: "Doubt, which saves both sides (believers and non-believers) from being shut up in their own world, could become a channel of communication. Doubt prevents both from enjoying complete self-satisfaction; it opens up the believer to the doubter and the doubter to the believer."[7] Francis Gonsalves says "Belief and doubt come and go, ebb and flow, like the tides of an invisible ocean."[8]

An acknowledgement that doubt and faith are common to all citizens provides a basis for conversation between church and society. It is grounded in our shared experience. This is an experience of G-d as present and absent. G-d is known as unknown; G-d un/known. It often just depends where one stands at any particular moment in time. In postmodernity our perspectives are frequently shifting. Holding the tension between church and society, present and absent, known and unknown is the place where we encounter the un/known G-d. To have experienced presence without

6. Ratzinger, *Introduction to Christianity*, 46–47.
7. Ibid.
8. Gonsalves, "The benefit of doubt."

absence, and faith without doubt is not to have encountered G-d. The church needs society to make it whole. Society needs the church to make it whole. Viva la reconciliación!

A/THEISM: OUR COMMON NEOTRIBAL FAITH

A/theism is the word that Pete Rollins has usefully coined to communicate that atheism and theism are neither mutually exclusive nor fixed states of mind. He writes: "This recognition of hyper-presence is what leads us to reconsider the traditional atheism/theism opposition, for if our beliefs necessarily fall short of what they attempt to describe, then it would seem that a certain atheistic spirit is actually deeply embedded within Christianity . . . we ought to affirm our view of God while at the same time realizing that that view is inadequate. Hence we act as both theist and atheist. This a/theism is not some agnostic middle point hovering hesitantly between theism and atheism, but rather actively embraces both out of a profound faith."[9]

There is also a biologically-based, visual perceptual shift that helps humans consider first one viewpoint and then the alternative. In psychology the visual illusion of the old hag/young lady, or the two faces/flower vase, illustrates this well. People see things one way and then another. Perception flits back and forth. This can also be applied as an analogy regarding faith and doubt. Pete Rollins has therefore commented that "to believe is human, to doubt is divine."[10] Our doubt leads us to question what leads to a clearer view of the way things are. Our view of life is always changing as we travel, read, experiment, test, experience, act, contemplate, change, and grow on our Cosmic-Earth journey. Postmodernity, globalization, and internetization have caused the kaleidoscope of reality to turn faster and faster. It has also exponentially turned up the volume and brightness of our shifting experiences. We are all on an a/theistic journey involving faith, doubt and un/knowing. It is a spiralling kaleidoscopic quest in which the journey itself is the destination: YHWH. My end is in my beginning and my beginning is in my end.

9. Rollins, *How (Not) To Speak of God*, 25.
10. Rollins, "A Miracle without Miracle."

A/THEIST RELIGION AND OUR UN/KNOWN G-D

This quest is where we can encounter once again the multi-voiced dancing G-d of reciprocity. Bede Griffiths has acknowledged that, "Atheism and agnosticism signify the rejection of certain images and concepts of God or of truth, which are historically conditioned and therefore inadequate. Atheism is a challenge to religion to purify its images and concepts and come nearer to the truth of divine mystery . . . It is no longer a question of a Christian going about to convert others to the faith, but of each one being ready to listen to the other and so to grow together in mutual understanding."[11] We are all in the same a/theistic neotribal society. It is on the basis of our common experience and common quest that church and society can journey together in conversation and reconciliation. We can affirm our common a/theism and our un/known G-d.

The apostle Paul recognized the unknown G-d of the Greeks as being the G-d of Abraham, Isaac, and Jacob. Within Greek culture he found the G-d of his own people. Jewish YHWH and the Greek unknown G-d were the same. He introduced this unknown G-d to the Athenians at Mars Hill. What followed was an eternal dialogue between Greek and Jew. Our Western societies are grounded in Greek ideas about how to approach knowledge and reality. The software our minds think in is Greek. Paul's recognition of YHWH, present in Greek culture as the un/known G-d ,echoes through the ages into our own neotribal and postmodern democracies. Western civilization has inherent within it the un/known G-d. That is how G-d is experienced for the majority. Alain de Botton's quest for a religion for atheists therefore resonates with a Western and a/theistic experience of G-d as un/known. Encountering G-d in this way is the experience of everybody in neotribal postmodernity.

Unlike its apostle and martyr Paul, the modern church is obtuse in its inability to recognize our un/known G-d. It lacks the dark-adapted eyes that are gained only through waiting in perplexing and atomized postmodernity. There are those who want to eliminate all paradox. Some have a desire to hold on to the dualistic certainties and safety of a one-way modernity. This may be as secular, scientific atheists or as protestant evangelical fundamentalists. The demand for one totalizing and invulnerable explanation and final social solution is the same in both. They are both creations of the ancient Greek philosophy that created such a crippling social myopia

---

11. Griffiths, *The Marriage of East and West*.

and inability to acknowledge the whole. Ironically, what is regarded as unequivocal strength in biblical or scientific belief turns out to be a smoke screen for a deeper kind of fear. This is a doubt so deep that it dare not speak its name.

SEEKING OUR COMMON GOOD IN A PLURALISTIC WAY

Recognizing our un/known G-d can lead people to seek the common good of our societies in a pluralistic way. Yet lack of common belief is not a barrier to people of all faiths and none to working together for the common good. Miroslav Volf of Yale has accepted that we live in a pluralistic world in which secular, Christian, Muslim, and others have a significant contribution to make to the common good. On the downside, faith can be inserted into society in a coercive, dominating, and sometimes violent, way. All fundamentalist religion has this fragmenting effect. This is fundamentally counterproductive to the common good. It is not authentic to the calling of all faiths to bring wholeness and peace. On the other hand, faith can take a passive role. It can capitulate to being marginalized and privatized. Then it does nothing. Neither coercion nor withdrawals reflect faith. Engagement in a mutual conversation in the public realm regarding human flourishing is therefore an essential activity. It is an expression of the vitality and social commitment for people of all faiths and none.

To be able to have such a rich and challenging conversation about human flourishing in the public realm Volf says that "We need faith friendly democracies and democracy friendly faiths."[12] He therefore proposes "engagement in the public realm of all religious faiths, mutual respect . . . in the search for common good . . . We need to find a middle road, which respects others, which treats others, as Jesus said, as we would want to be treated ourselves and does so in the public realm."[13] In a pluralistic democracy we need to formulate the common good together and this can be done by seeking a common set of values between people of all faiths and none. Volf cites the Arab Spring as an example of secularists, Christians and Muslims in engagement for the common good in the public realm in a pluralistic way. He says, "It holds a certain kind of promise. There are sufficient values there that can provide us with the possibility of envisaging a common future . . . There may be something we can formulate together . . . each speaking out

12. Volf, "A Public Faith 3."
13. Ibid.

of our own vision. This is a good example of what is possible within the Muslim cultural environment, Egypt, which is predominantly a Muslim country."[14]

John Milbank also writes of the way in which, "In the face of globalisation . . . we need to counterpose Augustine's counter-empire, the City of God. We may do this alongside many secular co-workers: socialists, communists and anarchists. We should not refuse their cooperation yet we should insist they have little grasp of the counter-empire."[15] His insight regarding cooperation with secular society for the common good reflects the companionship of empowerment, even though Augustine's City of G-d and the idea of counter-empire does not. This will be discussed in more detail in the next chapter.

The business entrepreneur John Spedan Lewis also understood that social empowerment is realized through genuine partnership. The John Lewis Partnership is an employee-owned UK partnership that operates John Lewis department stores, Waitrose supermarkets and some other services. The company is owned by a trust on behalf of all its employees, who are known as partners. They all have a say in the running of the business and receive a share of annual profits. This is usually a significant addition to their salary. The group is the third largest UK private company. John Spedan Lewis had this to say about the impact of genuine partnership in society:

> Partnership is justice.
> Better than justice it is kindness.
> Partnership is a matter of fact,
> Not of words.[16]

EMERGING INTEGRAL FAITH COMMUNITIES

What does overcoming the righteous mind, developing an empathic civilization, recognizing our common a/theism, and seeking the common good in a pluralistic way mean for the future of faith communities? They will need to shift from the practice of preaching to conversation, from missional practices to reconciliation, and from domination through management to

14. Volf, "A Public Faith 6."
15. Milbank, *Being Reconciled*, 210.
16. Plaque in John Lewis Partnership store.

mutual empowerment through small communities. The developments of emerging and integral faith communities are pivotal in facilitating this shift. Coming home is accepting where we are planted in the here and now without trying to manufacture an alternative map. This means grieving for the loss of an overconfident and polarized modernity and accepting our fragmented and darkened postmodernity. In this kaleidoscope of humanity church and society will together encounter in a new and living way; G-d as un/known . . .

12

G-d of Everybody

"God is not somebody else."
—Thomas Merton[1]

"I am that which I am seeking."
—Richard Rohr[2]

"I am ... the Way."
—Jesus Christ[3]

---

1. Mitchell and Wiseman, *The Gethsemani Encounter*, 214.
2. Rohr, *Franciscan Mysticism*.
3. John 16:4.

Part 4: Our Un/Known G-d

A JUSTIFIED REJECTION

The people of Europe and the USA have not rejected Christ. They have rejected a domination Christianity formed in the image of ancient Rome and perpetuated in Protestant bureaucratic management. Its inequity underpins the systems of government that have shaped the West. As our societies have grown more democratic it is no accident that church attendance has fallen exponentially. Hierarchy does not resonate well in postmodern democracies. Protestant and Catholic Churches have failed to grasp or express the egalitarian nature of Christ and the companionship of empowerment. It is not reflected in leadership structures or the ethos of the people. In Europe and the USA Christianity has capitulated wholesale to structural forms rooted in bureaucratized domination ideology. Such failure has alienated church and society from a G-d of reciprocal love. It has created suffocating institutions of prescribed and commoditized religion; the spiritual bankruptcy of the churches of the management-mission God. The seeds of the sower have been choked to death by the weeds of managerial efficiency and effectiveness. Such a church has lost its purpose and its reason. Ichabod, the Shekinah has departed.

Gordon Lynch describes the situation well:

> The form of religion that is most commonly rejected by progressive spirituality is, as we have already noted, hierarchical religion grounded in a belief in a personal God who is removed from the cosmos. William Bloom refers to such forms of religion as being based on the idea of God as "General in Command" or "Chief Executive Officer." Such religion, it is argued, is authoritarian—dictating what kinds of beliefs and lifestyles its adherents should follow. It is patriarchal—using its power structures to reinforce certain assumptions about who should hold power and what kinds of gender and ethnic identities, or sexual orientation, are more inherently valuable than others. It is rigid and inflexible—asserting timeless doctrines and moral codes without asking whether these are meaningful or constructive in a modern context. It inserts the need for religious authorities and institutions for mediating the divine rather than allowing people to pursue their spiritual search on their own terms. It devalues embodied experience and makes us suspicious and guilty about sexuality. It removes the sacred from the cosmos, and in doing so leaves a desacralized world ripe for capitalist, industrialist exploitation. It places salvation in a life and

context above and beyond this one, rather than seeing the cosmos as the only real context in which issues of life and death, salvation and grace are worked out. Because of this, it is argued, traditional hierarchical religion has little to offer by way of a framework for an authentic spiritual search or to inspire constructive responses to contemporary problems.[4]

ROME: THE BIRTH OF CHRISTIAN SOCIAL DOMINANCE

Where does Christianity or, more accurately, Christian social dominance formed in the image of Roman rule and leadership begin? When does the unChristlike idea of G-d's forceful saving love become the basis for Christian mission? It was the fall of Rome that created the social circumstances which caused Augustine (413–426 CE) to create the concept of the City of G-d. The fall of Rome was inconceivable to all Romans. Their image of G-d and Christ was tied into the idea of the supremacy of the Roman Empire. They believed G-d had chosen to manifest his kingdom on Earth through Rome. Therefore at the fall of Rome its populace believed that Christ, their domination king god had failed. The pagans had won. Surely this could not be the case? Augustine tried to salvage his G-d's reputation and restore hope to Rome by helping people to see the difference between the earthly city of Rome and G-d's City. The earthly city contains the damned that G-d has not saved. In contrast the City of G-d contains those who have been repaired by G-d's grace. They escape the vanity of the world and begin to love G-d as they should. These merit salvation. The City of G-d is not situated physically in heaven or earth. Instead, it is the collection of good people on the earth and the good society they can form among themselves.

The crux of the matter turns on the way Augustine imagined the City of G-d would be created. He thought force and coercion were necessary. His interpretation is Roman and therefore rooted in ideas of hierarchical domination. The City of G-d would be built through the use of external conformity to doctrinal creeds created by the Roman political elite and incorporation into the church. Consent would be manufactured in the population by use of doctrinal creeds and through social conformity to the state church. Augustine argued that Love will use whatever means necessary to achieve the greater good. If the building is burning people should use force to rescue those inside. This argument was then applied to saving people

4. Lynch, *The New Spirituality*, 63.

from hell. Augustine cited the example of Christ using force to convert Paul by saying that G-d even dashed him to the earth with his power. He also argued that a doctor will often have to hurt in order to bring healing and doctor always knows best. Love should therefore compel pagans, heretics, and schismatics to join the Roman Church. His idea is both patriarchal and paternalistic; a pseudo spiritualization of Roman military conscription. The doctrine of G-d's forceful saving love became the spirit in which Roman Christian mission was conducted. Augustine was seduced by a false vision of Christ as domination king god. He did not follow the Jesus way of reconciliation and reciprocity. This would have brought social empowerment, peace, and justice.

Ironically, contemporary health psychology is clear that the relationship between patient and doctor is equally as important as the advice and intervention of the doctor. Healing is holistic. To save and heal someone requires both consent and cooperation. This is an understanding basic to the Hippocratic Oath taken by all medical practitioners. Good medicine and good religion do not violate the sanctity of free will. It is the fundamental right of all human beings made in the image of G-d. Forceful saving love is in opposition to the apostle Paul's teaching, "Love is patient, love is kind. It does not envy, it does not boast, it is not proud. It does not dishonour others, it is not self-seeking, it is not easily angered, and it keeps no record of wrongs."[5] Love may reason, urge, and plead but it does not coerce, force, or violate a person's freedom and personal integrity. Augustine's love was used to justify Christian domination in true Roman style. This idea remains the basis for all imperial intervention in the West. As Noam Chomsky observed, the Monroe doctrine has functioned as a declaration of American hegemony. It is the basis for unilateral intervention over the Americas; a political rhetoric summed up in the jibe attributed to Captain Kirk in Star Trek: "We come in peace, shoot to kill."[6]

Perhaps it was forceful saving love that was the basis for the political cunning of Emperor Theodosius First. He lovingly saved the Empire by forcing it to become Christian in the fourth century. Under his rule it became compulsory to be a Christian in order to be part of the Roman Empire. He issued decrees that effectively made Nicene Christianity the official state church. Sacrifice to pagan gods and goddesses were outlawed. People had to be Christian to belong and to survive. This created the social

---

5. 1 Corinthians 13:4.
6. en.wikipedia.org/wiki/Star_Trekkin.

conditions for minorities who were not Romanized Christians to become marginalized and potentially persecuted. The obsessive Roman need to maintain power on the basis of religious uniformity created an oppressive power structure. Christian hegemony had been born. Belonging and social status became defined by allegiance and submission to the laws, regulations, and social expectations of the Imperial State and its church. Faith became a matter of conformity to the legal-rational codes of those in political power. Creeds became the basis of mind control and were used to reinforce allegiance to the Roman State and maintain Roman unity. Church and state became intertwined structures of power, control, and domination.

The Roman Church was not empowered by its encounter with G-d in community but by its hierarchical structure and the military state. Christian baptism became the way to become a citizen of the Roman Empire. Jesus is YHWH had been co-opted; it was the Emperor who was now Vicar of Christ. In their need to create and maintain Roman unity the ruling elite of the fourth century introduced the idea of one canon of Scripture, one Creed and one Roman Church. A domination of the populace through ideological and cultural means had been created. It utilized these social levers as instruments to create and reinforce consent. This was, in fact, manufactured by the creation of one church, one creed and one Bible in conformity to Roman political hierarchy.

This church-empire system continued in Europe into the Middle Ages and became the basis of unity in the Holy Roman Empire. The G-d of everybody that Jesus Christ exemplified had been annexed in order to serve the domination kings and popes of Europe. The Reformation just changed the rulers. It did not change the practice of hierarchical religious rule through justifiable force. In fact, forceful saving love and just war theory became Augustine's legacy; 125 years of Catholic and Protestant war in which eleven million people died. The command of Jesus to love your enemy meant nothing after that. The very heart of Jesus' non-violent way of sacrificial empowerment was totally erased in over a century of Christian bloodletting. Instead of following Christ by bringing reconciliation within society through the sacrifice of their own bodies, Christians sacrificed the aliens and the others. The others were either the pagans, the Catholics or the Protestants. The Christian state and church sanctioned and sanctified the doctrine of Christian just war.

Part 4: Our Un/Known G-d

FORCEFUL SAVING LOVE: ELEVEN MILLION WAR DEAD

Augustine was right when he saw the City of G-d as the good people on the earth and the good society. However his interpretation of planetary salvation was tribal. He saw the Roman Church as needing to incorporate pagan religions and tribes. His approach was essentially dualistic: join my Roman Church or be damned. Yet he was categorically wrong to assume that all the peoples of the Earth would all join uniform communities in conformity to one church. In stark contrast to Augustine the Bible speaks of the good people of the Earth being of every tongue, tribe and nation. In the teaching of Jesus those most in danger of damnation were religious hypocrites. Jesus makes no such warning for not joining the church.

Augustine was wrong when he saw the salvation of the planet coming to pass through uniformity and submission to one church, one creed and one Bible. The faith is one but the church is not one. It is a kaleidoscope of expressions in one faith. Salvation and wholeness are experienced in and through connected communities in worldwide diversity in unity. Reconciliation, mutual submission, and giving bring wholeness. Peace does not come from blind submission to church or state. That is a false peace. It results in the kind of totalitarianism described in Orwell's novel *1984*. Salvation and wholeness are never found in outward conformity to a meaningless uniformity imposed through forceful and paternalistic love; even when dressed up in Christian vestments and creeds that promise earthly immortality and worldly domination. There is nothing more Satanic. It is an unholy and blinding light—whether Protestant, Catholic, fascist, capitalist or communist. These are all ideological manifestations of the same spirit that motivated the domination system symbolized by the Tower of Babel. They seek to incorporate and enslave G-d's diverse peoples for their own glory, power, and prestige.

George Orwell saw clearly that, "Who controls the past controls the future, who controls the present controls the past."[7] Forceful saving love has been incorporated wholesale into the mindset and politics of the West. This is because Theodosius forced the Roman Empire to become Christian. The church-empire then formed the basis of Western civilization. History is shaped by the political and military winners. Forceful saving love is at the root of all toxic leadership in church and society. Something is made true or right because the king, priest, pastor, or manager says it is right. This is how

---

7. Orwell, *1984*, 35.

the West has been shaped. Reconciliation and love of neighbor are no longer needed when imposed doctrinal systems can be used to manufacture religious uniformity and consent. The use of thought control and the imposition of church law backed by military strength can manufacture consent in the population. In England after the Reformation the church continued the practice Theodosius started. It imposed a series of Acts of Uniformity. These regulated the religious life of England under one church, one creed and one Bible. Enforced creedal domination had effectively replaced reconciliation through eternal dialogue. Bowing to the state religion replaced discovering G-d together in a communal way of life. The need for national unity as a means of power saw the imposition of a highly prescribed one size fits all religion and G-d.

Following the Protestant Reformation in the pursuit of their one true church, Protestants and Catholics went to war for 125 years. "In Europe's wars of religion eleven million people would die."[8] The human cost in the pursuit of Augustine's City of G-d rivals the loss of human life under the regimes of Hitler and Stalin. This fact is a pernicious indictment of Protestant and Catholic mission. Augustine's idea of just war is in stark contradiction to Jesus' non-negotiable practices of non-violence and love of enemy. If the church had followed Christ in reconciliation and non-violence instead of forceful saving love, Europe would have been literally saved. Ironically, Catholic and Protestant religious wars actually led to the rise of secularism, which brought religious tolerance. Arguably, there is much in the secular solution that echoes the teaching of Christ far more than the intransigence of Protestant or Catholic dogma. Augustine's ideas of forceful saving love persist today. Redemptive violence is the foundation myth of the West. In great contrast the companionship of empowerment is established through justice and peace; the practice of reconciliation and reciprocity in community. The cost of real peace is not less than everything. It acts like yeast by loosening and eventually breaking the grip of the monolithic domination system upon all the peoples of the Earth.

BABYLON OR ZION

Babylon is not described in the Bible as a whore due to its mixture of peoples and religions, but because of its need to dominate through the hubris of hierarchical power. Hierarchy always requires unfaithfulness to the

---

8. Marr, "Age of Plunder–History of the World."

bond created through mutuality with brothers and sisters in community. This is symbolized in the Tower of Babel, which is in essence an expression of phallic narcissism. Its hubris is what makes it adulterous. What better image describes the skyscraper gods of capitalism that have seduced and failed the West? In our time capitalist social dominance has become Moloch; the king god who devours the flesh of innocent children, families, and livelihoods. Such a king god is violently rapacious and without mercy. It demands total allegiance and robs people of everything. The fact that four in every one hundred business leaders and CEOs have been recognized as corporate psychopaths reflects its true nature.[9] This is the toxic leadership of the domination system.

In great contrast Zion is a city not made with hands. All the peoples of the Earth gather freely from every tribe, tongue, and nation in freedom. They do not gather as one homogenized mass. They are not an enforced church, people, nation, or planet. Peoples gather to celebrate holding to their identities as well as being able to embrace a larger identity. Zion is non-hierarchical; neotribal; glocal. Elders are respected. Authority is mutual and maintained through loving sacrifice and self-evident wisdom. Zion does not need an egotistical or hierarchical system.

RIGHT DOCTRINE OR PRACTICES OF JUSTICE?

When Rome fell the population believed their domination king god had failed. They had mistakenly thought of G-d as being synonymous with their City and Empire. Unlike Rome, when Jerusalem was conquered Jewish community continued because they were the people of a shared history and experience. Their identity was not primarily tied to a city such as Jerusalem but was carried in their communal history. Jewish history was created through a series of experiences and encounters with their G-d: "I will be what I will be."[10] When the Temple in Jerusalem was destroyed they did not lose G-d. They were scattered abroad in other countries but their G-d went with them in their stories. P. Z. Myers describes it in this way: "They attached their sense of identity to a collection of laws and stories and commentaries and books. They acquired a persistence that cities could not have. When Jerusalem fell the Jewish people were not destroyed. It became

---

9. www.theguardian.com/science/2011/sep/01/psychopath-workplace-jobs-study, 1 Sep 2011.

10. Exodus 3:14.

a chapter in their books, a remembered part of their history. It strengthened their identity. A Roman could not be landless, city less or country less but a Jew could. You could take everything away from the Jewish people. You could make them homeless and scattered and still they knew who they were."[11]

Therefore the genius of Jewish community provides a great contrast to hierarchical Roman Christianity. Christ was Jewish. He was not the founder of Christianity in any of its forms. In the Gospels he clearly states his belief that salvation and social wholeness is from the Jews. Jewish community practices promote social wholeness and well-being, or Shalom. Unlike Roman Christianity the Jewish people did not require right belief. Wikipedia usefully discusses the differences between Judaism and Christianity:

> Since the First seven Ecumenical Councils, Christendom places emphasis on correct belief (or orthodoxy), focusing primarily on the New Covenant that the Christian Triune God made through Jesus Christ. Judaism places emphasis on the right conduct (or orthopraxy), focusing on the Mosaic Covenant that the God of Israel, made with the Israelites, as recorded in the Torah and Talmud. Christians obtain individual salvation from original sin through repentance of sin and receiving Jesus Christ as their God and Savior through faith and grace. Jews individually and collectively participate in an eternal dialogue with the God of Israel through tradition, rituals, prayers and ethical actions.[12]

Jesus the Jew practiced eternal dialogue, *ahava*, or mutual giving and covenant through communal life. In other words, he practiced conversation, reconciliation and empowerment. Eternal dialogue is mutual conversation and submission. He practiced reconciliation and reciprocity through exchanging his gifts with others in community. He practiced empowerment through finding strength in the mutuality of covenant relationships. This was his way of life and truth. Through following these practices people encountered YHWH: "I will be what I will be."[13] They also led to the realization for all who walked in them that "I am . . . the Way."[14] People today can also begin to realize that YHWH is latent in their own bodies and in people

---

11. Myers, "Sacking the City of God!"
12. en.wikipedia.org/wiki/Christianity_and_Judaism.
13. Exodus 3:14.
14. John 14:6.

of all faiths and none. YHWH is made real and given skin in communities that practice eternal dialogue, mutual giving, and covenant.

AHAVA: MUTUAL GIVING CREATES COMMUNITY

Ahava is central to the creation of social wholeness and salvation with/in society. This is another way of describing an exchange of gifts. It is the practice of reciprocal giving or reciprocity. The meaning of *ahava* is I give and also love. To give is to love. Giving creates a connection between the giver and the receiver. The more giving that one does the greater is the connection. Through the act of giving physical gifts or speech people give themselves to others. This is not just helping someone else or giving someone a hand out. It is choosing to take what could have been utilized for one's own needs and to use it for someone else. Giving becomes a way of living that creates and sustains love. Without mutual giving there is no connection that sustains. The relationships that take on meaning are those in which mutual giving takes place. The giving may be physical, emotional, or intellectual. Without this way of personal giving no relationship can be enduring.

This mutuality, which is practiced in Jewish communities, creates social cohesion. It expresses the mutuality inherent in the love of G-d, which we in turn experience through one another. There is no greater giving possible than the intertwined mutual submission and sacrifice that is made possible between husband and wife. Eternal dialogue and mutual giving lead to the creation of social bonds of loyalty and commitment to one another. They result in an ability to make covenants or binding agreements. For Jews, Christians, and Muslims the idea of covenant begins with Abraham. Yet, what makes covenant possible is what is eternally present before Abraham. This is what undergirds covenant. Jesus described what is eternally present when he said, "Before Abraham was, I am."[15] To say this is to realize the presence of G-d is latent and eternally present in all matter, including our own bodies. Ken Wilber has spoken of "I am" being that which is the same five minutes ago, 500 years ago and before creation.[16] This is what it means when we realize, "Before Abraham was, I am."[17] Covenant is built upon our common humanity and shared destiny. Without it we have no human future.

15. John 8:58.
16. Wilber, "I Am Big Mind."
17. John 8:58.

COVENANT: THE WHOLE EARTH BLESSED

Abraham is the common patriarch of the three Abrahamic religions. Jews trace their ancestry from him, through his son Isaac, and grandson Jacob or Israel. Christians and Muslims both claim descent from him in faith. G-d made a covenant with Abraham that promised, "in you all families of the earth shall be blessed."[18] In joining conversation in community there is also an implicit invitation to that same covenant that runs through Judaism, Christianity and Islam in the person of Abraham. A covenant is a binding relationship of commitment to one another. It is based on a shared agreement of goals, survival, and destiny. G-d invites everyone into that friendship. Friendship, however, is not just a fuzzy, warm, cuddly thing. It demands sacrifice in terms of loyalty, faithfulness, and integrity. In a covenant people make a binding agreement that they will no longer live for themselves but for others. This is a mutual agreement of the heart based upon faithfulness. It is never entered into under compulsion but always willingly, and is based in mutual concerns, destiny, and purpose. The philosopher Rousseau recognized that a nation or people group has a social contract or unspoken agreement with its rulers. If the rulers break the expectations of the social contract revolution can erupt. In our day divorce is so prevalent because people rely on legal contract to act as a socially binding force. Legal contract is an expression of commitment, but it is not what sustains a real marriage. Hearts of mutuality and reciprocity create that essential faithfulness which makes a marriage enduring.

Covenant reflects the mutuality inherent in the very nature of G-d. It is also found in people of all faiths and none as they journey together. Hierarchical dominance through bureaucracy and managerialism is a perversion of a covenant way of life; a corpse seeking to dominate the living. Covenant in community is the basis for all human growth and flourishing. Without this mutuality there is no human future. Yet covenant must be genuine. It can never be enforced or demanded but is expressed only in voluntary mutual submission. This can only be arrived at through conversation or eternal dialogue. Covenant also reflects the mutuality and loving commitment inherent in the Trinity. It is an expression of G-d's never ending and pervasive perichoresis. Without mutual love there is no obedience or faithfulness. It is never obedience that is lacking, but the mutual honor and love that creates obedience. This love is absent in the practices of all

---

18. Genesis 12:2–3.

church leadership structures. Bureaucratic hierarchy or ideological rule through creed or Bible is not love because it is not rooted in mutuality. There is no love without voluntary mutual submission. Bureaucratic domination violates equality, mutuality, and the law of love. In the Epistles the apostle Paul advocates voluntary mutual submission in the *koinonia* life of the communities of G-d. The G-d of Jesus, Scripture, tradition and community is a Trinity in unity of voluntary mutual submission. That is why G-d is love.

Voluntary mutual submission calls for risk and may involve failure. When Jesus said, "If you love me you will obey my commandments,"[19] he meant it as a promise rather than a command. Mutual obedience comes from mutual respect. The bonds of love are created by how we honor and give to one another. People do not have to be ordered, coerced, and deceived. Real obedience is always voluntary and comes from mutuality. Genuine obedience is in fact destroyed through hierarchical bureaucracy and managerialism. In a marriage love cannot be commanded or ordered. In fact, mature love only comes through mutual submission to one another. As C. S. Lewis said, "obedience is an erotic necessity."[20] One is obedient when one is loved. That is why voluntary mutual submission is the practice that Paul advocates for marriage in the Epistles. Faithfulness and obedience to one another is formed through the practice of mutual giving, which creates voluntary mutual submission. It is also exactly the case in the communities of G-d. Obedience and faithfulness to one another is born through mutual giving and submission to one another. This is what it means to love.

"I will be your God and you will be my people," wrote the prophet Jeremiah.[21] G-d is seeking to create covenants of mutuality with/in the neotribal communities in our postmodern democracies. Our un/known G-d will meet us and provide for our needs as communities if we choose to live for the needs of others. These are people of all faiths and none bound together in the covenant G-d made with Abraham. This is our un/known G-d as well as the G-d of Abraham, Isaac, and Jacob; YHWH. A covenant relationship is created in society as the communities of G-d begin to practice open source conversation, reconciliation, companionship and empowerment.

---

19. John 14:15.
20. Lewis, *That Hideous Strength*, 149.
21. Jeremiah 7:23

THE KALEIDOSCOPIC G-D

Missional Christianity has wisely looked to Jewish communities for inspiration concerning joining G-d in the neighborhood. Yet it has paid less attention to the kind of G-d that the Jewish people encountered there. In the Hebrew Scriptures G-d is experienced in a wide variety of ways. Understanding the implications of that encounter happened in and through their communities of eternal dialogue. The recorded history of the Jewish people reveals that G-d is experienced in ways that are beyond definition or the constraints of orthodox doctrinal faith. Secular and religious mysticism reflects the same dynamic. Yet common features can also be discerned. Such encounters with G-d only take on meaning after the experience. It is in the conversation community that our experiences find deeper clarity and take on meaning. Individual experiences become synthesized and take on greater significance. What no longer works for our time and place can be discarded.

A kaleidoscopic breadth and variety of human experience is illustrated in the names for G-d found in the Jewish Scriptures. This breadth confirms the indefinable G-d experienced by Moses in the unburning bush. When he asked for G-d's name he was told, "I will be what I will be."[22] Wikipedia outlines the sheer breadth of possible encounter:

> Seven names of G-d
> In medieval times, God was sometimes called The Seven. The seven names for the God of Israel over which the scribes had to exercise particular care were:
> 1. Eloah (G-d)
> 2. Elohim (G-d)
> 3. Adonai (Lord)
> 4. Ehyeh-Asher-Ehyeh (I am that I am)
> 5. YHWH (I am that I am)
> 6. El Shaddai (G-d Most High)
> 7. YHWH Tzevaot (Lord of Hosts: Sabaoth in Latin transliteration)
>
> Less common or esoteric names:
> - Adir—Strong One
> - Adon Olam—Master of the World
> - Aibishter—The Most High (Yiddish)

---

22. Exodus 3:14.

Part 4: Our Un/Known G-d

- Aleim—sometimes seen as an alternative transliteration of Elohim
- Avinu Malkeinu—Our Father, our King
- Bore—the Creator
- Ehiyeh sh'Ehiyeh—I Am That I Am: a modern Hebrew version of Ehyeh Asher Ehyeh
- Elohei Avraham, Elohei Yitzchak ve Elohei Ya`aqov—God of Abraham, God of Isaac, and God of Jacob
- Elohei Sara, Elohei Rivka, Elohei Leah ve Elohei Rakhel—God of Sarah, God of Rebecca, God of Leah, and God of Rachel
- El ha-Gibbor—God the hero or God the strong one or God the warrior
- Emet—Truth
- E'in Sof—endless, infinite, Kabbalistic name of God
- HaKadosh, Barukh Hu (Hebrew); Kudsha, Brikh Hu (Aramaic)—The Holy One, Blessed be He
- HaRachaman—The Merciful One
- Kadosh Israel—Holy One of Israel
- Magen Avraham—Shield of Abraham
- Makom or HaMakom—literally the place, perhaps meaning The Omnipresent[23]
- Malbish Arumim —Clother of the Naked
- Matir Asurim —Freer of the Captives
- Mechayeh HaKol —Lifegiver to All (reform version of Mechayeh Metim)

Mechayeh Metim —Lifegiver to the Dead

Melech HaMelachim or Melech Malchei HaMelachim—The King of kings or The King, King of kings, to express superiority to the earthly rulers title.

Oseh Shalom —Maker of Peace

Pokeach Ivrim —Opener of Blind Eyes

Ribono shel `Olam—Master of the World

Ro'eh Yisra'el—Shepherd of Israel

Rofeh Cholim—Healer of the sick

Somech Noflim —Supporter of the Fallen

Tzur Israel—Rock of Israel

Uri Gol—The new Lord for a new era (Judges 5:14)

---

23. See Tzimtzum in http://en.wikipedia.org/wiki/Tzimtzum

YHWH-Nissi (Adonai-Nissi)—The Lord our Banner (Exodus 17:8–15)

YHWH-Rapha—The Lord that healeth (Exodus 15:26)

YHWH-Ro'i—The Lord my Shepherd

YHWH-Shalom—The Lord our Peace (Judges 6:24)

YHWH-Shammah (Adonai-shammah)—The Lord is present (Ezekiel 48:35)

YHWH-Tsidkenu—The Lord our Righteousness[29] (Jeremiah 23:6)

YHWH-Yireh (Adonai-jireh)—The Lord will provide (Genesis 22:13–14)

Yotsehr Or —Fashioner of Light

Zokef kefufim —Straightener of the Bent[24]

A. W. Tozer said of Moses: "God wanted to show him who he was and bring him into an encounter by experience."[25] Genuine experience of G-d is discerned in the joys and challenges of community. One danger in this practice is in reaching conclusions too quickly. Relying on our own interpretation alone rather than entering into the process of mutual submission can lead us astray. However, we must also be wary of letting our experience be defined by what is handed down to us by one denomination or religion. G-d is beyond definition by religious institutions or their hierarchical leadership. Their offers are at best provisional. Putting G-d in a box just to please a leader, denomination, or religion should be rejected. G-d can be discerned in the journey of the group together in mutual conversation, reconciliation and companionship. What makes faith authentic, socially binding, and transformative is the G-d we encounter together. My G-d then becomes our G-d. This G-d is only discovered in eternal dialogue and the mutual submission and reciprocal giving that leads to covenant relationship and commitment.

G-D OF EVERYBODY

Jesus' conversation with the Syro-Phoenician woman in Matthew's Gospel opens up the reality of a G-d who is beyond boundaries. Encounter with G-d is beyond the limits prescribed by national identity, ethnicity, religion,

---

24. en.wikipedia.org/wiki/Names_of_God_in_Judaism.
25. Tozer, "The Man Who Met God in the Fire."

and gender. When pleading for the healing of her daughter she calls Jesus "son of David." In doing so she recognizes that he is called to serve Israel. Yet the woman is not from Israel. In refusing her Jesus says, "Why should I take the bread for the children (of Israel) and throw it to the dogs?" Then there is a shift in the conversation. Instead of referring to him as "Son of David" she calls him "Adonai" recognizing in him the G-d of Everybody. "Adonai," she replied, "even the dogs under the table eat the children's crumbs." Then he told her, "For such a reply, you may go; the demon has left your daughter."[26]

In that moment the Syro-Phoenician woman recognized that the mercy of G-d goes beyond the social barriers of nation, borders, ethnicity, religion, and gender. As Ronald Rolheiser puts it, she says in effect: "You are the God of Everybody and I am one of the Everybody!"[27] Therefore give me the children's bread because I am one of G-d's children too. It is in her recognition that G-d is merciful to all people that creates an encounter with the G-d of everybody. As socially constructed religious customs and boundaries are crossed this also becomes a healing moment. Through the challenge of their conversation she becomes reconciled with her brother from Israel even though she is a Samaritan. She recognizes that, in reality, they share one G-d and her social situation is transformed. As she goes beyond her religious and social customs she is made whole through reconciliation with the alien and the other. In her case these are the people of another tribe, the Jews. As she recognizes the G-d of everybody in her brother she is born again into a new and different social reality. It was reconciliation that was the doorway she walked through to arrive in a new place of peace and wholeness with others.

Jesus has a similar meeting with a Samaritan woman. The Samaritans were a mixed race people who had intermarried with the Assyrians. They were hated by the Jews because of their mixed culture. They also had different scriptures and worshipped at a different temple. Again, Jesus goes beyond the borders of gender, ethnicity, and the social and religious rules. He broke three Jewish customs. He spoke to a woman. She was a Samaritan. He asked her to get him a drink of water, which would have made him ceremonially unclean from using her jar. They have a conversation at the well. Out of this emerges a religious question; where is the right place to worship? In Rabbinic style Jesus offers an insight that is provoked by the situation. He replies that worship is not about the place, as in which Temple, but about

---

26. Mark 7:28–29.
27. Rolheiser, *Naming Our Moment*.

the state of a person's heart. What is important is to be in reality, honesty, and transparency with others. This is to be in spirit and truth.

Jesus defines worship as being in a place of reconciliation with people of all faiths and none. Of course, this also helps the woman to address her own situation. She is hiding away in shame from her own community by coming to the well at midday when no one else would be there. Once again, she is liberated by Jesus going beyond their social and religious customs in order to identify with her. As this happens she has a realization that worship is about being with others in a common spirit, regardless of differences. A new and more integrated way of life became possible for her. She realizes that religious customs can be transcended. This also enables her to return to her own community and be reconciled. The Samaritan woman recognized that G-d is found in spirit and truth. To translate this realization to our situation today, Jesus was saying that G-d can be encountered in mosque, temple, synagogue, or church. This is realized through being in a place of honesty, openness, and transparency with others and G-d. It is also the case that a person can be in any of these places of worship, but be far away from G-d. This is because they are not in a spirit of truth and reconciliation with people of all faiths and none. To the G-d of everybody what matters is the heart. The Samaritan woman is born again into a new and healed social situation with others. This happened through her realization that G-d is beyond religious divides, but present through an open, honest, and reconciled heart. This realization about G-d leads her to a place of reconciliation with the people in her village. Up to that point she had been avoiding them because she felt ashamed. Her encounter with Jesus enabled her reconciliation with her village and with herself.

Ahava is only experienced and communicated in and through communities who are journeying together toward covenant. In going beyond the separating borders of gender, ethnicity, and religion Jesus signals that G-d has left the building. The community conversation has gone from tribal to neotribal. G-d can now be encountered in the neotribal citizens' assembly, or *ekklesia*, in the public square. This is why Desmond Tutu is right when he says that G-d is not a Christian, a Jew, a Muslim, nor a Hindu. G-d through Christ is through all and in all: "I will be what I will be." In the same conversation Jesus is quite clear that salvation and spiritual and social wholeness is from the Jews. Jesus is made real and given skin in communities of eternal dialogue, *ahava* and covenant. This is where we encounter ourselves and others as YHWH.

"I AM THE DOOR . . . TO G-D; I AM THE WAY . . . TO G-D"

The real offence of the Gospel is that the way of Christ can be found in all religions and without any religion. In fact our own religion can become a barrier to discovering G-d as present in all and through all. YHWH is found through following the way of life and truth that Christ embodied and made flesh. Through this lifestyle people discover YHWH in themselves and all creation. This is why Christ said, "I am the Way" and "I am the Door." Also, this illuminates our understanding of the phrase Jesus is YHWH. It means following him as a way of life is the door to encounter with YHWH in our own bodies and minds. When Jesus said "I am the Way," he meant it as something true for all who follow his example of conversation, reconciliation, and empowerment. To follow this way of Christ is to begin to realize and live in an altered reality. It is in fact beginning to believe the truth about oneself that: "Before Abraham was, I am."

Abraham is the common patriarch of Judaism, Christianity, and Islam. To be before Abraham is to be before these three religions existed. Therefore to follow the way of life who is Christ is not to be Jewish, Christian, or Muslim, but to be in any—or all—of these religions and also outside them. This is what it really means to say Jesus is YHWH and to be a follower of Christ. Jesus is not making an exclusive claim for the truth of the Christian religion. He is simply recognizing YHWH as present in himself and people of all faiths and none. All who follow his way of life can say the same. Jesus is YHWH is a way of saying that human beings can realize that they too are YHWH. This has been made possible because Christ has exposed the illusory lies of the domination systems. It has nothing to do with Jesus being made a lord or a king through hierarchical, or ideological, or cultural domination. No one can make Jesus lord or king; he is already present as YHWH. When people realize they are YHWH, and that they are part of "the Way," they begin to believe. After such awakening they begin to manifest the way of life as a social reality. Relationships and communities of conversation, reconciliation and empowerment are the result. This is the Way of Life and Truth: YHWH. It is what happens when people realize Jesus is YHWH. Simultaneously they also realize "I am the Way."

Gandhi was therefore right when he said, "I am a Muslim, and a Hindu, and a Christian, and a Jew,"[28] as is Bellows when he says "God has no religion."[29] He was recognizing YHWH in himself and latent in all humanity. In doing so he is echoing Christ, who also recognized in himself that "I am the Way." This is a recognition that all humanity has always existed and still exists in YHWH. G-d is present and abides in the eternal star stuff of which human beings are made. "I will be what I will be" has existed and will go on existing. All humanity also abides with/in G-d. As the apostle John said, "without him was not anything made that has been made."[30] G-d's great river is manifested in the tributaries of our religious and human traditions. Jesus is therefore not claiming divinization is only possible through Christian religion. He is pointing to the reality that YHWH is latent in the very flesh of all people regardless of religious affiliation. G-d's energy and power is realized and then manifested in people when they wake up to their true nature. That only happens when they see through the domination systems that blind them and choose to live beyond such illusions. YHWH is the sleeping giant present in the very star stuff that makes up our bodies. Richard Rohr has understood this reality in the life of the Franciscan mystics as the realization that "I am that which I am seeking."[31] Thomas Merton put it this way: "God is not somebody else."[32]

Unlike the church, Jesus did not demand right belief through submission to creeds, doctrines, or church leadership as the door to eternal life. Salvation is not found in this way. What mattered to Jesus was how people lived. He taught a way of life through the practice of eternal dialogue and conversation in community. Christianity took a devastatingly wrong turn when it began to demand right belief (orthodoxy) instead of creating practices of social justice through reconciliation in community (orthopraxy). The need to conform to right belief as a basis for unity is intrinsic in the church created by Rome and perpetuated by Protestantism. The Rabbi Jesus did not come with a tick box of doctrines for people to join his movement.

28. Sen Gupta, *A Man Called Bapu*, 5.
29. Bellows, *Re-statements*.
30. John 1:2.
31. Rohr, *Franciscan Mysticism*.
32. Mitchell and Wiseman, *The Gethsemani Encounter*, 214.

He did not run an Alpha course or an RCIA program, but affirmed faith where he found it: in Roman commanders, Syro-Phoenicians, Samaritans, Pharisees, soldiers, women, fishermen, and tax-collecting bureaucrats.

In following Jesus people entered into the Jewish practice of eternal dialogue with G-d and one another. They began to practice conversation with G-d and one another in community. It was not the G-d of imposed state or church belief. This conversation was informed by the history of the community. It emerged in the context of tradition, rituals, prayers, and ethical actions. The eternal conversation happened in the context of what the faith community already knew. Yet the tradition was always dynamic not static. Faith was not a pre-packaged deal you signed up to. It was a dynamic quest in the context of a shared journey. Jesus saw the key to righteous living as the heart and not the mind. What changed the heart was a way of life in small communities of companionship and empowerment. Salvation and wholeness is found through this way. It is not in blind and unthinking submission to state or church authorities, or their doctrines and systems.

I WILL BE WHAT I WILL BE: G-D UN/KNOWN

G-d is beyond names. No person, church, denomination, religion, or nation can name or contain YHWH. This leads people of all religions and none to an honest and openhearted a/theistic experience of G-d as un/known. Moses had a defining moment of encounter with YHWH as a G-d beyond names. His inability to name or contain G-d is what defeated him. It beat him. Our own encounters with G-d will also be beyond names and beyond definition or creed. The encounter with "I will be what I will be" altered Moses. It literally changed his physical and mental make up. When people encounter "I will be what I will be" they are empowered to set their brothers and sisters free. Today, those in bondage are systemically enslaved through managerialism and bureaucracy in the modern domination systems of state, church, and business. This expresses itself in pseudo-Christian corporate capitalism or the bureaucratic machinery of centralized atheistic communism.

Encountering "I will be what I will be" is liberating. This G-d saves us, makes us whole, and empowers us. When Moses met G-d in the fire he was beaten down and defeated in the encounter. We also have to meet G-d in the crisis of encounter and be decisively defeated. Then we become real and truly generative in society. We are born again in the wrestling of conversation, community, and the journey toward mutual covenant. Ironically, the imposition and easy answers of a paternalistic and hierarchical leadership nullifies this essential alchemical process. It seeks to remove the struggle with our own darkness and dirt that we see projected in others. In doing so it also robs people of their identity and purpose. The grit of encountering G-d in community creates the pearl of great price. We are cleansed and purified in the fiery heat. In our struggle with "I will be what I will be" we are transfigured and made beautiful. The prayer of Moses was, "Let the beauty of YHWH be upon us."[33] It is not the vain and empty beauty of a sterile and manufactured perfection but an earthy humility of holy dirt. Through the encounter Moses also became a catalyst of liberation for G-d's people, who were under Egyptian domination. In encounter we also become empowered agents of liberation in the bureaucratic domination systems oppressing society in state, church, and business.

G-D: RECIPROCAL RECONCILING LOVE

Our encounter with G-d as presence and absence authenticates and authorizes our community and religion. It is what the history of the diverse encounters with G-d, recorded in the Hebrew Scriptures, point to. The myriad experiences of both secular and religious mystics reflect G-d's inability to be put in anyone's pocket. We communicate the G-d that we encounter. What we gaze longingly and lovingly upon will transform us. If we gaze upon the religious and financial machine we will become a machine; unholy necrophiliacs. If we gaze upon a G-d of mission we will become technical pragmatists. If we gaze upon a G-d of reciprocal love we will become love. As the apostle John said, "God is Love."[34] The world does not need more bureaucracy, management, money, ideology, or pragmatism. It thirsts for reconciliation and encounter with the G-d of reciprocity in community.

Gods consume people and demand sacrifice. A god is an energy that gives life force, motivation, power, and meaning. When in adversity it is on this force and energy that people rely. They turn to it for salvation. It is where people invest their time, money, energy, effort, blood, sweat, and tears. They worship there. The capitalist god is money and management. The communist god is bureaucratic ideology. Modern men and woman worship these forces. The roots of our nihilism lie in them. They render

33. Psalm 90:17.
34. 1 John 4:8.

Part 4: Our Un/Known G-d

life worthless and pointless. The Protestant and Catholic mainline churches worship a management god. The missional movement worships a mission god. People seek to exert ideological power through mission, leadership, map-making, and planning. The missional movement believes that devotion to pragmatism will enable Christianity to remake the New Christian West.

"When I heard about this matter, I tore my garment and my robe, and pulled some of the hair from my head and my beard, and sat down appalled."[35] G-d is not a management god or a mission god. Modern Christianity is enthralled by these twin idols. Such worship makes it impossible for those enmeshed in their false and blinding light to follow the liberating example of Jesus. Communities of reconciliation have been rendered void by an idolatrous addiction to a modernist story of domination through hierarchy and bureaucracy. We need to be appalled at our complicity and the blindness and self-deception of the church. What is needed is a holy bonfire for the destruction of these corporate vanities. Real mission consists not in seeking new people or new territory but seeing with new eyes. It is about becoming a new kind of people together through the reconciling way of Christ.

"When they said 'repent' I wonder what they meant?" wrote Leonard Cohen.[36] In a neotribal society his words take on new meaning. The true enemy of the egalitarian kingdom of G-d is mission itself. Catholic and Protestant domination christianities must stop their intransigent stand off. Mainline churches must stop their strategic missions of bureaucratic and managerial hubris. Missional Christianity must stop its covert cold war of trying to win back a Christian West. It is a just act of penance to lay down all hierarchical dominance, missional plans, and maps. This is a time of reconciliation between neighbors of all faiths and none as we recover together a way of life and truth. The dawn will break in small communities of conversation, reconciliation and empowerment.

Hafiz knew G-d. His words are an invitation to dance with people of all faiths and none on our journey toward covenant. There we will meet the G-d of everybody.

> "Every child has known God,
> Not the God of names,
> Not the God of don'ts,

35. Ezra 9:3.
36. Cohen, *The Future*.

Not the God who ever does anything weird,
But the God who knows only four words.
And keeps repeating them, saying:
Come dance with me
Come dance."³⁷

---

37. Hafiz, *The Gift*, 270.

Glossary

Ahava: mutual love that is expressed, fostered, and strengthened by giving. It creates interpersonal social and emotional bonds through the practice of exchanging gifts: personal, social, intellectual, physical, spiritual, and verbal.

A/theism: "we ought to affirm our view of God while at the same time realizing that that view is inadequate. Hence we act as both theist and atheist. This a/theism is not some agnostic middle point hovering hesitantly between theism and atheism, but rather actively embraces both out of a profound faith."[1]

Atomization of society: breaking down natural bonds of duty and responsibility between individuals and replacing them with a reliance on the corporations and institutions of the state/corporate religion.

Authority in equality: authority is equally held. There is no first among equals. Mutual submission is practiced toward others in their areas of natural authority. Authority is mutually recognized by the group according to an individual's sphere of influence, maturity of character, and gifts. This charismatic authority is always undermined and distorted by the hierarchical, organizational, or bureaucratic exercise of power over others. Authority in equality is always power with others.

Charismatic authority: power legitimized by personal abilities and gifts that inspire devotion and obedience.

Christian hegemony: leadership or dominance by one Christian country or Christian social group. "The everyday, pervasive, and systematic set of Christian values and beliefs, individuals and institutions that dominate all aspects of our society through the social, political, economic, and cultural

1. Rollins, *How (Not) To Speak of God*, 25.

Glossary

power they wield. Nothing is unaffected by Christian hegemony (whether we are Christian or not) including our personal beliefs and values, our relationships to other people and to the natural environment, and our economic, political, education, health care, criminal/legal, housing, and other social systems. Christian cultural dominance achieved through the mechanisms of state and church hierarchy, bureaucracy and management."[2]

Church: mainline churches practicing and promoting Christian hegemony through bureaucratic management and leadership practices: Anglican, Catholic, Methodist, Baptist, Pentecostal, Brethren, and evangelical house churches (Pioneer, New Frontiers, Vineyard).

City of God: St Augustine's idea that the earthly city contains the damned, which G-d has not chosen to save, the *massa damnata*. The City of God contains those who have been repaired by G-d's grace, and who are therefore able to escape vanity, to love G-d as they should, and therefore merit salvation. The City of God is not situated physically in heaven. It is not even a single physical city, like London or New York, instead it refers to the collection of good people on Earth, and the good society they can form among themselves.

Community of G-d: *ecclesia*, or citizens' assembly; the people of community/neighborhood. A people of all faiths or none in genuine conversation practicing reconciliation, companionship and empowerment in the Way of Christ

Companionship of empowerment (Aramaic: *malkuta*): a way of living in society that emphasizes empowerment through companionship rather than domination through hierarchy. Translated in the Bible, through the lens of Romanized Christian hegemony, as "the kingdom of god."

Constructionist: the ways in which individuals and groups participate in the construction of their perceived social reality. The ways social phenomena are created, institutionalized, known, and made into tradition by humans. The social construction of reality is an ongoing, dynamic process that is (and must be) reproduced by people acting on their interpretations and their knowledge. Because social constructs, as facets of reality and objects of knowledge, are not given by nature, they must be constantly maintained and re-affirmed in order to persist. This process also introduces the

---

2. Kivel, "Challenging Christian Hegemony."

possibility of change, for instance what justice is and what it means shifts from one generation to the next.

Conversation: open source mutual reflection on human and religious experience.

Domination Christianity: Corporate Protestant and Catholic Christianity, which promotes Christian hegemony though the practice of hierarchy, bureaucracy, and management.

Empowerment: increasing the spiritual, political, social, educational, gender, or economic strength of individuals and communities.

Globalization: innovations in communication, manufacturing, and transportation. A force which has driven the decentralized modern life, creating a culturally pluralistic and interconnected global society lacking any single dominant center of political power, communication, or intellectual production.

G-d: G-d is beyond names and naming. The English words God (used for the Hebrew *Elohim*) and Lord (used for the Hebrew *Adonai*) are often written by many Jews as G-d and L-rd as a way of avoiding writing in full any name of God. In postmodernity I am suggesting it may also be used as a way of acknowledging that no one person or religion has the definitive last word regarding our un/known G-d. G-d is not Jewish, Christian or Muslim, but all in all. In that sense G-d is experienced in a kaleidoscopic and mysterious way. This reflects the experience of Moses who, when he asked G-d for his name, was told, "I will be what I will be."

G-d un/known: G-d experienced by all people as present and absent, in some ways known and in some ways unknown.

Hegemony: leadership or dominance by one country or social group.

Legal-rational authority: bureaucratic authority; power is legitimized by legally enacted rules and regulations through institutions and governments.

Management: the act of getting people together to accomplish desired goals and objectives, using available resources efficiently and effectively. Management comprises planning, organizing, staffing, leading or directing, and controlling an organization (a group of one or more people or entities) or effort for the purpose of accomplishing a goal. Resourcing encompasses the deployment and manipulation of human, financial, technological, and natural resources.

Glossary

Misseo Dei: mission of G-d

Mission: New Testament usage is sent. Modern usage is important assignment carried out for political, religious, or commercial purposes, typically involving travel; methods of cultural dominance maintained through management and leadership practices.

Missional: practices of collaborative Christian leadership, engaging in community/neighborhood conversation, using map-making skills and non-strategic planning to form Christian missional communities with the end goal of remaking the New Christian West.

Modernity: capitalism, industrialization, secularization, rationalization, the nation-state and its constituent institutions and forms of surveillance. Tendencies in intellectual culture, particularly the movements intertwined with secularization and post-industrial life, such as Marxism, existentialism, and the formal establishment of social science.

Necrophilia: sex with the dead/love of what is dead.

Neotribal: human beings have evolved to live in tribal society, as opposed to mass society, and thus will naturally form social networks constituting of new tribes. Theorists such as Michel Maffesoli believe that postmodernity is corroding the circumstances that provide for its subsistence and that this is resulting in the decline of individualism and the birth of a new neotribal era.

New Christian West: new society that is Christian.

Perichoretic: dancing mutual exchange of loving gifts with/in the Trinity in community, who is Father, Son, and Holy Spirit.

Postmodernity: dominance of television and popular culture, the wide accessibility of information and mass telecommunications. A greater resistance to making sacrifices in the name of progress discernible in environmentalism and the growing importance of the anti-war movement. Increasing focus on civil rights and equal opportunity, as well as movements such as feminism and multiculturalism, and the backlash against these movements. The postmodern political sphere is marked by multiple arenas and possibilities of citizenship and political action concerning various forms of struggle against oppression or alienation (in collectives defined by sex or ethnicity), while the modernist political arena remains restricted to class struggle.

Glossary

Economic and technological conditions of our age have given rise to a decentralized, media-dominated society in which ideas are only simulacra, inter-referential representations and copies of each other with no real, original, stable, or objective source of communication and meaning. The postmodernist view is that inter-subjective, not objective, knowledge will be the dominant form of discourse under such conditions and that ubiquity of dissemination fundamentally alters the relationship between reader and that which is read, between observer and the observed.

Practices: spiritual life skills that create a structured and common way of ordering and replenishing life.

Reconciliation: making peace through naming the truth/reality and injustice in a social situation, which enables the embrace of the stranger, enemy or other.

Retrograde: reverting to an earlier or inferior condition; motion in the opposite direction.

Romanization: way in which cultures took on Roman practices, such as maintaining order through hierarchical structures that promote dominance.

The medium is the message: "a medium affects the society in which it plays a role not only by the content delivered over the medium, but also by the characteristics of the medium itself."[3] The message of the medium of preaching is: words are power (use words to dominate others). The message of the medium of mainline corporate church is: management is power (you can use management to dominate others). The message of the missional medium is: leading, mapping, planning. The message of the medium of conversation is: mutual exchange of words and ideas brings mutual power.

Traditional authority: power legitimized by respect for long-established cultural patterns.

Trinitarian: G-d as Trinity in community and authority in equality—Father, Son and Holy Spirit.

Voluntary mutual submission: people submit to one another out of free will and not by compulsion or in deference to the demand of leaders, bureaucracy, hierarchy, or management.

---

3. en.wikipedia.org/wiki/The_medium_is_the_message.

Bibliography

Allan, Kenneth D. *Explorations in Classical Sociological Theory: Seeing the Social World.* Thousand Oaks, California: Pine Forge Press, 2005.
Auden, Wystan H. *A Certain World; A Commonplace Book.* London: Faber and Faber, 1970.
Bataille, Georges. *L'Expérience Intérieure.* Paris: Gallimard, 1943.
Bellows, Henry W. *Re-Statements of Christian Doctrine, in Twenty Five Sermons.* New York: D. Appleton, 1860.
Bonhoeffer, Dietrich. *Life Together.* London: SCM Press, 1954.
Borg, Marcus. *Jesus at 2000.* New York: Basic Books, 1996.
Börne, Ludwig. *Gesammelte Schriften von Ludwig Börne, Volume 6: Fragmente und Aphorismen (Collected Writings of Ludwig Börne, Volume 6: Fragments and Aphorisms).* Hamburg: Hoffmann und Campe, 1840.
Bromiley, Geoffrey W. *An Introduction to the Theology of Karl Barth.* Grand Rapids, MI: Eerdmans, 1979.
Brueggemann, Walter. *Psalms and Life of Faith.* Philadelphia: Fortress, 1995.
Chomsky Noam "Domestic Constituencies," *Z Magazine,* (May 1998).
Coakley, Sarah. "Has the Church of England lost its Reason?" *ABC Religion and Ethics,* (November 23rd 2012).
Cohen, Leonard. *The Future.* Audio CD, 1997.
Coupland, Douglas. *Marshall McLuhan: You Know Nothing of My Work.* New York: Atlas Books 2010.
"Crimson Tide." DVD, 1995.
"Dalai Lama Says Secularism Is The True Route To Happiness." National Secular Society. No pages. Online: http://www.secularism.org.uk/dalailamasayssecularismisthetrue.html.
Davies, J. G. *Christians, Politics and Violent Revolution.* Online: en.wikipedia.org/wiki/Jesus_is_Lord.
De Chardin, Teilhard, Hymn Of the Universe, New York: Harper & Row, 1965.
De Saint-Exupery, Antoine. *The Little Prince.* Hertfordshire: Wordsworth Editions, 1995.
Dostoevsky, Fyodor. "The Grand Inquisitor." In *The Brothers Karamazov,* 1880.
Eisenstein, Charles. *Sacred Economics; Money, Gift and Society in the Age of Transition.* Berkeley, California: Evolver Editions, North Atlantic, 2011.
———. "Sacred Economics with Charles Eisenstein–A Short Film." Online: http://youtu.be/EEZkQv25uEs.

Bibliography

Foucault, Michel. *Society Must Be Defended: Lectures at the College de France 1975–76.* London: Penguin, 2004.

Francis, Robert. *Collected Poems 1936–1976.* Massachusetts: University of Massachusetts Press

Fromm, Erich. *The Anatomy of Human Destructiveness.* London: Pimlico, 1973.

———. *To Have or to Be?* London: Continuum Publishing, 2005.

Godin, Seth. *Tribes: we need you to lead us.* London: Piatkus, 2008.

Gonsalves, Francis. "The benefit of doubt." *The Asian Age* (November 18, 2013). No Pages. Online: archive.asianage.com/mystic-mantra/benefit-doubt-618.

Griffiths, Bede. *The Marriage of East and West.* Norwich: Canterbury Press, 2003.

Habermas, Jurgen. *The Philosophical Discourse of Modernity.* Cambridge: Polity Press, 1990.

Hafiz. *The Gift-Poems by Hafiz the Great Sufi Master.* Translated by Daniel J. Ladinsky. Penguin Books Australia, 1999.

Haidt, Jonathan. *The Righteous Mind : Why Good People are Divided by Politics and Religion.* Great Britain: Allen Lane, 2012.

Hedges, Chris. "I Don't Believe in Atheists." *Yurica Report* (May 23, 2007). No pages. Online: http://www.yuricareport.com/Religion/ChrisHedgesI_DontBelieveInAtheists.html.

Heidegger, Martin. *Basic Writings: Martin Heidegger.* London: Routledge, 2010.

Hirsch, Alan. "Defining Missional." *Leadership Journal* (Fall 2008). No pages. Online: http://www.christianitytoday.com/le/2008/fall/17.20.html.

Hirsch, Alan. *The Forgotten Ways: Reactivating the Missional Church.* Grand Rapids, MI: Brazos Press, 2006.

Izzard, Eddie. "Cake or Death." Online: www.youtube.com/watch?v=rMMHUzm22oE.

Jung, Carl G. *Modern Man in Search of a Soul.* London: Routledge, 2001.

Jung, Carl G., et al. *The Red Book: Liber Novus.* New York: W. W. Norton & Co, 2009.

Kim, Sung Ho. 'Max Weber.' *Stanford Encyclopedia of Philosophy.* August 4th 2007. Online: plato.stanford.edu/entries/weber/, retrieved 17th February 2010.

———. *Max Weber's Politics of Civil Society.* Cambridge: Cambridge University Press, 2007.

Kivel, Paul. "Challenging Christian Hegemony." *Alternet,* (February 26, 2010). Online: http://www.alternet.org/speakeasy/2010/02/26/challenging-christian-hegemony.

Lewis Clive S. *That Hideous Strength.* New York: Scribner Paperback Fiction, 1996.

Lynch, Gordon. *The New Spirituality, An Introduction to Progressive Belief in the Twenty-First Century.* London: I.B. Tauris & Co. Ltd, 2007.

Machado, Antonio. *Selected Poems of Antonio Machado.* Translated by Betty J. Craige. Louisiana State University Press, 1979.

Marr, Andrew. "History of the World." Eight episodes broadcast on BBC 1 (September–November 2012). Online: http://www.bbc.co.uk/programmes/p00xnr43/episodes/guide.

McLuhan, Marshall. *Understanding Media: The Extensions of Man.* Massachusetts, MIT Press, 1994.

McMaster, Johnston. "Living in tomorrow's world–globalisation and beyond." *Moot* (May 26, 2012). No pages: Online: http://www.moot.uk.net/2012/05/26/johnston-mcmaster-living-in-tomorrows-world-globalisation-and-beyond/.

Merton, Thomas. *Conjectures of a Guilty Bystander.* New York: Bantam Doubleday Dell, 1968.

Bibliography

Milbank, John. *Being Reconciled: Ontology and Pardon.* London and New York: Routledge, 2003.

Mitchell, Donald W. and Wiseman, James. *The Gethsemani Encounter: a dialogue on the spiritual life by Buddhist and Christian monastics.* New York: Continuum Publishing, 1999.

Morrell, Michael. "God in the Material World: Altizer and Žižek in the 'Wake' of the Death of God." No pages. Online: www.mikemorrell.org/2012/11/.

Myers, P. Z. "Sacking The City Of God!" A Celebration of Reason—2012 Global Atheist Convention, Melbourne. Online: http://youtu.be/2-CJojL4ZfA.

Newbigin, Lesslie. *The Gospel in a Pluralist Society.* Grand Rapids, MI: Eerdmans Publishing, 1989.

Nin, Anais. *The Diary of Anais Nin Volume Two.* New York: Harcourt Brace, 1967.

O'Murchu, Diarmuid. "Christian Life (Essay 2)." Diarmuid (2010). No pages. Online: www.diarmuid13.com/christian-life-essay-2.

———. *Christianity's Dangerous Memory: rediscovering the revolutionary Jesus.* New York: The Crossroad Publishing Company, 2011.

Orwell, George. *1984.* London: Penguin, 1949.

Pagola, Jose A. *Jesus: A Historical Approximation.* Miami: Convivium Press, 2009.

Palmer, Parker J. *Let your Life Speak: Listening for the Voice of Vocation.* Jossey-Bass, 1999.

Ratzinger, Joseph C. *Introduction to Christianity,* San Franscisco: Ignatius Press, 2004.

Rifkin, Jeremy. *The Empathic Civilization.* Cambridge: Polity Press, 2009.

Rilke, R. M. *Letters to a Young Poet.* New York: Vintage, 1986.

Ringma, Charles. *Resisting the Powers with Jaques Ellul.* Colorado Springs: Pinon Press, 2000.

Rohr, Richard. *Franciscan Mysticism: I AM That Which I Am Seeking* CD, October 2012 http://store.cac.org/Franciscan-Mysticism-I-AM-That-Which-I-Am-Seeking-CD_p_85.html.

———. *Things Hidden, Scripture as Spirituality.* Cincinnati, OH: St. Anthony Messenger Press, 2008.

Rolheiser, Ronald. *Naming Our Moment Biblically* CD, Loud and Clear Conference , Exeter 2004. ww.ccr.org.uk/archive/gn0409/tapes.htm.

Rollins, Peter. *How (Not) To Speak of God.* London: SPCK, 2006.

———. "A Miracle without Miracle." Blog online: *peterrollins.net/2010/09/to-believe-is-human-to-doubt-is-divine/.*

Roth, G. and Wittich, C. *Max Weber: An Outline of Interpretive Sociology.* Berkeley, Los Angeles, London: University of California Press, 1978.

Roxburgh, Alan J. *Missional: Joining God in The Neighborhood.* Grand Rapids, MI: Allelon, 2011.

———. *Missional Map-Making: skills for leading in times of transition.* San Francisco: Jossey-Bass, 2010.

———. "Practices of Christian Life–Forming and Performing a Culture." *Journal of Missional Practice,* Missional Network (Issue 1, Fall 2012). No pages. Online: www.themissionalnetwork.com/index.php/practices-of-christian-life-forming-and-performing-a-culture.

Sacks, Jonathan. "The Future of Judaism with Chief Rabbi Lord Jonathan Sacks." Online: http://youtu.be/tH4_mtXF7qE.

Bibliography

Schmid, Peter F. *In the beginning there is community: implications and challenges of the belief in a triune God and a person-centred approach.* Norwich: Norwich Centre, 2006.

Sen Gupta, Subhadra. *A Man Called Bapu.* Bangalore: Pratham Books, 2008.

Shaw, George B. *On the Rocks: A Political Comedy.* A Project Gutenberg of Australia ebook, 1933.

Sim, Stuart. *The Routledge Companion to Postmodernism.* New York: Routledge, 2011.

Steigmann-Gall, Richard. *The Holy Reich: Nazi Conceptions of Christianity 1919–1945.* New York: Cambridge University Press, 2003.

Steindl-Rast, David. "Beyond Religion: Ethics, Values and Wellbeing." The Dalai Lama Centre for Ethics and Transformative Values, Massachusetts Institute Of Technology (2012). Online: http://youtu.be/llaiMoCfFGk.

Tolstoy, Leo. *A Confession.* London: Penguin Group, 2008.

Tozer, A. W. "The Man Who Met God in the Fire." KC21 (September 27, 2013). Online: http://www.kc21.net/2013/09/27/a-w-tozer-the-man-who-met-god-in-the-fire/.

Tutu, Desmond. *God is not a Christian: And Other Provocations.* Reading: Rider, 2011.

Volf, Miroslav. "A Public Faith 3." Online: http://youtu.be/Ax7mgkewucM.

———. "A Public Faith 6." Online: http://youtu.be/BqVg2tq_DiM.

———. "From Exclusion to Embrace: Reflections on Reconciliation." No pages. Online: http://www.ce-un.org/resources/speeches/20010911-exclusion-to-embrace.pdf.

Voltaire. *La Pucelle D'Orléans: Poëme Héroï-Comique. En Vingt-Quatre Chants.* Ulan Press, 2011.

Walker, Reginald. *The Methodist Preacher.* Association of Conservative Evangelicals in Methodism.

Ware, Kallistos. *The Orthodox Way.* New York: St Vladimir's Seminary Press, 1982.

———. *The Power of the Name: Jesus Prayer in Orthodox Spirituality.* Oxford: SLG Press, 1986.

Wells, Stuart. *Choosing the Future: The Power of Strategic Thinking.* Oxford: Butterworth-Heinemann, 1997.

Whyte, David. *Crossing the Unknown Sea: Work as A Pilgrimage of Identity.* New York: Riverhead Books, 2001.

Whyte, David. "Life at the Frontier: The Conversational Nature of Reality," TEDx. Online: http://youtu.be/5Ss1HuA1hIk.

Wiens, Delbert. "Mennonite Brethren: Neither Liberal nor Evangelical," *Direction Magazine* (Spring 1991). No Pages. Online: as referenced in comment on www.themissionalnetwork.com/index.php/practices-of-christian-life-forming-and-performing-a-culture.

Wilber, Ken. "I Am Big Mind." Online: www.youtube.com/watch?v=BA8tDzK_kPI.

Williams, Harry A. *Living Free.* London: Continuum, 2006.

Wittgenstein, Ludwig. *Philosophical Investigations.* Oxford: Blackwell Publishing Ltd, 2009.

Woodward, James and Pattison, Stephen, Eds. *The Blackwell Reader in Pastoral and Practical Theology.* Oxford: Blackwell Publishers Ltd, 2000.

About the Author

FRANCIS ROTHERY IS A New Monastic and a Community Franciscan in the European Province of the Anglican Communion. His mission experience emerges from delivering leadership training and development with Partners in Mission International. In collaboration with leaders and churches in Russia, Africa and Pakistan he exercised a ministry of teaching, guidance, governance and spiritual companionship for over ten years. From 2008, in partnership with the Nightchurch Community, he developed an ecumenical and contemplative Fresh Expression based in Exeter Cathedral. In this sacred space he initiated new approaches to conversational learning and communal spiritual development. In 2012 he co-started the South West Emergent Cohort as a conversation hub for people of all faiths and none. Francis is also rooted and connected with/in the Simply Hub, a movement for the development of small communities. Alongside spiritual teaching and development Francis has a lifelong involvement in professional social work, counseling and psychotherapy as a practitioner and in management. He has also lectured in Philosophy and Religious Studies in Further Education and Psychology and Counseling in Adult and Higher Education.

www.ingramcontent.com/pod-product-compliance
Lightning Source LLC
Chambersburg PA
CBHW070248230426
43664CB00014B/2453